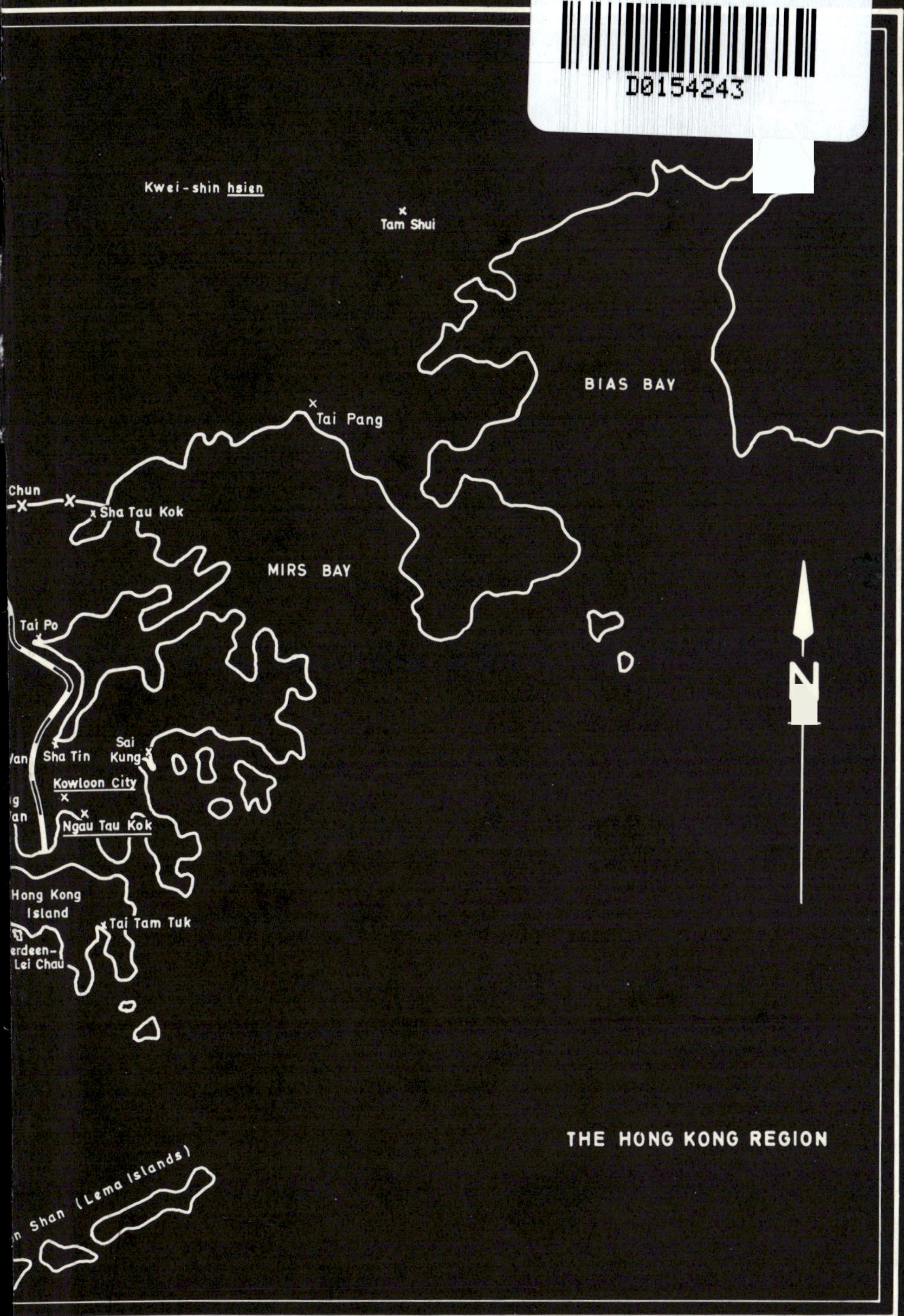

Kwei-shin hsien
Tam Shui
BIAS BAY
Tai Pang
Chun
Sha Tau Kok
MIRS BAY
Tai Po
N
Sha Tin
Sai Kung
Kowloon City
Ngau Tau Kok
Hong Kong Island
Tai Tam Tuk
erdeen-Lei Chau
n Shan (Lema Islands)

THE HONG KONG REGION

The

Hong Kong Region

1850–1911

Aerial view of the northeast part of Tai O Market, Lantau island, Hong Kong.

At the top of the picture at the foot of the *feng shui* hillock next to the sea is the Hau Wong temple with salt fields opposite. At bottom right is part of Tai O Creek with anchored craft and houseboats. At bottom left is that section of the village which contains the Kwan Tai-Tin Hau temple and the former Chinese military office (yamen). *Courtesy of the Hong Kong Government.*

The Hong Kong Region *1850–1911*

Institutions and Leadership in Town and Countryside

by

James Hayes

Archon Books • 1977 • Dawson

First published in 1977

Archon Books, The Shoe String Press Inc
995 Sherman Avenue, Hamden, Connecticut 06514 USA

Wm Dawson & Sons Ltd, Cannon House
Folkestone, Kent, England

Archon ISBN 0-208-01626-0
Dawson ISBN 0 7129 0768 8

Set in ten point Monophoto Plantin light on twelve point by
Asco Trade Typesetting Ltd of Hong Kong

Printed in the United States of America

Library of Congress Cataloging in Publication Data

Hayes, James, 1930–
The Hong Kong region, 1850–1911.

Based on the author's thesis, University of London.
Bibliography: p.
Includes index.
1. Hongkong—Social conditions. 2. Social institutions
—Hongkong. I. Title.
HN761.H62H39 1977 309.1′51′2503 77-6756

For Maurice Freedman

Contents

List of Maps

Preface

THIS BOOK, and the doctoral thesis on which it is based, arose from my fascination with the Hong Kong scene and the character of its people, especially with those of the New Territories where I served as district officer south 1957–62 and to which, under the vastly changed physical and demographic circumstances accruing from twenty years of intensive industrial, commercial, and residential development, I am again posted as town manager and district officer of the Tsuen Wan district. Its genesis lies with the late Maurice Freedman who, during a field trip to Hong Kong in 1962, suggested to me that the historical inquiries I had already begun should take the shape of a formal study. I have therefore dedicated the work to him because, in addition to setting the course, he maintained a continuous interest in my work and became a valued friend and counsellor.

In the course of the field work, particularly in the early stages, I was helped by a number of friends and colleagues who, in their private capacities, assisted with interviews (their assistance was always necessary where Hakka speakers were involved) and, in part, with translation: also I owe a debt of gratitude to many friends among the leaders and elders of older communities in Hong Kong, Kowloon, and, especially, the New Territories. Space does not permit me to list them all, and I hope that this general acknowledgement will not obscure the very real appreciation I feel for their help and encouragement. Two persons, however, must be named; Wan On 溫安 of Pui O, Lo Wai, and Chan Yiu 陳耀 of Tai O, to whom I am deeply grateful for twenty years of cheerful friendship and much enlightenment of the local scene. I first met Wan On when he was chairman of the newly formed South Lantau Rural Committee and I was district officer, and together we had to deal with the land resumptions, grave removals and agricultural compensation for the first road on the Island and the construction of catchwaters for its first reservoir. He was a great help in dealing with his fellow villagers, and taught me one basic fact of village life that has stayed with me ever since. One day I got rather testy with him about his grumbles and argumentativeness. "You're lucky" he said, "you've only got me to deal with. *I've* got a hundred angry villagers, and don't forget that I have to live with them!" As for Chan Yiu, now eighty-four and a former Chairman of the Tai O Rural Committee, he has always been an interested and helpful adviser, as well as a courteous host and a cook who does his own marketing!

On the library side, the registry staff of the district land offices of the New Territories Administration, and of the Registrar-General's Department, and the librarian of the Colonial Secretariat Library, Mr. Douglas Cheung Yuk-ming 張旭明; have helped with inquiries. Other friends, the librarian of the University of Hong Kong, Mr. H.A. Rydings and the head of its Chinese library, Mrs. Sydney Fung 馮陳善奇, have also given much assistance; which I gratefully record here.

I must also thank Francis Sham Shui-yu 沈瑞裕 my teacher and friend over many years, for help and advice; and my charming wife, Mabel Chiu-woon Wong 黃超媛, who has been another great support. She has retyped innumerable passages, has put up with all the demands of scholarship, and has run a home for us both in the course of her own duties in a busy post.

I wish, too, to express my appreciation to the American publishers, and to Asco Trade Typesetting Ltd. of Hong Kong, for much courtesy shown during preparation of this book.

Finally, in the midst of my preoccupation with China and the Chinese and their passion for social organization and good works, it was salutary for me to see on a horse trough on the outskirts of my home in Cheltenham Spa the words "Presented to the Leckhampton Local Board by the Cheltenham Ladies' Society for the Protection of Animals, 1889". I hope this will raise a smile among fellow toilers, and remind them, as it did me, not to get too immersed in the activities of one race, however numerous and compelling.

Hong Kong, April 1977 JAMES HAYES

INTRODUCTION

Local Leadership below the Gentry

THE PROPOSITION that gentry participation was essential to the management of local affairs in imperial times has been long regarded as a theorem of Chinese political and social existence. John Fairbank's classic statement of the position was first made nearly thirty years ago:

> [The] relative smallness of the imperial administration no doubt reflects the fact that it depended upon the gentry to lead and dominate the peasantry in the villages[1]

and again:

> The imperial government remained a superstructure which did not directly enter the villages because it rested upon the gentry as its foundation. The many public functions of the local degree-holders made a platform under the imperial bureaucracy and let the officials move about with remarkable fluidity and seeming independence of local roots.[2]

More recently, Kung-chuan Hsiao has restated this thesis in a major work of great authority:

> The gentry (persons with official or academic titles) seem to have constituted the most active element in whatever community life was displayed in the Chinese village. . . . There is some indication that the gentry were more active and

> exerted more influence in the southern villages than the northern ones.... Villages owed a great deal to the leadership supplied by the gentry—retired officials and titled scholars—for their limited organization and activities.... It is not an exaggeration to say that the gentry constituted the keystone of rural organization. The village could and did exist without the gentry, but villages without gentry could hardly show any high degree of organized community life or any considerable amount of organized activity.

and again:

> Although organization appeared in many villages, it did not appear in all, and even in those where organizations existed, communal activities were limited in scope and were rarely if ever conducted by all the inhabitants on a basis of equality. It is difficult to find an instance in which associative efforts were coordinated by a village-wide organization for the welfare of all inhabitants. Most of the organizations were set up only for special purposes and often merely to meet temporary emergencies. Their membership usually included only a segment of the inhabitants of a given village. Commoners were not precluded from participation or even leadership in village undertakings, but the gentry usually dominated them. It was the gentry that determined to a large extent the pattern and direction of organized village life.[3]

Etienne Balazs carried the prevailing view to an extreme in an article on tradition and revolution in China, written in 1954. Describing "the scholar–official gentry" he stated:

> By exploring the nature and role of this peculiar class we may find the key that will explain the structure of every regime, past and present, of eternal China...it was not landownership, nor even heredity, that conferred upon it its special position and its extraordinary power; it was its indispensible social function.... Thus we find that, at bottom, Chinese society consisted of a vast majority of illiterate workers without legal rights, and a tiny minority of culti-

> vated literati who planned, directed, supervised, and officered the work of others—in short, who assumed all the tasks of organization, coordination, and administration, and without whom the social organism could not have functioned at all.

At the same time, Balazs admitted to having drawn an "incomplete and one-sided—if you like, tendentious" picture of Chinese society.[4]

In contrast, the richness of local community life in China has also been noted. Huc commented that communal organization "is perhaps nowhere else as perfect as in China,"[5] and in an important passage in his major work S. Wells Williams remarked upon the "tendency to associate...a fertile principle applied to every branch of life."[6] It is, of course, easier to see the peasant contribution to communal organization from a field study than from a documentary one, and since the opportunities for the first are very limited, it has seldom been stated in explicit terms and for a particular area. However, it has not gone unremarked. C.P. Fitzgerald, for instance, has noted the Chinese peasant's "great capacity for organization, usually of a clandestine kind."[7]

The proposition that gentry participation was essential to the management of local affairs has, therefore, puzzled me. Using the opportunities for study arising from twenty years' local residence, I have examined the management of local affairs in some of the villages and townships of the Hong Kong region, with special reference to the second half of the nineteenth century. I have come to conclude that undue emphasis has been given to the role of the gentry, especially at the subdistrict and village levels. This study is therefore an attempt to provide new perspectives.

The Hong Kong Region: The Nature of Local Society

The Hong Kong region, as I have defined it, and as shown in map 1, takes in the present British crown colony and those adjoining areas in which the colonial authorities and others have shown an interest from time to time, as shown in government papers and the writings of naval and military officers, missionaries, naturalists, businessmen, and others. It includes the Portuguese enclave of Macau, formerly part of Hsiang-shan county. Hong Kong itself constituted part of the Hsin-an county of the Kuang-chou (Canton) prefecture, to which Hsiang-shan also belonged.

The main historical and geographical facts of the Hong Kong part of the region may be summarized as follows: a continuing influx of different dialect groups from Sung times on; a reconstruction of local society in the later 17th century following drastic depopulation during the upheavals of the Ming–Ch'ing changeover and the Evacuation of the Coast 1662–69; a reliance on farming and fishing as the principal means of livelihood; the vagaries of an exceedingly destructive climate; endemic disturbance caused by feuds between inhabitants or attacks by robbers and pirates from outside; ownership of land by a few major families up to the British takeover of Hong Kong Island (1841), Kowloon (1860) and the New Territories (1899), with a two-fold division of the soil which placed peasant cultivators in a position of near independence; and, finally, the rise of Hong Kong to a position of economic importance.[8] My study is concerned only with the final stage of this long evolution, the nature of local society in the late Ch'ing. As I see it, this was determined by four main factors: the local system of land tenure, the absence of gentry leadership from most villages, the prolonged mixed settlement, and the place of the sea in the economic life of the region. These produced a distinct form of local society which we may call Pao-an, after the name of the larger *hsien* to which it had belonged before the mid-T'ang, and with which it was retitled in the early 20th century, in a general revision of county names to avoid similarities and confusions.[9]

Pao-an rural society was essentially peasant, and generally fits the four-fold categorization outlined by Teodor Shanin in his important restatement (1971) of what constitutes peasant society; namely, the "peasant family-farm as the basic unit of multidimensional social organisation; land husbandry as the main means of livelihood directly providing the major part of the consumption needs; specific traditional culture related to the way of life of small communities; and the 'underdog' position, the domination of peasantry by outsiders" (though here, as I shall show, less in degree and practice than in other places). It was also characterized by a variety and complexity of settlement found alike in village and market and by a flourishing rural organization under indigenous leadership. Other notable features included a diversified economy; a good standard of domestic housing; and a conspicuous expenditure on folk religion, the ceremonies of family life, and a variety of essential services that were often provided by itinerants on circuit. These common elements are detailed in chapter one.

This study demonstrates the variety of settlement, the diversity of institutions, and the extent of local leadership through an examination of six places in the Hong Kong region, for convenience underlined on map 1. They include an island market town with a mixed population including boat people (chapter two) and another older example of the kind, with long-established salt pans and an adjacent farming community (chapter three). These small towns are styled coastal market centers to distinguish them from G. William Skinner's standard market centers, from which they differ in certain particulars. The other four areas of detailed study comprise a multilineage Cantonese farming village (chapter four), a linked group of mixed Cantonese and Hakka villages (chapter five), a multilineage Hakka settlement of specialist artisans (chapter six), and a standard market center located outside a subdistrict magistracy (chapter seven). A summary and discussion chapter follows the six individual studies, while the postscript suggests a possible classification for the local political systems of Hsin-an at this time.

The main point to emerge from this survey is local competence on the part of a community of peasants and shopkeepers. Local management was left to resident peasants and shopkeepers who had to deal virtually unaided with routine management in villages and market towns, and with every form of disaster, natural or man-made. There were long-established nonresident gentry landlords in these areas, but owing to a local division of the soil into surface and subsoil rights between tenants and owners respectively, the latter had come to be concerned only with the collection of rents or other levies on land and made no attempt to control routine local affairs.

The genius to devise, and the capacity to operate, many

different kinds of organization designed to meet local needs were clearly present, without gentry initiative or guidance. Thus the dynamics of Chinese society in this part of Kwangtung did not derive as directly from the gentry as is maintained in the general surveys of Hsiao, Balazs, Michael, and Fairbank, and owed more to peasants and shopkeepers than has been apparent from individual village studies.

It follows that the maintenance and exercise of imperial control also leaned more on these classes than has been hitherto allowed in the literature on this subject. If, as is generally accepted, the officials were largely dependent upon the cooperation of the gentry and county elites, it appears that they, in their turn, were dependent upon the innumerable leaders of large and small communities up and down the subdistricts. It is this sub-gentry and local management of affairs that comes out in any area examination of community organization in town and country in the Hong Kong region in the late Ch'ing.

The Choice of Location and Extant Literature

The field research for this study was carried out in both urban and rural areas of Hong Kong. The community studies are mostly of places in the Southern District of the New Territories, where I was district officer from 1957 to 1962, and much of the additional information comes from villages in Hong Kong Island and Kowloon where my government service from 1962 to 1974 has provided contacts helpful for the study of the pre- and post-1841 settlements there. The documentary evidence comes from the New Territories as a whole and from Macau.

I undertook the work because I was interested and because I soon found, at that time in the late 1950s, that very little modern research had been undertaken in the Hong Kong region. Apart from Barbara Ward's published articles on the Kau Sai boat people and Maurice Freedman's notices of the New Territories in his *Lineage Organization in Southeastern China* (1958), Hong Kong was, as Freedman put it a little later, regarded by scholarship as "no more than the railway route into Kwangtung."[11] Little attempt had been made to study the area for its own sake and for what it might tell us about other parts of South China.

The position has greatly changed since that time, but far less in the historical field than in sociological and anthropological studies.[12] Historians have not yet thoroughly studied what may be styled "the Chinese side of British Hong Kong" and the Chinese past before 1841 on Hong Kong Island, 1860 in Kowloon, and 1899 in the New Territories. As recently as 1958, G. B. Endacott took for the introduction to his history of Hong Kong a passage from E.J. Eitel, "And Men had to come from the Far West to give it a name in the history of the East."[13]

Generally speaking, there were few serious prewar contributions made to the study of local history, and we must look to the postwar period for the beginning of sustained study of the region.[14] On the Chinese side, Lo Hsiang-lin, Jen Yu-wen and Jao Tsung-i have made useful contributions to Hong Kong's Chinese past in the course of wider studies of Chinese history and society, and other scholars have written on particular aspects of it. However, the bulk of their work is less than the contributions to the study of contemporary and traditional society made by Western anthropologists who, in their study of the present, have found it necessary to investigate what has gone before, and have cast a backward eye that, in some cases, has lingered for more than a glance. H.D.R. Baker's work on the Liao lineage[15] of Sheung Shui is a good instance of the kind and an excellent example of the assistance that the anthropologist who is also a sinologue can give to historical work. Jack M. Potter has provided a study of part of another major lineage, the Tengs of Ping Shan, that, as in the Sheung Shui case, takes us back to the early days of the permanent settlement of the region, though he has given less attention to history than has Dr. Baker. Cornelius Osgood's contemporary and monumental three volume study of an island community off Hong Kong Island has been the most recent major addition to anthropological and ethnographic studies of the region. Other scholars have worked among lesser and newer lineages and village settlements, and in the market towns, but only a portion of their work has yet been published.

Some students in related fields have produced work that thickens the village cover provided by the anthropologists. Barbara Ward, Eugene Anderson, and Hiroaki Kani have studied the past and present of the Tanka, the native boat people of

Hong Kong. K.M.A. Barnett, a former career officer of the Hong Kong Civil Service, has made thoughtful and stimulating contributions to the linguistic and ethnological background, and John McCoy of Cornell and Armando da Silva of the University of Hawaii have also published on these fields. Marjorie Topley's work is of great help in unravelling the past and assessing its relevance for the present; while Carl Smith's painstaking research into original sources is a major contribution to historical studies of the local community.

However, much of the detailed work has related to one lineage or village; and although some of the scholars involved in these studies have attempted to place their communities within the general context and background of the Hong Kong region, the lack of work on the smaller settlements, and on a wider basis than the village or the lineage, has led to an imbalance. There were nearly 700 villages within the present New Territories of Hong Kong in 1899,[16] with many other old settlements in Hong Kong Island and Old and New Kowloon. Published research has not yet done justice to the number and variety of rural and market settlements with their long history of continuous residence, to either the details or the broader aspects of land ownership and tenurial arrangements, or to the social and political institutions of the region and their leadership patterns; yet these studies are required to place the lineage strongholds of the Liaos, Tengs, and others in context and perspective.

An interim statement on the wider basis of historical development in the Hong Kong region is clearly overdue. Although this study is far from being comprehensive, it does go beyond the confines of the village. It takes us away, too, from the gentry leaders of the lineage villages to the peasants and shopkeepers who manned the institutions that managed the lesser villages and coastal market towns.

Other Sources

In the effort to provide a wider view, I have, as stated, taken a number of settlements and market towns and used whatever local documentary sources and opportunities for recording oral history have been available. On the documentary side I have consulted the Chinese district, prefectural, and provincial gazetteers and similar works, together with the printed and manuscript reports of the Hong Kong government and other Western bodies with an interest in South China.[17] However, these usually produced only occasional and fragmentary information for my purposes.

In the case of Hsin-an, especially at the subdistrict and village level, information in the gazetteer is often scanty, and field work is required to supplement the written record. For instance, the list of temples in the last edition (1819) does not include all that were then already in existence.[18] The list of markets lacks the important information on schedules necessary to construct a model of marketing along Skinner's lines,[19] and this information must be sought in the field. The history of settlement, by time and dialect group, must also be constructed from field research. The relations between large and small villages, great and minor lineages, landlord and tenant, as well as information on rents and tenure systems, must be obtained largely from local sources. In this situation local records like lineage genealogies, shop accounts, rent books, land deeds, and inscribed tablets in temples and other buildings[20] are all essential adjuncts to the construction of a fuller picture than that provided by the local gazetteer. Although much of the less durable historical material has already been lost due to the ravages of the climate, the devaluing effects of modernization, and to the direct and indirect effects of the Japanese occupation of the colony between 1941 and 1945, I have used these records wherever they have been available to me.

Fortunately, another major source of information, able to serve as a base line for many inquiries and for checks on the results of field work, is still available. This is the survey and settlement of titles to land undertaken by the Hong Kong government after the lease of the New Territories, which provides ownership schedules and demarcation sheets showing fields and houses in towns and villages existing in 1899. (However, the schedules are not necessarily an accurate guide to the pre-1899 situation and should be used with caution: see n. 129 to chapter one).

Even with these sources, I have faced major difficulties in

recovering sufficient material for a serious study. As Ramon Myers has affirmed, this problem is likely to affect most researchers who attempt to reconstitute the social community and structure at village and town level in China before this century.[21]

I have mentioned the use of oral history, which I soon found was essential in the village and town studies, both for the recovery of material and for anything like an understanding of the period. This was begun in 1959–60, before too many of the old persons who had spent their youth in the last decades of the 19th century had passed beyond my reach. Like any other form of historical research, oral history has its own rules and requirements.[22] These are, and must be, especially rigorous in view of its obvious dangers. I shall therefore explain in detail the techniques used in over ten years of interviewing, so that the reader can assess the degree of accuracy reached by this line of inquiry.

I first obtained the life history of new informants to check local birth and to find out if, when, and for how long they had been absent from the village, as it is little use asking questions that are outside personal experience. Wherever possible, questions were related to information obtained from printed or manuscript material and to the statements made by other old persons in the same or a neighboring village. Replies were tested at intervals to note any variations or additional material. Where possible, old persons were brought together for discussion to check facts and reactions, views and opinions.

This is, of course, a recital of perfection. Interviews did not always proceed as planned. They were nearly always conducted in company in small houses, and family members were sometimes a handicap in proportion to the interest they showed. Occasionally a younger and more voluble member of the family would try to give answers or to influence, put off, or weary the old person. Sometimes the elders or committeemen who on many occasions came with me would hold the floor, with frustrating or disastrous effects on the interview. At other times, the problem would be the old person himself, who was too old, too weak, or too deaf to provide anything worthwhile.

Fortunately, in my experience the majority of those interviewed have had something useful to offer. Some old people are veritable "National Treasures," as they would be styled in Korea or Japan.

They impressed with their quiet dignity, sincerity, gentleness, and knowledge. Though possessing little education—very few of the women had even the rudiments of an education in the written language—many of them had intelligent minds that retained facts and impressions from earlier days. They had lived, too, through a period when the rural villages, although surrounded by change, retained their isolation until very recently, and with it reliance on the village as a source of entertainment and instruction. Through abundance of leisure time and want of much else to do, these old persons had been in direct and attentive contact with their fathers, uncles, and grandfathers. They were the last generation to have absorbed the accumulated lore and legend of earlier times and to have lived in a style similar to that of past centuries. Because of this, their like will not be seen again. I have been handicapped in having come almost too late to the task,[23] since a person who was 20 years old in 1899, the terminal date of my thesis, was about 80 years of age when I began my interviewing in earnest and with some knowledge of what I was about. I have been fortunate in finding persons with this background and, in many cases, of this caliber. Moreover, I have had the advantage of being able to go back many times.

Since the material from interviews has extended over a period of fifteen years and more, it has been necessary to devise a system which gives the reader the age of the informant and the time that he was interviewed. An entry with (1883; 1961–65) after it means that the informant was born in 1883 and gave this information at various times between 1961 and 1965. Unless otherwise stated it should always be assumed that the informant was a native of the village or market town concerned. I have used this method sparingly, to indicate important material: otherwise the work would be full of such interpolations.

An unavoidable weakness, due to the length of years separating the period of study from the time of the interviews, is that it has often been necessary to rely on the evidence of a very few persons, and sometimes on only one. Where this is so an effort has been made to supplement their testimony from written sources or to reinforce it with hearsay evidence from responsible people who have understood, say, from their fathers and uncles, that such and such was the state of affairs at the time in question.

Nonetheless, it is difficult to conceive of this study without the help and stimulus given by old people. They provided information too commonplace, or too specialized, to be recorded in books and reports. Some chance remark has frequently made me see something in a new light,[24] or has confirmed hints or statements given in historical sources.[25] Often, the manner of a remark was as revealing as the content.

A study such as this puts me in the debt of many people. Besides the old persons who allowed me to ask them so many questions, to cross-examine them and to return to the same subjects with a different approach on later occasions, I have received a great deal of help from friends among the village representatives and rural committees of the New Territories and the Kaifong and other local associations in the older parts of Hong Kong and Kowloon. Many of them took an interest in the work and did all they could to locate and introduce likely informants and to smooth the way for satisfactory interviews. Without their help, the task would have been more difficult. There would have been a greater barrier of noncomprehension, reserve, and sometimes suspicion to break down. Their skillful handling of old people, and in many cases, their long acquaintance with them, reduced to a minimum difficulties of this sort.

I was aware initially of some disadvantages of being an official: suspicion as to my motives for inquiry and, in some cases, a degree of apprehension at my presence in a house (sometimes for reasons that had nothing to do with the interview, as when I sat on top of a tin of gelegnite intended for illegally dynamiting fish). However, these obstacles were much less apparent than the benefits from having first-class contacts, and as my historical interests became established they were almost entirely removed.

Abbreviations Used in the Text

(For details see under relevant headings in the Bibliography.)

ADR	Annual Departmental Report
AR	Annual (Colony) Report
ARDONT	Administrative reports by District Officer, New Territories
AU	Authorities—correspondence between departments and the Colonial Secretary's Office 1857–87
BB	Blue Books of the Hong Kong government
BCL	Block Crown Leases issued in 1904–1905
CO	Colonial Office record series in the Public Records Office, London
CR	Colony Report
CSO	Colonial Secretary's Office
CSO Ext	CSO files dealing primarily with land matters in the New Territories 1899–1907
CSP	China Sea Pilot
CSWT	Ch'ing-shih wen-t'i
DAR	Departmental Annual Report
DCNT	District Commissioner, New Territories
DD	Demarcation District
First Year	Report on the New Territories in the First Year of British Administration
FO	Foreign Office record series in the Public Records Office, London
GN	Government notification
Gazetteer	A Gazetteer of Place Names in Hong Kong, Kowloon, and the New Territories, 1960
HAN	Hong Kong Hansard

HKGG	Hong Kong Government Gazette (in the nineteenth century, "Hong Kong" was usually spelled as one word, "Hongkong")
HKLR	Hong Kong Land Registry
HKN	The Hong Kong Naturalist
HNHC	Gazetteer of the Hsin-an district 1688 or 1819 editions, as specified
HNTES	Hong Kong and New Territories Evangelization Society
IMC	Imperial Maritime Customs
JHKBRAS	Journal of the Hong Kong Branch Royal Asiatic Society
JOS	Journal of Oriental Studies
KCFC	Gazetteer of Kuang-chou prefecture, 1880 edition
KTTC	Gazetteer of the Kwangtung province 1935 reprint of 1823 edition
KTKKCY	Summary of historical researches on Kwangtung, 1894
KTTS	An Atlas with Commentary of Kwangtung, 1865
Lockhart	Report on the New Territory at Hong Kong, 1898
NT	New Territories (originally used in the singular)
NTA	New Territories Administration
Nathan	Correspondence in Eastern No. 88
New Atlas	New Atlas of the Chinese Republic, by T'ung Shih-hsiang
Orme	Report on the New Territories, 1899–1912
PRO	Public Record Office (London and Hong Kong, as specified)
PSN	Peasant Studies Newsletter
SP	Sessional Papers, Hong Kong
TCBRAS	Transactions of the China Branch Royal Asiatic Society
TCITC	The General Gazetteer of the Ch'ing Dynasty
TCITCCY	The Concise General Gazetteer of the Ch'ing Dynasty
TMITC	The General Gazetteer of the Ming Dynasty
YCKC	Notes on the History of Canton, 1806–1807
YLTT	Yung Lo Encyclopedia, 1403–1408
YTPC	Sketches of Kwangtung, c. 1780

I

A General Account of the Hong Kong Region

Peoples and Settlement of the Hong Kong Region

There is no satisfactory full length account available in Chinese, English, or any European language which takes in all the complexities of the population and settlement of the Hong Kong region.[1]

The Hong Kong region was occupied in prehistoric times by persons whose origin and racial affiliations are, despite plentiful evidence, still uncertain.[2] It is not clear whether these early inhabitants are the progenitors of the Yao and other tribes who are believed to have occupied the area before the period of intensive Chinese settlement, or of the Tanka boat people who formed a major part of the indigenous local population in the 19th century. The only certainty is that this region was inhabited from an early date.

The first regular settlement of the New Territories by the Chinese was during the Sung dynasty. Prior to this, Kwangtung was only Chinese in patches, with scattered military and agricultural settlements and a few towns and cities. In the Hong Kong region, the oldest of the major lineages still living here, the Tangs of Kam Tin, was firmly established by A.D. 1100.[3] From about this time Cantonese and Hakkas,[4] the two main groups of Chinese to settle in the district, moved there in an influx that continued through the centuries up to and beyond the British occupation of Hong Kong in 1841 and the extensions of the area under their rule in 1860 and 1899.

Besides the land population of Hakka and Punti, there were the Tanka and the Hoklo boat people. Barnett traces the origin of the Tanka in Chinese sources and believes that it was during

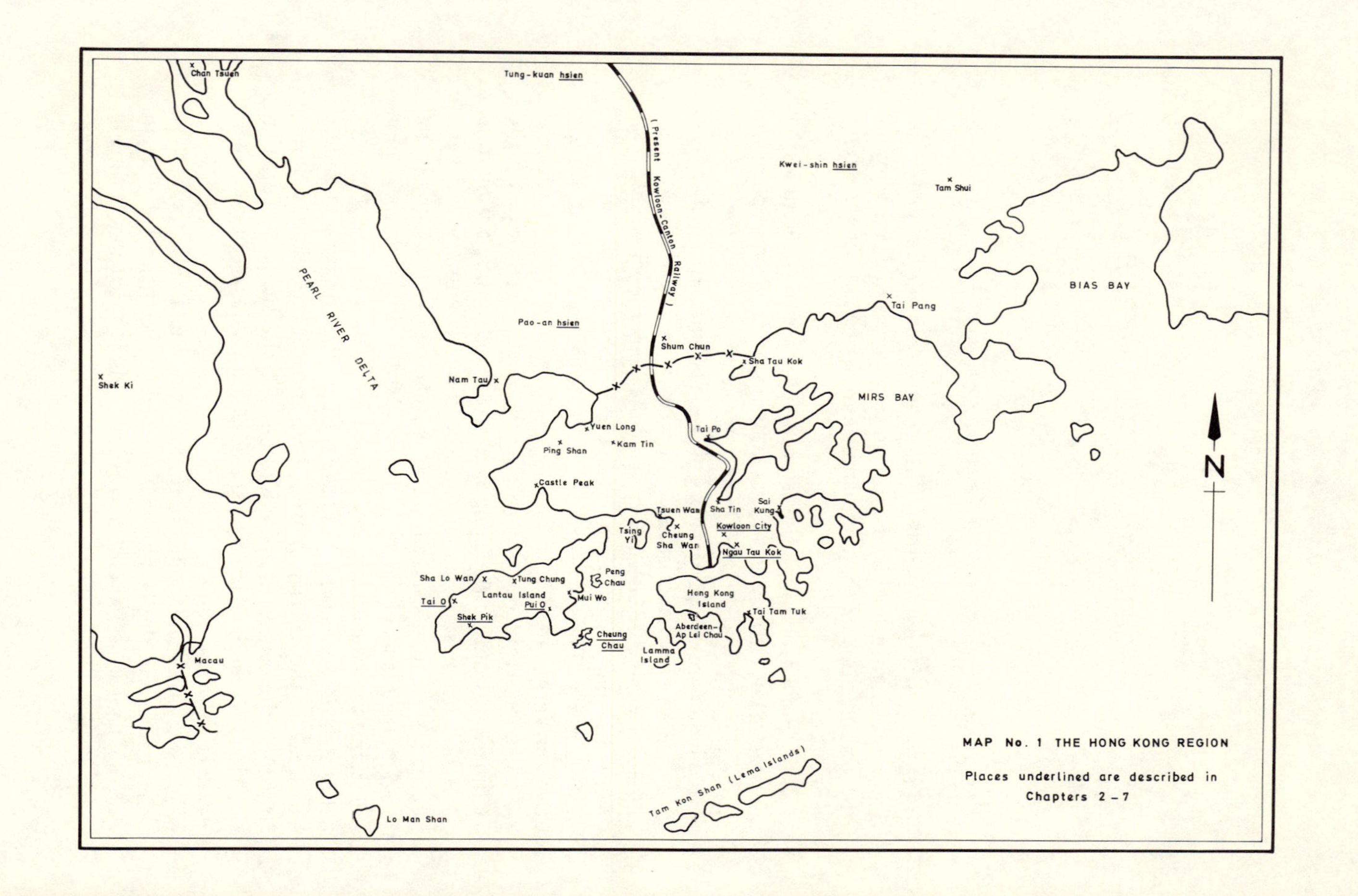

MAP No. 1 THE HONG KONG REGION

Places underlined are described in Chapters 2 – 7

the Yuan dynasty that they began to speak the dialect of Cantonese which they use to this day.[5] They live mainly afloat although some of them have long dwelt in pile huts with thatch roofs erected on stilts in a creek or on boats drawn up on land, from which they go off to sea in their fishing boats.[6] Such huts and boats are shown in several early 19th century paintings of the Canton River, Macau, and Hong Kong area.[7]

The Hoklo people have also been long in the region,[8] but they are not native to it, coming mainly from northeast Kwangtung and Fukien.[9] They were commonly found in early Hong Kong and the adjoining districts. Letters and reports now preserved in the archives of the American Baptist Board of Foreign Missions at Valley Forge give detailed evidence for this in the 1840s and 1850s.[10] They appear to have been more nomadic than the Tanka boat people; by the late 19th century, and probably much earlier, they came yearly into the Hong Kong region for the seasonal fisheries, especially for shrimp and prawns.[11]

Among them, these four Chinese-speaking groups appear to have accounted for the fifth, the aboriginals mentioned above.[12] The several tribes have long disappeared. They were probably dealt with by a process of assimilation and elimination that has left little trace of them as a separate people in the Hong Kong region, though they still exist as independent groups in other parts of the province.[13] The time scale for this local operation is still unclear. Barnett considers that it did not begin until the Yuan dynasty at the earliest, and it must have continued for centuries if material from nearby districts is any guide.[14] Indeed, Barnett observes that when the first edition of the Hsin-an gazetteer was printed in 1587 "there must have been several villages which preserved their former language, dress and customs."[15]

The Chinese movement into Hsin-an, which may be described as a small part of the Han Chinese move to the South chronicled by Wiens,[16] is established as a time sequence in the genealogies and memorials of the many lineages who inhabit its villages today. I have examined as many as I could from the old Southern District, and these show as varied and lengthy a time scale as is required to prove continuous ingress. The present families have come at various times from the Sung and Yuan onwards.

Naturally, these records only relate to lineages that have survived to the present and take no account of those that have vanished in the course of nearly a thousand years. The severe break with the past that occurred in mid-seventeenth century during the Evacuation of the Coast 1662–69 must have disposed of many old families. It is clear that no dogmatic statements can be made about the age of any particular settlement, while other villages may have disappeared without trace or recollection.

However, there are other aspects to be explored. They are less straightforward than the history of this regular incursion, but equally important for an understanding of the peoples of the region. What are the local characteristics of the settlement of Punti and Hakka? Which came into the area first? Did they settle together or separately, and how did they stand one to the other? What were their social and political relationships over the years, as reflected in intermarriage, economic and other interaction, the occurrence or absence of hostility, and the influence of one speech upon the other? These questions apply also to the Tanka, in their relationships with Hakka and Punti land people and with visiting and resident Hoklos.

Taking up these points in turn, it has long been assumed that the Hakka came later into the area than the Cantonese. Both Lockhart and Orme considered that the Punti were the older inhabitants.[17] It was presumed, too, that the Hakka's late arrival in the region led to their having to make do with the poorer land and to their being generally in a subordinate position to the longer-settled Cantonese lineages.[18]

Barnett has been responsible for correcting the long established view of the latecoming Hakka settlement of the New Territories. With facts almost certainly supplied by him, the 1957 issue of the colony annual report contained an authoritative statement to the effect that the Hakka began to enter this region at about the same time as the first Cantonese or even before; that the Cantonese were the more successful settlers, and in the areas where both groups live side by side the Hakka are always found upstream, along foothills, and in general on worse land; that at an early stage they seem to have become dependants or serfs of the powerful Cantonese families, but that the balance was later restored by heavy immigration from the East River districts in the 17th and 18th centuries. The report also stated that the Hakka's origin is unknown and their traditions contradictory, pointing to both a northern and a southern origin, and that certain New Territories villages which show indications of being of non-Chinese origin are invariably Hakka speaking.[19]

Barnett had by 1967 developed the last of these proposals to the point of stating, "The Hakka are descendants of the hill people, with or without Han admixture, who adopted a Chinese way of life about the same time."[20] For him the Hakka riddle, as he called it, had this explanation. If this is so, the Hakka settlers of the Hong Kong region are to be numbered in two groups: those whose origins are old and uncertain and are perhaps to be ascribed as Barnett suggests; and those who came more recently and whose immediate origins are known, or at least attributed.

Earlier I advised caution in making statements on the age of local settlements. My research experience also leads me to make reservations about the classification of villagers as being either Hakka or Punti; even among the later group of Hakka arrivals. I have sometimes met with the curious statement that a lineage is "Hakka, now speaking Punti," implying that the family group, originally regarding themselves as Hakkas in the place from which they migrated, had now become Cantonese. I have recorded such statements from lineages in several villages on or near Lantau and elsewhere in the Southern District, and with one or two exceptions in which length of settlement was not known, the statements came from lineages claiming a mere three to eight generation stay. The same process can be found operating in reverse among lineages who tell one that they were formerly Cantonese but are now Hakka.[21]

Some likely explanations for these assimilations, and even changes of classification, among the local, long-established population would include mixed settlement over the centuries, intermarriage, and the incorporation of persons of one lineage into another of the type reported from Shek Pik and elsewhere. It is to be expected that in areas of mixed settlement the minority group, especially if small, will intermarry and in time produce descendants who, through living and working in the same place for generations, will gradually conform in speech and customs to the majority. This is especially likely where, as in many local cases, there does not appear to be a history of animosity between the two groups. In such places, too, the local educational arrangements would have helped to accelerate the process, as at Pui O, where the Punti minority educated its children in the school provided by the leading Hakka lineage.

Inevitably, this confusion is reflected in local speech. A mixed Hakka–Punti language is still to be found in some areas of the New Territories among the older generation, known to its speakers as *wai tau wa*.[22] However, it would be wrong to conclude that it will be found in all areas of mixed settlement, since conformity to one speech or the other is more usual, I believe. Like Hakka, and Pao-an Cantonese, it is rapidly dying out in the face of intensive standard Cantonese teaching in all local schools.

Another aspect of Hakka–Punti relations that requires attention is a general assumption that the two dialect groups have always lived in separate villages, and in a state of mutual animosity.[23] Detailed investigation shows that separation does not always occur. There are, as Balfour wrote before the war, "many cases of Punti and Hakka sharing villages."[24] This mixed settlement is often of long standing. The good relations, or at least peaceful coexistence, that seem to have characterized it, modify the uniformly hostile picture of Hakka–Punti relationships in the province that may be assumed from the literature. Kung-chuan Hsiao's statement, "the line of demarcation between the *pun-ti* (natives) and the Hakkas—the *k'e chia* (stranger-families)—that lived in some parts of Kwangtung, Kwangsi, and Kiangsi, was particularly rigid,"[25] was apparently not specially applicable here.

To conclude this outline of Hakka–Punti relationships I turn to the former's reputed subordination to the major Punti lineages of the area. Orme writes of the Hakka in particular as being "released" from the "former exactions" of many Punti villages.[26] Barnett writes that, by 1899, in some places in the New Territories the Hakka appear to have fallen into the position of "dependants, clients, tenants or serfs of the Tang clan."[27] Schofield has a note in his manuscript papers "Hakkas employed as serfs (farm slaves) by Puntis are colloquially termed *kang tsai*."

My inquiries show that while these assertions are true, Puntis as well as Hakkas found themselves in a client relationship to the big lineages.[28] Recent research in the mainland New Territories also confirms that the serf families of the major Cantonese lineages were not restricted to the Hakka population. At Ping Shan, one of the main villages of the Tang lineage, they came from minor Punti families.[29]

The same complexities attend the Hoklo group, whom my limited inquiries show to be an interesting group deserving fuller investigation.[30] Because of their main occupation, I have put them in the boat category, though I am not sure how they lived in their own districts in between their seasonal incursions into the Hong Kong region.

As Orme remarks, they appear to have settled locally in small numbers.[31] The 1911 census lists 1,444 of them as presumably permanent residents of the New Territories.[32] This is a lower figure than my inquiries lead me to expect, as Hoklos seem to have been much in evidence in the Southern District. The reason probably is that, continuing with their fishing, they have lived on or near beaches in temporary structures or on boats, thereby avoiding the census. It may be only recently that, as on Cheung Chau, they have changed to the more solid structures favored by the Punti and Hakka population.[33]

In this area they are difficult to classify, as they exhibit variations within their own group, Some have settled on land but have continued to gain their livelihood from the fisheries. Others, even before 1899, seem to have changed to or always had a type of craft more akin to that used by the Tanka, and lived upon it rather than on shore. It is also necessary to separate them into those who settled here with their families and those who came into the area, seasonally and without their family members, to fish or work. Hoklo laborers seem to have been particularly attracted to work at the lime kilns.

The Hoklos appear not to have been on good terms with the land groups. They have long had the reputation of being difficult and pugnacious.[34] However, they appear to have felt their separateness then as now, and their reported combativeness may have arisen from this sensitivity.

The Hoklos often shared the sea and anchorages with the Tanka. Their social relationship is an interesting one. It was apparently closer and more amicable than with the land people, since in addition to the floating existence of some Hoklos there has been intermarriage with Tanka traceable in some families for one hundred years.[35]

This brief review turns last to the Tanka and their relations with land people. It is important to note the great differences in the life style of local Tanka, from the small families in fishing sampans to the assemblies of forty to forty-five persons of all ages in the larger craft. The former were generally tied to local anchorages, while the latter customarily roved far and wide from a home base.[36] The traditional view is that all such persons were subject to economic and social disabilities consequent upon their way of life and were oppressed by the land population in many petty ways.[37] John Davis wrote in 1836 that the Tanka of Canton were "considered as a distinct part of the population, being under a separate regulation, and not allowed to intermarry with those on shore."[38] Judging by the entries in various official papers and my inquiries into the subject in the ports and villages of the region, this concept of the day-to-day relationships between the land and sea communities must be modified.[39]

The foregoing account implies that the Hong Kong region has long had this admixture of people—in its old established settlements, in passage and in seasonal incursions—with all the variations in speech and life style that one would expect to find in such a situation. A knowledge of these complexities is necessary background for the study of institutions and local leadership.

Rural Economy at the End of the Nineteenth Century

There are three easily accessible sources of information, all in English, about the economy of the New Territories, the major and most typical section of the Hong Kong region. These all date within a few years of 1900. The first is Stewart Lockhart's report of August 1898; the second is contained in a dispatch of 11 January 1905 from the governor of Hong Kong on the subject of alternative routes for the proposed Kowloon–Canton railway;[40] and the third is Orme's report on the New Territories for the years 1899 to 1912, dated 9 June 1912.

Put together, and augmented from other sources, they give an impressionistic, seldom quantitative account of the economy, but one suited to serve as background to a study of the people and institutions of the area and to help gauge whether it was conducive to mental energy or lassitude.

The British reports show that the region's main activities were agriculture and fishing. Rice was widely grown and the crops eaten by the grower or sent for export, Hong Kong imported rice being often consumed instead.[41] Coastal fishing by villagers and deep water fishing by the floating population was, and had long been, a major activity.[42] In consequence, salt fish was another of the principal exports. Lockhart wrote: "The trade in salt fish is one of the most important, and employs a large number of persons."[43] Arlington's description of contemporary Cheung Chau, where he was in charge of the Imperial Maritime Customs post, 1893–99, also illustrates its importance at this time.[44]

Lockhart mentioned that lime burning was "an important industry, coral and oyster shells being burnt in the place of limestone...it is understood that a great deal of the lime used in Hong Kong is imported from the San On district."[45] This was, indeed, a sizable industry, carried on in several places.[46]

Lockhart also stated that pigs and firewood were items of trade. "In almost every village is carried on the rearing of pigs, large numbers of which are exported annually." On firewood he wrote, "Pine trees are grown, and cut down for firewood, which is an important article for export." The valuable enclosures to Governor Nathan's dispatch quoted above provide supporting evidence.[47]

Sugar was widely grown. The foreman forester estimated in 1900 that there were around 7,000 acres under sugarcane in the New Territories.[48] It was, in part, exported to Hong Kong.[49]

Salt pans have long been worked in the region. Lockhart mentioned this industry briefly. Orme said rather more on the subject, and listed five places where salt pans took up 82 acres.[50]

Quarrying is another old Hong Kong activity. Charles Gutzlaff, as chinese secretary to the government of Hong Kong, styled it as long ago as 1846, "the only produce of Hong Kong for exportation"; and reported that there were seldom less than a hundred craft of seventy to one hundred tons leaving Hong

Kong each month fully laden with stone for the interior.[51] Orme mentioned it also, and stated that the two New Territories' quarries sold their stone to Canton and the West River, while the famous east Kowloon quarries, of which there were a large number, supplied most of the granite used in Hong Kong.[52]

Boat building and ancillary manufactures like rope, oar, and sail making have long been carried on in this coastal region, and were to be found in all market centers located on the sea or on navigable streams.[53]

Several species of hemp were grown in the villages of the region to produce grass cloth for local wear. The production of indigo was directly linked with it. Lockhart stated, "The indigo grown in the district is used for dyeing cloth, both men and women being engaged in the work of dyeing." Its cultivation until fifty or sixty years ago is remembered in many villages and dyeing and calendering were done in the market towns.[54]

Wild tea bushes were long tended for local use—the Clear Water Bay villagers were using tea from their own bushes as late as the 1960s—and apparently large scale cultivation was practiced on many of the mountain slopes of the New Territories. From the wide extent of the terracing work done for this purpose a commercial crop seems to have been intended, and perhaps was realized for a period.[55]

Peanuts were widely grown in the villages at the turn of the century, but by all accounts were mainly for home consumption. However, in 1905 the crop was still important enough to be listed as one of the chief agricultural products, coming after rice, sugar, and sweet potatoes.[56]

Brick and tile works are mentioned by Lockhart and Orme.[57]

There was only one pottery works in operation at the turn of the century. Located at Wun Yiu near Tai Po, it is mentioned by all three authorities.[58]

Silver and lead had been mined in the territory in the late 19th century.[59]

Miscellaneous manufactures reported at this time included bean curd which "chiefly at Tsuen Wan, dates back more than 50 years"[60] and of joss sticks. The latter was a flourishing industry at Tsuen Wan, of special interest because the pounding hammers producing the necessary incense powder were operated by water wheels.[61]

Soy manufactories and distilleries were also found in the New Territories. Orme states: "Distilleries for the making of native liquor are numerous in all parts of the New Territories. . . ."[62] The revenue from licensing these establishments soon formed a considerable part of the income of the British administration.[63]

Fruit cultivation was a cash crop in some areas. Krone mentioned that "large quantities of different fruit are grown. . . in the more mountainous parts of the interior of the district" which supplied the markets of Canton and Hong Kong. Pineapples were extensively cultivated in his time and later.[64]

Herbs and other items of Chinese medicine were another old trading commodity in steady demand, and there were herbal doctors and apothecaries in the market towns.[65]

Oysters probably have been farmed in Deep Bay for centuries, and there were extensive oyster beds at two places outside British territory.[67] The oyster beds at Deep Bay have long been a fertile source of disputes between the various individuals and villages interested in their cultivation.[68]

How much of this economic activity had been stimulated by the rise of Hong Kong? My impression is some, but perhaps not quite as much as was suggested by the glowing reports of early colonial administrators.[68] Nor, I believe, does this review support the view that the old economy had been as sluggish as Lockhart stated in his report,[69] or the place as "primitive" as one of his fellow members of the Legislative Council of Hong Kong recalled some years later.[70]

There are various indications that there was a degree of trade and exchange before 1841. Salt making and the export of granite were two well-established local industries. Lime burning may also have been a well-established activity, with an exported product. The pottery kilns at Wun Yiu had probably been in existence for several hundred years and may have been exporting their wares before 1841 as they were still doing in 1899. Another local export that had flourished up to the time of the Evacuation of the Coast 1662–69 and, on a diminished scale, lingered on until the 18th century was incense. Its production seems to have been an important economic activity, for incense was sent as far away as Soochow and Sungkiang.[71] Oyster farming and all kinds of fisheries were clearly old forms of local economic activity. Some of these products were included in the tribute items required of Kuang-chou fu in the late 18th century.[72]

The entries in the Hsin-an gazetteers of 1688 and 1819 are another indication of a considerable activity within the district, while various sources give an impression of lively internal trade and barter in the 1850s. The movement of villagers between their homes and the markets was considerable. Krone mentions, for instance, that "Shum Chun is the chief place of export from the villages occupied by the Hakkas, who are often met with in long trains of from 400 to 600, conveying produce to that place."[73] This internal trade was in goods that had a mainly local distribution, such as agricultural produce, farm implements, local cloth and items of clothing, Chinese *materia medica*, some foodstuffs, oil for lamps and cooking purposes, and livestock, especially pigs.

Another indication that internal trade flourished before the rise of Hong Kong is provided by the age of the local markets.[74] A stone tablet in the Tai Wong temple in Yuen Long Old Market states that the market was established in the early years of the K'ang Hsi reign by a member of the Tang lineage.[75] Another inscription formerly in the Man Mo temple in Tai Po records the grant of market rights there to another branch of the Tang lineage in K'ang Hsi 11th year, (1672–73).[76] Cheung Chau is described as a *hsü*, or market, in an inscription of Ch'ien Lung 50th year (1785–86) on an old incense burner at the Tin Hau temple at Pak She, and is listed as such in the Hsin-an gazetteer of 1819.[77] Other market places, old and new, can be shown to have existed in 1841 and before, though none of them were styled *hsü* and included in the gazetteer.

There were numerous shops in some of these market centers. According to a report of 1905, Yuen Long had seventy-four shops, of which twenty-five were large and dealt in rice, oil, samshu, and other products. The remainder belonged to barbers, doctors, jewellers, vegetable sellers, piece goods dealers, and so forth. Tai Po market consisted of twenty-three large shops and fifteen smaller ones.[78] Some of these local shops were flourishing and long-established concerns. Their proprietors were often outsiders who had been attracted to these places by business opportunities.

The local markets fit into the framework suggested by Skinner,[79] except for a particular variation that is examined below. This I have described as a coastal market center. In the old Southern District of the New Territories, such centers included Cheung Chau, Peng Chau, Tai O on Lantau Island and Sai Kung in the eastern New Territories. The first three were located on islands, and the last was situated on the coast. The coastal market centers characteristically served a resident and visiting boat population, as well as their own inhabitants and villagers from surrounding settlements on the mainland and islands.

The coastal market center was different in other ways from the market towns designated *hsü*. In the first place it had its daily or twice daily *chieh shih* in one or more parts of the town. (*Chieh-shih* were the street markets of the kind described by Sung Hok-p'ang as "'Kaai shi' . . . the place in a town where fish, vegetable etc. are sold every day.")[80] Secondly its shops were open every day.[81] There were no "cold" market days as reported by Skinner from Szechuan.[82] Activity continued daily at the same pace, varied only by the numbers of fishing boats in the anchorage at any one time and, of course, by bad weather and typhoons in summer. This was the situation throughout the New Territories, and it was not an innovation of the 20th century. Interviews with the oldest inhabitants of these places shows there was not, in the years before 1899, a periodical market at any of them, nor any remembrance that there had ever been.

There was another novel feature about these coastal market centers. In all such places the floating boat people did not generally come ashore to the streets where the morning and afternoon markets were in progress to buy food and vegetables, but relied mainly on marine hawkers who went among the craft moored in the anchorages in their sampans. This situation can be observed to this day at Cheung Chau, Aberdeen, and Shau Kei Wan on Hong Kong Island, where this class of hawker has long had its own associations for welfare and business protection. It was noted by observers in the 19th century also.[83]

The reasons for these divergences from the standard market

center are obvious enough. With land and sea people to supply with daily needs of all kinds, and both land and sea hawkers to assist in distribution, the shops and providers of perishable commodities in the local coastal towns had no need of periodic marketing arrangements to bring together producers and consumers. Also, the number of persons to be supplied was sufficient to warrant daily transactions in those towns and large villages where resident land and boat people were always present. Thus Professor Skinner's classification should be expanded to take into account this particular type of marketing community.[84]

The Sea Fisheries

Commissioner Lin once recorded two Kwangtung sayings. "Three parts mountain, six parts sea" and "Seven go to the fishing, three go to the plough."[85] In 1964, I called this "an exaggeration which nevertheless makes its point."[86]

In this review of the Hong Kong region in the 19th century, it is necessary to stress the importance of the sea, for coastal dwellers and for the big clans which got a sizable revenue from leasing fishing stations and beaches to villagers and boat people.[87] I have gained this impression from documents, from visual evidence along the coastline and from conversations with old residents in many places on Hong Kong Island, the islands, and parts of the mainland New Territories.

Space permits only a brief statement of the variety and extensiveness of the local fisheries. Shek O on Hong Kong Island used large seine nets, each manned by 30 village men and a large sampan. Many Lantau village families owned boats for shrimp fishing, and smaller ones for cuttlefish and pomfret. The Clear Water Bay villagers operated three separate types of craft for seasonal fishing, working in pairs or groups of four. About one-third of the families in two Tsuen Wan villages owned boats manned by three men, with others helping to crew them. A special type of fishing canoe was favored by the villagers of the Castle Peak and Deep Bay areas, and was also found at Tung Chung on Lantau. In addition, wherever the terrain made it possible, villagers operated stake nets from suitable points on the coastline, and many used throwing nets in the shallows, dug up shellfish from the foreshore, and at low tide collected anything edible. A variation on the stake net was the fishing stake set out in the sea and attached to the sea bed. No account of the local fishing would be complete without mention of a quicker technique, more harmful and wasteful for the fish and more dangerous for the user. Dynamite was used by land and sea fishermen from at least the turn of the century,[88] and I saw several limbless villagers in the Sai Kung district in the late 1950s who had been maimed in this way.

Punti and Hakka alike took a full and active part in the local fishing.[89] In some recorded cases it constituted the sole economic activity of the men, rice and vegetable farming and stock rearing being left to their womenfolk. This was a common situation in the South Lantau villages. The Shek Pik village head, born in 1899, has said that he did not know how to cultivate the fields, that this was typical of Shek Pik men and that the women did all the farming work. On one occasion when I asked the elders for a list of types of seed used in rice planting, the answer had to be secured from two old female villagers. Locally based Hoklos showed an even greater concentration of effort, amounting to a total involvement with the sea. There were large communities of these persons at Peng Chau and Cheung Chau, some of them living in boats.

All this confirms Governor Sir Henry Blake's statement, "To the produce of the land must be added the result of the fishing in which a considerable number of the inhabitants are engaged for a portion of the year,"[90] and helps to explain the large and important trade in salt fish in the region.

As a postscript, it is interesting to compare the Hong Kong situation with the contents of a report on the fisheries of Swatow, published by the inspector general of customs in 1883 in connection with Chinese exhibits sent to the International Fisheries Exhibition in London in that year.[91] There is a striking similarity between the two regions in the type and variety of fishing operations, though this is not very surprising as Swatow is only 120 miles east of Hong Kong and many of its natives have come regularly into this region for the seasonal fishing.

Itinerant Specialists and Self-Sufficiency

Another aspect of 19th century rural life and economy of the Hong Kong region evident from my many conversations with old villagers was the important part played by itinerant workmen and other specialists on the local scene. It is something of a paradox that, at a time of comparative self-sufficiency in the rural economy, outsiders should have played such a major role in village life. This was so even in main activities like farming and fishing. Despite the emphasis still placed on fishing in the economy of coastal villages at the end of the 19th century, villagers wanting a new boat had to order it from boatyards in the various fishing ports of the region, and nets, though sometimes made up at home, were generally made from material purchased in Hong Kong and other market and fishing centers. Where farming was concerned, none of the many villages where I have made inquiries had their own blacksmiths to make and repair iron farming implements such as ploughshares, harrows, hoe heads, and the like. Villagers' wants were met in the market centers or by itinerant workmen.

The practice varied from place to place. In some areas farm tools had to be purchased and repaired in the market towns and villages, whose businesses always included several blacksmiths. In villages at a greater distance from market places, specialist workmen found sufficient customers to itinerate on a more or less regular schedule, particularly in the winter months.

Besides the blacksmiths, the workmen in the building trade—known locally as *san-hang* or *ni-shui-lao*[92]—were also largely itinerant. Whole villages engaged in this work, some of them within the Hong Kong region.[93]

Weavers provided another important group of traveling specialists. As late as the early years of this century, all village families usually grew their own hemp, but they relied on outside help for weaving. The hemp thread was prepared by the village women and handed to the weavers to spin into cloth. This seems to have been an old practice, observed in the last century by one of the leading missionaries of the Basel Mission, and confirmed by my local inquiries.[94]

All the blacksmiths, builders, and weavers of whom I have heard from old villagers were said to be Hakkas. They seem to have been specialists in these trades, were usually itinerant, and often came from long distances. This is confirmed in various articles written about the Hakkas in the later 19th century.[95]

Villagers also relied on the services of two other kinds of specialist for assistance. Itinerants were frequently employed in such important matters as siting graves and burial urns, and in the education of village children. The geomancers, who gave advice on the siting of graves and on all matters of *feng-shui*, were not all local people. Graves on Lantau Island and elsewhere show this clearly. The tablets often list the name of the geomancer responsible for siting the grave and add the characters indicating his native district of Kwangtung or even of another province.[96]

The profession of teacher, like that of geomancer, was also staffed in part by persons who were prepared to travel to obtain employment. Inquiries on Lantau about the village schools at the time of the lease show that whilst many teachers were local people—either clansmen, fellow villagers or members of a neighboring settlement—there were also persons from outside the island.[97]

It is well to remember that village people were themselves accustomed to a degree of travel on account of long established lineage connections and keenly felt family obligations. Settlers in new villages and new arrivals in old villages long kept up a connection with their old homes and made regular visits, often over long distances, to their native villages in other parts of the Kwangtung province.[98]

The economic and demographic implications of the intensive village fisheries and the dependence on outsiders for specialist services of the kind mentioned above is important to an understanding of the strength of the rural economy. The fisheries undoubtedly helped to provide a part cash economy to pay for these services which, in their turn, increased the standard and sophistication of rural life. This favorable situation provided optimum conditions for the exercise of village initiatives.[99]

Village Housing, Hygiene, and Climatic Conditions

Evidence for a relatively high standard of local building is found in the countryside, in documents, and in other source material.

In the 1840s an English officer remarked on the "exceeding neat" appearance of the villages on the south side of Hong Kong Island "with blue-tiled and white-walled houses."[100] At the end of the century Stewart Lockhart wrote in his report:

> The houses in these villages are, as a rule, well and solidly built. The foundations and lower courses of their walls are, in many cases, of granite masonry, the upper courses being made of blue or sun-dried bricks. The door posts and lintels are dressed granite slabs with tiled roofs on rafters made of China fir. The floors are generally concreted, and frequently paved with red bricks or with granite.[101]

Such houses were described locally as *ch'ing-chuan shih chiao*, "blue bricks with stone footings." Nineteenth century deeds of sale and mortgage for houses and farm buildings often include descriptions of the property, and underline the findings in Buck's later survey, 1929–33, that 98% of the buildings in the localities studied in the double cropping rice region area had tiled roofs.[102]

Besides being substantially built, village dwellings, even those of modest size, often had external fittings of considerable visual appeal. Besides designs or pictures executed in stucco,[103] work of similar artistry is found on carved wooden boarding hanging under the eaves or above the entrances of old houses. Walls in small ancestral halls were often finished below the roof line in black and white scrolls, 12 or 18″ deep,[104] and such buildings, large and small alike, invariably had carved and painted main cross beams, with other simple inscriptions, tastefully executed, on wooden fittings such as the altar (*shen t'ai*).

Village houses were thus built and fitted by craftsmen with a sure sense for material and a considerable skill in its use. Although the poorer of them later drew down the criticisms of Western medical staff and field workers for their lack of light and the dampness of their rammed earth walls and floors, they had, when kept in repair, a degree of solid comfort allied to a charming appearance in keeping with their rural surroundings. They were practical, too: old villagers say that earth brick was cool in summer and warm in winter.[105]

There is, however, some contradiction between the relatively high standard of individual housing and the uncleanliness of the average rural settlement. Western observers were quick to notice their low standards of sanitation.[106] Conditions in Chinese territory apparently continued in this way right up to the Pacific War. An escaped British prisoner of war from Hong Kong who spent some time in the coastal villages just north of the Sino–British border at Sha Tau Kok in 1944 described them as being "utterly devoid of any knowledge of hygiene."[107] According to the reports of the St. John Ambulance Brigade, the situation was no better in the Hong Kong villages before the war.[108]

Other sources add to the impression of a low standard of health. Village wells were often badly sited, being "usually close to the houses or pig-sties, unlined, and receiving all the surface washings and sewage."[109] In places where water was scarce, as on the many smaller and flatter islands of the region, residents suffered the more. In the case of Cheung Chau, up to as late as 1955 there was a chronic supply situation that had to be relieved by water boats in the dry season.[110]

Besides complaints resulting from contaminated water and chronic illness due to unhygenic food storage and preparation, other debilitating disorders resulted from a lifetime's work in flooded paddy fields. In South China diseases such as malaria and hookworm were endemic and, on a diet allowing no emergency reserve, contributed with malnutrition to reduce mental and physical vigor in the villages.[111] The result of these accumulated ills, in extreme cases, matched the description of her condition once given to me by an elderly village woman, drained of vitality and humor, of being "live and not alive, dead but not dead," able to carry out farm work and household duties but only with an effort.[112]

The destructive nature of the climate in the Hong Kong region contributed to the hardships of rural life and therefore to poor health. Typhoons were a special hazard. It was with good reason that the Royal Society, when submitting a proposal to establish an observatory in Hong Kong in 1879, informed the secretary of state that the colony was "favourably situated for the study of meteorology in general and typhoons in particular."[113] Scarcely a summer passes without a hit or near miss by a typhoon, and sometimes these are attended with enormous damage and much loss of life.[114]

The boat people have always been especially vulnerable. Local tradition on the island of Peng Chau, situated off south-east Lantau, credits the disastrous typhoon of 18 September 1906 with the virtual extinction of the island's trawler fleet of Tanka fishermen, which since 1857 had been large enough to have established its own community organization, the Peng Wo Tong. The boats were mostly at sea and were lost in the storm, and the Tong ceased to exist thereafter.[115]

The land itself did not escape damage on these occasions. The Shek Pik papers contain evidence of this kind. A rent book entry of a sale of three plots of land in 1865 adds "All these fields were totally destroyed by floods in Kuang Hsü 4th and 11th years." Destruction by floods is also recorded of six out of seven plots included in another transaction, and there are other references of the kind in the rent book. These entries do not surprise me as I saw in 1957–58 how quickly the Shek Pik stream could rise in heavy rain and become a raging torrent. Calamities were not confined to floods. Droughts, also, were experienced from time to time and are mentioned in the district gazetteer.[116]

Later, the administrative reports of the early British administrators of the New Territories contain valuable entries that show the vicissitudes of farming life in the region on account of weather.[117] Such losses and disasters were among the facts of life for local people[118] and must have added to their strength of character and the force of their religious beliefs.

Village Religious Beliefs and Fengshui

The rigors of the South China climate, the poor state of health of many villagers, and their consequent acquaintance with disease and early death nourished the growth and persistence of superstition. The narrow confines of village life conserved the strength of these beliefs. In the minds of village people there was a direct and powerful connection between religion and health, expressed in visits to shrines and temples and in consultations with geomancers, fortune-tellers, and women mediums.[119]

Human activities had to be conducted in accordance with the almanac. Lucky days had to be selected for anything out of the ordinary, and advice sought from persons skilled in the practice of divination and geomancy.[120] The erection of a new house was taken especially seriously. It was not only necessary to begin any interference on an auspicious day, but also to make certain, in advance, that it would not affect the favorable balance of the elements that made up the local *fengshui*.[121]

Much has been written on the theory and practice of *fengshui*; I am here more concerned with showing how widespread and concentrated an influence and following it had in the Hong Kong countryside. A plentiful crop of *fengshui* stories, old and new, can be produced from all the areas known to me.[122] I am certain that the greater part has never been recorded, and has been lost through succeeding generations and the disappearance of clans in periods of war and depopulation by disease. However, sufficient cases remain to sustain an impression of the very great importance attached to such considerations in this region.

It is clear that *fengshui* made villagers nervous and afraid. "To we men of Tang *fengshui* is *the* important thing," declared one of the Lantau elders. Consequently, anyone who disturbed the *fengshui* of a place was immediately condemned to be a bad character. Extravagant language was, and still is, used to recount their enormities.[123]

In response to the general uneasiness that ensued, and in which they naturally shared, the village leaders took preventive action whenever necessary. At Shek Pik this took the form of erecting, long ago, inscribed stones at three places in the valley where the *fengshui* influences were held to be especially important. These stones prohibited burials, grass and tree cutting, and any interference with these places. Any infringements would come before the village elders. In another case, in the village of Lin Ma Hang, near the present border with China, an inscribed tablet, dated 1894, recounted various measures that had been taken to preserve the *fengshui* of the village—including the purchase and demolition of offending structures—and stated that should there be any willful offender all members of that village would be summoned by the beating of drums to launch an attack on him.[124] The Lin Ma Hang tablet, it is stated thereon, was prompted by the decline that had overtaken the village by depopulation and a lack of male children, where previously there had been prosperity and a large and flourishing population.

Fengshui considerations led other villages to take severer remedies as a way to end such problems: namely, removal to other locations.[125] The great disruption and considerable expense involved in moving to new sites and building new houses there proves the compelling nature of the experience that prompted them.

In the Pui O group, three of the ten villages are known to have effected these removals in the past 100 years. The process began at Lo Wai in the second half of the last century when families moved down to occupy existing farm huts on the threshing floors a hundred feet or so in front of the old walled village, and later built new houses there. The village of Shap Long moved down to the sea about 1931, and the smaller settlement of Shan Shek Wan moved back from the coast a few years later. The new dwellings were not built to the same number or standard.

Shek Pik is the classic local example of concern with bad *fengshui* because the decline in its population was more dramatic and the final removal came after a longer endurance of decline. The onset of disease and death was traced to interference with the village *fengshui* through the cutting of a rock at the anchorage near the Hung Shing temple about the mid-19th century, but the village did not remove itself until after a violent attack of disease in about 1936.[126]

Despite their isolated situation, the peasantry of Lantau were not more than usually narrow-minded in matters arising out of *fengshui* and other local superstitions, or more than ordinarily turbulent and difficult over them. For them as for most rural Chinese a "unified cosmic eco system," as da Silva styles it, was the arbiter of daily life and fortune.[127] If a part of it got out of joint and manifested itself in disease and death, it was truly a matter of the deepest concern and required putting to rights, by whatever means were available. Wells Williams was not exaggerating when he described *fengshui* as "a source of terror."[128]

Land Tenure in the Hong Kong Region

The land tenure system is vital to the emergence of leadership because, according to its nature, it provides or denies the basis for social organization, especially in an agricultural society. Rigorous or lenient by law or by practice, it helps to determine the spirit of the people. In my view, the local situation developed over many centuries in the Hong Kong region was very favorable to tenants and was directly responsible for the flourishing social organization and self-direction evident there at the close of the 19th century.

It has taken me years to unravel the realities of the local land tenure arrangements. This is somewhat paradoxical since, at first glance, the survey sheets and ownership schedules of the Block Crown Leases completed by the N.T. Land Court in 1900–1905 would appear to give a complete guide to the situation. In fact, they are a great stumbling block. The pre-1899 situation was vastly different, yet it is difficult to untangle because the land court's printed papers are insufficient for the purpose and few of its Ms papers remain. There is, moreover, a great dearth of land deeds bearing on the earlier period, because they appear to have been handed in to the land court and have subsequently disappeared.[129] However, evidence has gradually been assembled from various sources, and the major documentary discoveries of a friend, Rev. Carl T. Smith, have been very kindly put at my disposal.

The subject can best be understood if described for one place. I have chosen Lantau for an exposition of the pre-1899 situation, because I have more information on it than for other places and because my sources have historical depth.

Land Tenure on Lantau Island

Lantau had been in the possession of a single non-resident gentry family since it was granted to them in late Sung times.[130] Its family trust, styled the Li Kau Yuen Tong, had issued leases and collected rents that, by the 19th century, represented the income of three main branches of the clan. It may also have owned the adjoining island of Peng Chau; but for 200 years before 1899 this had been controlled by another gentry family.[131]

The family, and its rents, are listed in old land deeds which have been made available to me by Lantau people. By good fortune, two of its printed leases to tenants are included in these papers. Chinese printed books provide other information. There is also an 18th century commemorative tablet in the Yeung Hau Wong temple at Tung Chung on north Lantau that describes the family's relations with its tenants.

At the land settlement of the New Territories, the Li family claimed the whole of Lantau. However, this claim is not substantiated by the surviving land deeds and tax papers. These show that whilst many fields at Shek Pik and Pui O carried an obligation to pay rents to the Li family, which so far as we know was liable to pay taxes on them to the Chinese government, other fields in these areas were not held from them and their owners paid the land tax direct to the district magistrate.[132]

The surviving printed leases, one dated 1727 and the other 1806, state that the grant of the estate was made in late Sung times to Li Chung-kan, also rendered Li Man-kan, who is identified as an official named Li Mau-ying. He took his *chin-shih* degree in 1226 and was later appointed to the magistracy of P'an-yu where he was given an appanage.[133]

The two printed leases that have survived are printed from woodblocks. They are not identical in that there are extra conditions in the later text, which is more explicit and sharper in tone than the earlier one. They are each valid for ten years and are renewable on expiry. Rent is to be paid in two equal payments of silver every year, in the early and late seasons, subject to the threat of re-leasing to someone else if rent is not settled for any one year. There are prohibitions on subletting, and in both deeds there is a clause that "in accordance with the usual practice, the lessee shall be responsible to receive, to send off, and to provide meals for the rent collector sent by the Tong to his farm."

The Lis did not live on Lantau, but maintained houses at various places on the island, in which their rent collectors stayed when levying charges. These men were sometimes very unpopular: the use of charms (*fu*) to drive one of them from Lo Wai, Pui O, was still recalled in the 1960s.

The family's dealings with its tenants were not always amicable. There was at least one major dispute over rentals in the long relationship between the two parties. It is recorded on the memorial tablet referred to above. The dispute was mainly over the amount of rent that tenants in certain parts of Lantau were to pay to the Lis, but it also involved the extent of the taxable areas which determined the amount of land tax that was payable by the Li family. (I presume from the situation of the Li and Tang families that they, as general owners of a wide area, paid the land tax on fields brought under regular cultivation by themselves and their tenants, but not on undeveloped land.) This matter had been brought up by certain parties to embarrass the Tong.

Tenant farmers coming into Tung Chung after the Evacuation of the Coast 1662–69[134] took land on lease from the Li family. In time the area under cultivation grew, and with it an increased liability for land tax for the Li family. Tenants who were paying the Li rents knew that the district land registers, on which the tax assessments were based, were out of date, and "in the 41st year of K'ang Hsi (1702–1703) an inhabitant of the Hsin-an district accused the landlord of deceitfully concealing the taxable land." Thereupon, the district magistrate ordered an inspection and measurement of cultivated land to be made. The tablet does not record his decision on the area of taxable land and the amount to be paid in tax by the Lis, but states that he ruled that their tenants should continue to pay the old rent.

The tenants may be presumed to have remained dissatisfied, and after nearly fifty years the rent dispute was again brought before the district magistrate who directed (1750) that rents should remain at the old rate. The case came up again in 1768 and a new measurement was ordered, with whose results neither tenants nor landlords agreed. The case then lingered on and passed through the hands of many senior officials without being settled.[135] At last, in 1775, through the mediation of certain parties rather than by official decision, both sides agreed to a compromise. This was approved by high authority. The tablet stated, "The landlords and tenants became harmonious: the former agreed to collect, and the tenants to pay, the fixed rent. Neither increase nor reduction will be made. After putting up this tablet we will follow the judgment which will in turn be perpetuated by our descendants."

One hundred and twenty-three years later, at the time of the British takeover in 1899, the tenants of the Li family's lands were still paying their rents.[136] However, the local land deeds show that payments were not being calculated at a uniform rate and were sometimes below what had been agreed in 1775. The variations are perhaps the result of later compromises agreed to by the Li family's tax collectors.

The next move in the relationship of landlord and tenant was determined by the latter's reaction to the British takeover and the decision of the land court in the matter of registering ownership of the land. Along with other cultivators in the mainland New Territories, Li tenants at Mui Wo on Lantau told Bruce Shepherd, the deputy land officer, that "the land is and always had been theirs absolutely free from rent, and that the amount paid by them to the clans was the Government land tax which they claim to pay direct to the Hong Kong Government without the intervention of the clans. The clans and farmers agree," wrote Shepherd, "that the farmers are absolute owners of the soil in perpetuity, but have been paying money or produce to the clans for generations." But where the farmers called their payments the land tax, the clans considered them to be rent.[137] As a result of the stand taken on this occasion, the Hong Kong authorities were prompted, even pushed, towards their decision to register fields in the names of tenants. With trifling exceptions the Lis' tenant farmers and shopkeepers were everywhere registered as owners.

How could tenant strength have developed within less than a century of the Li family's uttering strong prohibitions on subletting without authority, and after it had reworded and reissued its previous form of lease to take account of this unwelcome trend? This point introduces the perpetual lease and the "one field two lord" system of tenure in operation in the Hong Kong region at the time of the lease of the New Territories, and for a still undetermined time before then.

Two-fold Division of the Soil and the Perpetual Lease

In a recent book, Evelyn Sakakida Rawski describes the "one field two (or sometimes three) lord" system of land tenure and peasant agriculture in 16th century Fukien.[138] Briefly stated, it was the division of land into top and sub soil and the existence of separate alienable rights to each. This division was also a feature of land tenure in the Hong Kong region. In its local form it was described by Stewart Lockhart as follows:

> The relation between landlord and tenant is often a complicated one, chiefly owing to the system of perpetual lease. The landlord is called the owner of the *Ti Kwat*, which may be termed the right of receiving rent. The tenant is said to possess the *Ti P'i*, or right of cultivation. Under such leases the landlords have practically renounced all rights to the exercise of ownership and are contented to do nothing further than to receive a yearly rent.[139]

Cecil Clementi refers to it in a minute of 5 August 1904 on claims in New Kowloon, but uses the term *ti min* and *ti tai*.[140] F.H. May also notes this customary system in an official paper.[141]

This situation had not arisen in the course of a day. Another official report states:

> For generations landowners have been content to collect their rents without ever having taken the trouble to enquire into the land itself, which has been left entirely under the control of the tenants. These tenants have changed from time to time; sub-leased the land; sold the right of cultivation or mortgaged that right, without consulting the landowners who were quite satisfied as long as the rent was regularly paid.[142]

Though curious, these situations were real. The Tang clan was unable to show boundaries to substantiate an otherwise valid claim to land held since Ming times on Tsing Yi Island.[143] Many landlords on the Tai Po side of the New Territories could not supply an accurate list of their tenants and often included nicknames or the name of a deceased person.[144] Another example of the ignorance of landlord and tenant alike is given in a Kowloon case where some of the land in question had been let since 1737.[145]

Against this background the Li family leases of 1727 and, particularly, of 1806 strike a discordant and unrealistic note. In their insistence that tenants should not sublease, let alone "sell," they appear to ignore the local practice of recognizing two rights to land, and tenants' freedom to deal with their portion.

The custom of perpetual lease was practiced by another large landlord family that, like the Lis, was absentee over the centuries in much of its holdings. I refer to the Tangs of Kam Tin. They were the ground landlords of Hong Kong Island before 1841 and were found to be such in many parts of the Kowloon peninsula in 1860 and 1899 when the British authorities took over those areas and settled the land registration.[146]

The Tangs' position was confused by sales of land to other parties over the centuries, by disputes on ownership between different branches of the family, and by alienations of the top soil by the original tenants and their descendants. Nonetheless, it can be shown that the Tangs were or had been the registered owners, responsible for payment of the land tax to the Chinese authorities, and that much of their land was let out on perpetual lease for centuries before 1899.

The taxlord dispute may well give the erroneous impression that perpetual leases were the attribute of wide ownership, but in fact the perpetual lease was not characteristic only of big landlords. There is evidence that petty landowners in small villages also gave perpetual leases, and had long done so.[147] The widespread application of perpetual leases is substantiated by the fact that as late as 1910 the consolidated New Territories Land Ordinance, Cap 97, provided for their continued redemption.[148]

Rawski ascribes the origin and evolution of the "one field two lord" system to the labor intensive work required to develop and farm rice fields.[149] In the Lantau situation, and in the region generally, Rawski's work helps to explain the emergence of strong tenant rights and weak landlord control which, in turn, is so relevant for any discussion of institutions and leadership. Whether under Lis, Tangs, or small landlords, the local system accustomed the peasantry to virtual independence, and provided an excellent preparation for self-management. In particular, the unilateral disposition of their fields by sale and mortgage, through the "white deeds" so common in the region, must have encouraged the growth of that independent spirit discernable at the time of the British takeover.[150]

Another feature of this system made an equal contribution to the growth of local initiative. The landlords' sole concern with the collection of their rent charges, and their apparent abstention from intervention or direction in the management of local affairs, left the peasantry and shopkeepers to their own devices, and was thus another weighty factor in the development of local self-management.

The discovery of a similar situation in Formosa shocked the Japanese administrators who settled the land question there after 1895. After describing the local system, one of them felt "justified in asserting that in Formosa the inherited rights of the landowning class have been compelled to give way before the efficiency and diligence of the tenants—a strange phenomenon indeed which we, Japanese, have never either seen or heard of before."[151]

A final factor in these developments, adding to the consequences of the perpetual lease and the vaguenesses that appear to have so often accompanied it, was the general confusion of the land situation. This is well brought out in Sir Hercules Robinson's exasperated incredulity at the failure of the Anglo-Chinese Land Commission of 1862 to give him what he wanted to settle land in newly acquired Kowloon: namely, "a Schedule of every Proprietor, Tenant and Squatter in the Peninsula, showing the extent of the holding in each case, and the value of the claim." Robinson was reduced to repeating the difficulties enumerated by his commissioners, all able, experienced men, and to regretting the "somewhat rough and ready mode of proceeding" by which he proposed to sort out the confusion.[152]

This local situation appears to fit into a general pattern whereby, as noted by Mark Elvin, by the beginning of the nineteenth century "the Chinese countryside was becoming predominently a world of smallholders, that is to say of peasant owners and of petty landlords who owned on average only a little more land than a well-off peasant."[153] The relevance of both the regional situation and the national trend for the development and practice of local leadership is obvious.[154]

Other Preparations for Self-Direction in Rural Life

No general description of the background of the peasant and shopkeeper communities and of the factors that stimulated and encouraged their emergence as self-managing bodies may be closed without some statement of the contribution of these classes to their own continuance as an organized and organizing society. It has long been customary to credit the class of scholar gentry with the major role in carrying on local government. W.W. Rostow noted this tendency and queried it in his *The Prospects for Communist China.* "It is conventional," he wrote, "to ascribe to the scholar gentry class the major role in preserving the shape of Chinese society; but the other element in the relationship, the peasant, was likewise a very powerful conservative force."[155] However, Rostow does not credit the peasantry with the activist role which I have detected among the villagers and shopkeepers in the Hong Kong region, whereby, at need, they could manage their own affairs wherever gentry were absent.

Putting aside for a moment the favorable circumstances described in the earlier sections of this chapter, what other factors may have prepared the people for this self-sufficiency in local organization? I attribute it to a variety of causes. First on the list must come continuous preoccupation with family and family organization. The Confucianization of the rural communities had been completely and thoroughly done.[156] The preoccupation with family can be shown to exist very strongly at the ordinary level among lineages who, through two to three centuries of local residence, have never had gentry members. Genealogies and family records, usually of a very modest type, are common among the small peasant lineages of the Hong Kong region.[157] Many families in the villages of the Southern District still preserve their genealogies, and many more claim to have destroyed or lost them during the Japanese occupation, or in floods, fire, or house collapses since the war. Such casualties must be commonplace over the region; but despite this, Baker has been able to collect for the British Museum family records from (at the last count) over 80 small clans, living mostly in the northern districts of the New Territories.[158]

A second major contribution to self-direction was the persistence of other institutions of rural life that provided a keen sense of continuity and initiative in the community. I have often heard from old men of the Hong Kong region how village lore was transmitted by the elders when they were boys, but it was only recently that I found a written statement from the autobiography of a Hawaiian Chinese, born in 1865, whose family home was in another part of the Pearl River Delta.[159] This man describes the village tales, poetry recitations, and guessing games of his youth and the visits from itinerant storytellers and ballad singers, and praises their part in keeping alive China's great cultural tradition.[165]

There were, too, other major influences at work in the villages, perpetuating a knowledge of the history and mythology of the country and, through them, its ethical standards and terminology, and thereby encouraging emulation and self-help. Chief among them were the stories of the puppet and man opera, transmitted in regional traditions by performers using the local dialects.[161] Such performances, especially of puppets, were a regular feature of the protective rites considered so essential by country folk and of the celebrations of the birthdays of gods in the local temples.[162] The stories were well known and greatly loved, and made a direct impact on impressionable audiences. As C.P. Fitzgerald comments, "Through this medium even the illiterate could claim their share in the heritage of the ancient Chinese civilisation."[163]

Less compelling, perhaps, but equally formative were the paintings of historical and religious scenes and themes that, together with verses, were to be found on the external walls of many houses and public buildings.[164] Together with the fine wordings on memorial and presentation boards in temples, ancestral halls, schools, and other buildings, and the felicitous sentiments written on the specially prepared red papers used at New Year and birthday and other family occasions, the village boy was surrounded with reminders of the value system.[165] This could not fail to make a deep impression on the more receptive and energetic youths, to further a sense of continuity, and to develop a sense of self-direction and personal contribution within a great tradition.

Thus powerful influences at home and from outside provided one of the bases on which peasant initiatives were founded.

2

The Community of Cheung Chau

> It is considered that it needs basket after basket of earth to form a mound, and that unity is strength. Our forefathers came and lived in Outer Cheung Chau several hundred years ago. It is indeed a paradise for the common people who have come from other parts of the state to plough its fields, fish in its waters and start their businesses.[1]

The Town

Cheung Chau is a small island situated just over five miles west-southwest of Green Island, at the western end of Hong Kong harbor. Its total area is 0.925 square miles.[2] The island is 2.25 miles long at its greatest extent, and takes the form of a three-ended dumbbell whose arms radiate about a mile from the low beach area in the center on which the town is built. The northern arm is the highest and rockiest, attaining a height of about 300 feet. The other two are flatter and more fertile and contain most of the agricultural land. Because of its small size and its low features, the island has an insufficient supply of water. This has often been a problem for local people; yet surprisingly enough has not hindered its development as a fishing port.

The island settlement has long served as a home base for a large fishing fleet. The floating population was probably greater than the total number of land people at the time the island passed under British rule, since a decade later the census of 1911 listed 4,442 persons afloat and 3,244 on land.[3] This floating population

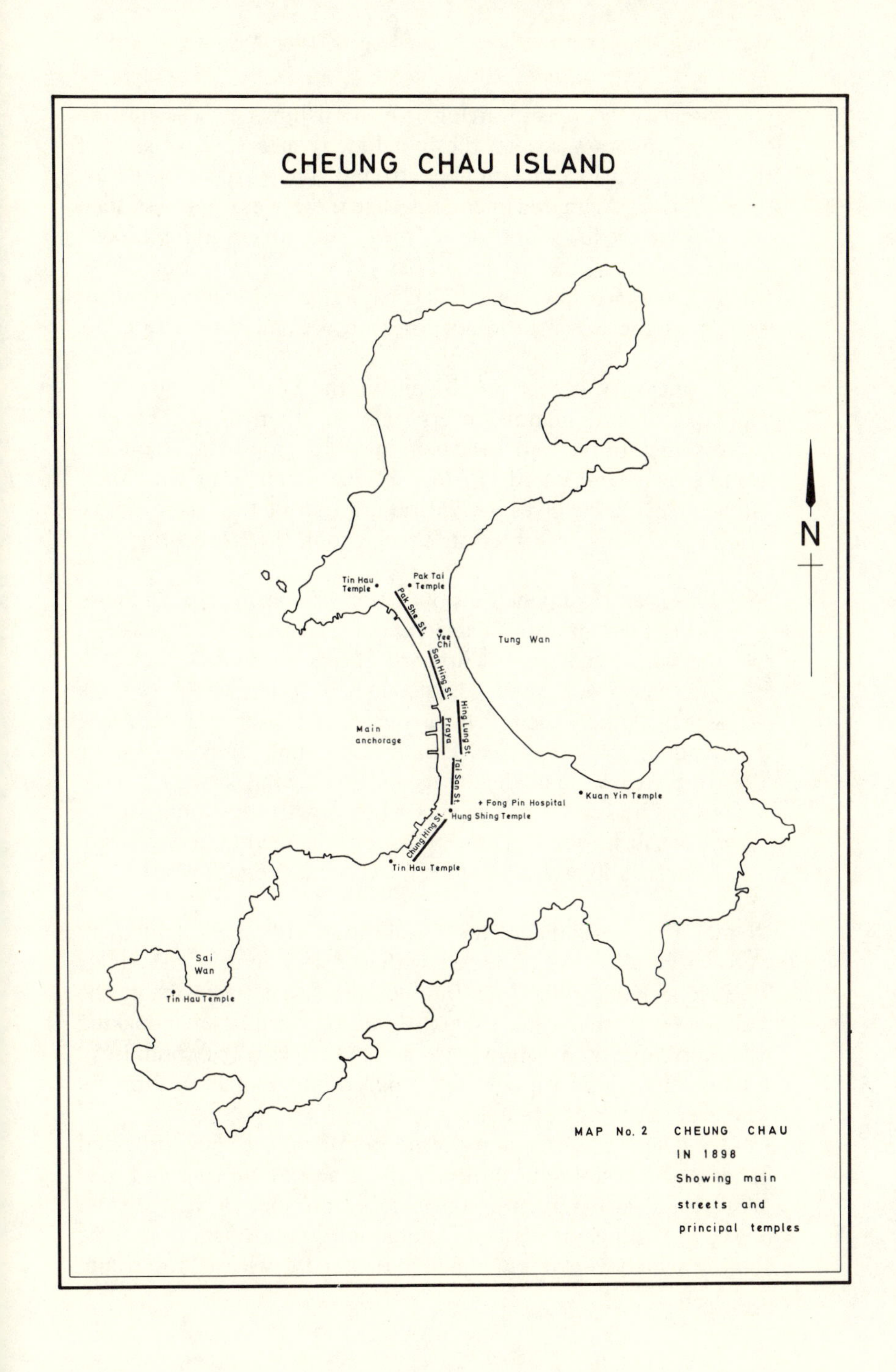

MAP No. 2 CHEUNG CHAU IN 1898 Showing main streets and principal temples

consisted largely of people living on board fishing boats. According to a contemporary report, these included "at certain seasons of the year. . . considerable numbers from distant parts of the China coast."[4] L.C. Arlington mentions that there were "no less than 900 junks in the harbour at one of the festival times" in the 1890s.[5] Even in normal times it was a busy place. A later edition of the *China Sea Pilot* states that "The bay. . . is generally so full of junks that there is little room for even a small vessel [to come in]."[6]

The majority of persons living on the island in 1899 were shopkeepers and manufacturers who together with their employees met the varied needs of the junk population and the island's own land-based Hoklo fishermen, and dealt with their catches. Arlington gives a vivid description of the island population's main business interests at the end of the last century:

> The island contained a population of some 5,000 Chinese, most of whom were engaged in manufacturing shrimp sauce, the vile stench of which nearly drove us frantic. Added to this there were hundreds of salt-fish drying establishments which spread their fish all over the island and on every available rock and tree. Hundreds of junk loads of fresh or rotten fish were landed daily, and after being sorted out were set in the sun to dry; this, combined with the odious stench of the shrimp sauce, may be better imagined than described. It was six long years before I saw the last of the place.[7]

Besides these establishments for dealing with the catch, there were various works connected with the servicing of the junks. The Hong Kong Blue Book for 1906 lists what are probably the main ones at that time: 5 boat-building yards, 3 oar-making works, 2 rope and sail works, and 3 blacksmiths' premises.[8] Finally, the island supported a small number of local farmers, who grew rice and vegetables.

The Cheung Chau shops were numerous.[9] They provided goods and marketing facilities for the island's own land and boat people, and also served a considerable number of villages and boat populations on adjacent Lantau and other offshore islands, some of which were not included in the territory leased to Britain.

Together this scattered population and the local fishing grounds provided the basis for what was, in 1899, a very flourishing coastal market center.

The land population was very mixed in 1899. No breakdown by dialect groups is available until the 1911 census, and then the figures are for the Cheung Chau census district which included neighboring Peng Chau and Nei Kwu Chau.[10] These give: Punti, 2,443; Hoklo, 957; and Hakka, 564.[11] My inquiries have shown that there were very few Hakka on Cheung Chau at that time, so that the island's population mainly comprised Punti and Hoklo speakers. The Punti element comprised sections from different counties of Kwangtung, notably from Hsin-an, Tung-kuan and Ssu-i. There were also people from the Hoklo-speaking areas of Ch'ao-chou and Hai-lu-feng in northeast Kwangtung.

The various district groups of Cantonese speakers came chiefly for business. The tablet commemorating the repair of the Pao-an Study in the T'ung Chih reign states that this was a time when "our native Tung-kuan people are flowing in for business."[12] The majority of the shopkeepers were from the Punti population. The Hoklo group were mostly occupied in fishing in local waters, with a few of their number engaged in small businesses connected with the catch.

Local Land Tenure and the Wong Wai Tsak Tong

Before 1899 the whole island of Cheung Chau belonged to the Wong Wai Tsak Tong.[13] The Tong was the organization that managed the ancestral estates and properties of a family of scholar gentry long established in the Hsin-an district, with its seat at Nam Tau, the district city.[14] The Tong originated from an eighth generation ancestor, a scholar of the *chin shih* degree. He had six sons, giving the Tong six branches, of which the first and third are today represented on Cheung Chau.

Various papers point to the Yung Cheng and early Ch'ien Lung period as the time from which the administration of the Cheung Chau properties, and responsibility for paying the land tax on them, were given to one branch of the lineage. About that time, it seems, the main lineage organization acquired, repossessed, or bought back the ownership of many fishing stations, oyster beds, hills, and beaches in the Hong Kong area, some of which were also given to this branch.[15]

Whatever the date and origin of its claim to the whole island, the Tong was firmly in control there at the time of the British occupation of the New Territories. All building and agricultural lots were leased from it,[16] and the Tong's managers also collected dues from the fishing stations and let out the local beaches to fishermen for breaming boats and drying nets.[17] The house leases applied to the land only; the superstructures were the property of their lessees.

Although some members of the lineage resided on the island, the Wongs were plainly "taxlords"—that is, rent charge owners—and as such it was likely that they would be dispossessed by the Hong Kong government. To the disappointment of the inhabitants, they were, against expectation, confirmed in their holding. This situation resulted in a petition from the Cheung Chau community in 1905 in which its leaders asked that owners be allowed to pay crown rent direct to the government.

The petition explains the relationship between the Wong family and its tenants and indicates how the Tong behaved before the lease. It includes the following statements:

> that the amounts payable to the [Hong Kong] Government are small while the amounts they [the Tong] collect are several times larger;
>
> that in cases where one's business prospers and where there is any ill feeling between any one and the Wongs, the latter always endeavour to raise the land tax...etc. that the said Tong does not concern itself with the welfare of the inhabitants and that therefore there is no reason why the inhabitants should pay tax to the Tong and submit to its interference.[18]

To confirm the first point, it was reported to the governor that the Wong Wai Tsak Tong paid crown rent of $550.65, while the petitioners stated that it collected something over $1,000 from tenants. No evidence in support of the second and third points was produced by the petitioners or provided in the official comments on the petition, but they probably give an accurate enough representation of the facts.[19]

When forwarding the petition to his superiors, a secretariat officer minuted briefly:

> This is a case in which Taxlord rights awarded by Mr. Gompertz were dealt with by recognising the taxlords as landlord.[20]

Despite the implied criticism, this decision was not reversed, and an entry in one of the early administrative reports confirms the extraordinary situation which continues to this day.[21]

Local Group Associations

The mixed island population and its nonlocal origin often led to the formation of local group associations.[22] On Cheung Chau, the Hoklo group and the several main sections of Cantonese had long been sufficient in numbers to have each established its own community organization some time before 1899.

Four organizations known as the Wai Chiu Club, the Po On Shue Shat (the present Tung Kwun Wui Sho), the Yik Shin Tong, and the Po On Wui Sho, looked after the interests of natives from different parts of Kwangtung as follows:

Wai Chiu Club	persons of Hui-chou and Ch'ao-chou origin (mostly described locally as Hoklo)
Tung Kwun Wui Sho	persons from Tung-kuan
Yik Shin Tong	persons from Ssu-i (i.e., En-ping, Hai-ping, Hsin-ning and Hsin-hui)
Po On Wui Sho	natives of Hsin-an (of which county Cheung Chau was itself a part)

The actual names by which they were listed in the ownership schedules of the Block Crown Lease as owners of premises used for community purposes are shown, with explanations, in table 1. There were probably persons from other districts resident on the island in 1899, but not in sufficient numbers to have their own associations. This development has come in the post-1945 period with the creation of district bodies to take in Ch'ao-chou (as a splinter group from the old combined Hui Ch'ao association.), Wu-i (i.e., the Ssu-i plus Hao-shan), Shun-te and Chung-shan (formerly Hsiang-shan) natives.

The older associations have a long history. The record of the Tung Kwun Wui Sho puts its establishment in 1800–1801. The Wai Chiu Club elders claim 200 years for their association, and may be right, as a private record in the possession of a long-established Hoklo family states that the Pak Tai temple was founded by Wai Chiu natives in 1783, when they were already a distinct, numerous, and flourishing group on the island. The Sei Yap Yik Shin Tong claims over 100 years, and traces its origin to the recovery of the ship wrecked body of a returned emigrant from San Francisco who had on his person a sum of money sufficient to construct premises for the new Tong. A date in the 1850s to 1860s is likely enough for the establishment of this association, as there is an inscribed stone lintel recording the repair of the Tong's building in 1897–98. Lastly, the Po On Wui Sho's claim to be of some age is substantiated by the reference in the Tung Kwun association's record to its having existed in the Ch'ing dynasty.

These four bodies are now categorized under the name of *t'ung-hsiang-hui*, or associations for persons from the same native place or district. Such organizations are common in present-day Hong Kong and Macau and in places all over the world where Chinese have settled for business.[23] Their purpose is two-fold: to provide community services not rendered by government, and to look after the interests of members within the settlement in which they exist.

In the Cheung Chau case, inquiry has shown that the four associations probably provided similar services to their fellow natives in the 19th century. However, historical evidence of these activities is largely confined to the Tung Kwun association, which is the only one to retain a written record. This was compiled by its leaders in the 1920s to take the place of earlier papers that had been lost or were no longer available. The record indicates that, at the time of the British lease, this association provided a community office, and school[24] for its members. It supplied free medicine and coffins for poor natives of the district, and had established a charity grave for paupers. There was a small building housing a memorial tablet (*shen-chu-p'ai*) repository for members. Judging from an inscribed incense burner dated Hsien Feng 9th year (1859–60), this tablet repository and worshipping hall had apparently been in existence for at least forty years before 1899. At certain times of the year, the association also carried out religious observances intended to benefit past members of the Tung Kwun community living on the island.[25]

The district associations relied upon the donations of their leading members for funds to carry out their activities; but also had a more regular income from shop premises bought by, or presented to, them. At the time of the lease, the Tung Kwun association owned five shops, office premises, and the small worshipping hall referred to above. The Chiu Chau and Wai Chau Club owned several premises. The Po On Association, though not registered as the owner of the property in 1904, is said to have always managed the premises at 99 Tai San Street which housed the Chan On She or Security Bureau that operated in the 1850s and 1860s. The Yik Shin Tong owned the premises in which its office and meeting hall were located and probably let out part of the premises for commercial and residential use, as it does today (see table 1).

Participation in the activities of these associations was extended to all persons of home district origin living on, or coming to, the island. It is unlikely that there were regular yearly subscriptions for members in the manner that has become common today. Leading members who directed association business would expect to give generously, and to be active in collecting funds from less active but prosperous merchants and shopkeepers. Ordinary members attending dinners at the main festivals observed by the associations would be expected to pay at least a minimum charge towards the cost of the entertainment and ritual services.

Members and leaders benefited according to their needs and station in the association. Ordinary members received help in time of trouble; the leaders and organizers who devoted much time, money, and effort to maintaining the work and well-being of their associations were rewarded with public acknowledgment,

TABLE 1

LOCAL GROUP ASSOCIATIONS ON CHEUNG CHAU

LOT NO.	ADDRESS	ASSOCIATION	DESIGNATION (in Wade-Giles)
229	94 San Hing Street	Chiu Chau & Wai Chau Club	kung-so
379	2B Tai San Street	"	"
421	67 Hing Lung Street	Po On Shue Shat[1]	shu-shih
482	100–102 Hing Lung Street	"	"
599	202 & 208 Tai San Back Street	"	"
502	58 Hing Lung Back Street	"	"
402	36 Praya	Yik Shin Tong[2]	t'ang
436	99 Tai San Street	Chan On She[3]	she

SOURCE: These entries are given as they appear in the BCL registers, in Cantonese romanization. The Chinese characters are given in the glossary. The variations in the English spelling, shor and sho (= *so* in Wade-Giles) are in the land records.

1. The Po On Shue Shat was renamed the Tung Kwun Wui Shor on a change of names registered at the District Office, South on 16th September, 1926.
2. The Yik Shin Tong was for Sei Yap (ssu-i) people.
3. The Chan On She or Security Bureau was managed by members of the Po On Wui Sho, the association for natives of the Hsin-an district.

NOTE: The Po On Wui Sho (Pao-an hui-so) did not own any property. Its existence is stated by all residents, and confirmed by the record of the Tung Kwun Wui Shor. This states that there was a Po On Wui Sho in the Ch'ing dynasty, that the possession of the same name by the two bodies led to confusion, and that in the 12th year of the Chinese Republic (1923–24) the Po On Study was therefore renamed the Tung Kwun Wui Shor.

enhanced status, and general respect. At times of foundation, extension, or major repair of association premises, the assistance of leaders and major subscribers was recognized by placing tablets in commemorative shrines inside the building. There were shrines in the Sei Yap Yik Sin Tong[26] and in the Tung Kwun association premises. The tablet of 1866–67 commemorating the repair of the latter's Po On Study states that "a small fixture known as the Tun Sin (promote charity) shrine has been placed at one side of the hall, where wooden tablets bearing the names of the organizers are placed therein, in commemoration of their devotion to the cause."

The Cheung Chau Kaifong

The Kaifong of Cheung Chau was the community organization responsible for island affairs. Kaifong (*Chieh-fang*) is a general term often used to describe the residents of an area as a group. It is also applied, more specifically, to their leaders who are usually the local shopkeepers. In order to differentiate between the two, I shall use "kaifong" for the first, and "Kaifong" for the second. For instance, the kaifong of Cheung Chau was the whole island community and the Kaifong were their leaders, the persons who gave public service to the community and acted in its name.

Kaifong are rather difficult to detect at work and have made little appearance in the literature. However, they are essential to the proper understanding of organization and management of the coastal market centers of the Hong Kong region. A good general description of Kaifong is given in a postwar Hong Kong government departmental report:

> "kaifong" is a Cantonese expression meaning the residents of a particular street or locality. Under one name or another kaifong have been known in South China for a very long time, and have existed in parts of Hong Kong throughout the Colony's history. At its best a kaifong was always something more that a chance collection of neighbours. It had its own spontaneous leaders who for all practical purposes were the Kaifong. These unofficial Kaifong of old had very practical social responsibilities, which included repairing bridges, mending roads, promoting educational facilities, providing free medical aid for the poor, and providing free coffins for the indigent dead. Another undertaking which fell to the Kaifong was the organization of holiday festivals on the birthday of a popular local god, and of processions to avert or diminish the effects of a disaster attributable to a god's negligence or anger.[27]

Though a late statement, this covers very well the main functions of the traditional Kaifong.

Illustrative material on 19th century Kaifong is also available from the region. On Hong Kong Island a Kaifong was early in evidence among the new population that flocked there after its occupation by the British in 1841. The committee which, up to the time of the opening of the Tung Wah hospital in 1872, managed the affairs of the local Chinese community from the

Man Mo Temple in Tai Ping Shan may be so described. This body erected its own meeting hall next to the temple in 1862.[28] In Yaumati in Old British Kowloon it was a Kaifong of local shopkeepers that erected the Tin Hau Temple and a community school there in the 1870s and provided a meeting hall in 1894.[29] There are other examples from early urban Hong Kong.[30]

However, none of these are as clearly documented as two Macau examples. A tablet inside the Fuk Tak Chi (Fu-te ts'u) or temple to the earth spirits at Ha Wan in the main harbor area, dated in 1873, records the reconstruction of the temple at that time.[31] It had been built in 1868, but had been destroyed by a typhoon in 1871. The tablet states that "we the Kaifong of the Lower Bay street" were the movers in the business, and that the temple, when first built, included "a public hall as the Kaifong's meeting place." The second example is detailed in a tablet in the Pau Kung Temple there. It relates how, when a great many people were dying of plague, the Kaifong of the Sam Pa Mun, the area near the ruins of the Saint Paul's Church,[32] arranged a procession round the town with an image of Pau Kung, a loyal minister of the Sung. Since this had an effect, the Kaifong obtained land, collected subscriptions, and built the present temple in gratitude for favors bestowed. The tablet is dated 1896.[33]

In Cheung Chau no inscriptions have survived from the 19th century that state clearly the existence, aim, or functions of the Kaifong. I have therefore to rely on indirect sources and second-hand information. From what elders have told me, there is no question that the Kaifong was in existence long before the lease of the New Territories. It appears that this body then provided the same range of services as the four district associations. It distributed relief to the poor; established a free grave or *i-chung* in 1873;[34] was interested in furthering education, especially for poor children, including those from the boat population;[35] and took part in the organization of religious and social celebrations on major festivals.

In what, then, lay the difference between the Kaifong and the local group associations? It was in the community served, which in the case of the Kaifong was the whole body of residents (the kaifong), but in the case of the district associations was only their own particular section of it. Generally speaking, the Kaifong undertook communitywide duties, of a kind and on a scale that a district association, in view of its basically sectional interest, could not expect to handle and finance. Included in such functions were duties of watch and ward. The Kaifong is said to have made the arrangements for policing the main streets by night. It was responsible for maintaining the wooden bars and gates that divided the main streets, and for ensuring that they were closed each night and opened each morning, and with subscriptions collected from shopkeepers it provided a building for the watchmen.[36] The Kaifong elders were also responsible for maintaining relations with the local officials who would, when necessary, enlist their support and cooperation. The many names of officers of the naval and military forces and the customs service that appear on the tablets and memorial boards commemorating the repair of local temples in the 19th century testify to this close connection.

The Kaifong seems to have been a very useful peg on which to hang schemes of benefit to the whole community, and to which to attach management and control in the public interest after the realization of any project. For instance, a charitable hospital and dying-house was established on the island in 1878.[37] This project is described in a commemorative tablet of 1906 which relates the origins of the scheme in the 1870s. The credit for it is given on the tablet to a local merchant, a native of Tung-kuan. He was supported in his project by the military official in charge of the Kowloon garrison at the time, who wrote a eulogy for the occasion that is included in the text of the memorial tablet. He explains how he heard about this man and his charitable projects, and decided to visit him. "I found him," he relates, "to be a merchant with an untiring devotion to philanthropic works, so I compiled a subscription book, urging contributions by officials, gentry, scholars and merchants to help make this scheme a success."[38]

This is too simplistic an account to be taken at face value. Despite individual inspiration and official support, it is hard to see how the scheme could have been realized without the foreknowledge and active assistance of the Cheung Chau Kaifong and the shopkeepers of the place. It is likely, too, that as a person interested in public service and a man of energy and ideas, the originator was himself a leading Kaifong. After its completion, management of the new hospital appears to have passed to the Kaifong. This is confirmed at the land settlement in 1904, when the premises were registered as public property and the trustees were persons who have been identified as leading Kaifongs of the time.

The same pattern of aftercare was not observed in another communitywide undertaking, the Security Bureau established in the 1850s and 1860s to protect the island from attack in troubled times, although the Kaifong's share in the enterprise is clear enough. The commemorative tablet of 1870 placed in the building, which is still standing, shows that its origin was due to united effort against a common danger. It states that four graduates, three of them named Wong, together with the proprietors of four shops, petitioned the district magistrate for permission to recruit "brave and strong village guards," *yung-chun tuan-lien*, for the defense of the island. The three Wong graduates were probably members of the Wong Wai Tsak Tong which owned the land on which the bureau was constructed. The shopkeepers were almost certainly leading members of the community, since men and funds were required from the whole island. Thus it happened that the Tong's "interest" with the *hsien* authorities as scholar gentry, its assistance as ground landlord, and the Kaifong's powerful influence over fellow shopkeepers and other residents, were combined to secure approval for the scheme and bring it to completion.[39]

Management of the bureau was not, in this case, left with the Kaifong. The Tong appears to have retained control of the land and building in its own hands, but by report allowed the premises to be let out for commercial and residential use to assist the Po On Wui Sho of Ch'ing times, in which the leading men of the Tong, as good Pao-an people, appear to have played a major role as they do to this day.

In considering the Kaifong's role in local schemes it is, I think, necessary to place more emphasis on the men than on the institution. The Cheung Chau leaders acted in a variety of roles: as leading individuals of the island; as heads of the Kaifong or of the district associations; as leaders of a temple committee or street worshipping group, and so on. Local leaders played many parts, and there seems always to have been interaction of personnel and institutions. Schofield put his finger on this when, describing the Kaifong's various activities and means of financing them in the 1920s, he drew attention to the "inextricable mixing of finances" that seemed to him to characterize its operations.[40] Men and finances went together, and since men played many parts, money matters tended to become rather involved also. After realization, communitywide schemes were managed as seemed most practical and convenient, perhaps also as dictated by local rivalries and compromises between rival factions. The Tong was a strong influence, and its relations with its tenants, the shopkeepers who collectively made up the Kaifong, were not always amicable. This might explain how an otherwise communitywide scheme like the Security Bureau was not retained under Kaifong control like the charity hospital.

Whatever the variations shifting forces imposed, the Kaifong was an important institution in the 19th century Cheung Chau.[41] It took in all the leaders from the different dialect groups who cared to act in the common weal, and it represented the sum of the whole community. That it met a vital need is proved by its continuance into the period of British rule, by the use made of it by the Japanese military authorities during the wartime occupation of Hong Kong 1941–45 (when it was restyled the Cheung Chau Residents' Association), and by its conversion to the Cheung Chau Rural Committee in 1960.[42] Through these changes of name the source of its personnel and its functions have remained the same.

Street Groupings and Religions Association

There was yet another type of community formation on the island. Besides the Kaifong and the four district organizations, the principal streets formed loose groupings for social and religious purposes. These developed into clubs and associations in the years just before and after the Japanese Occupation,[43] but in the 19th century these developments lay in the future.

There was a general connection between location and dialect. The different speech groups had been long settled in the several main streets and areas of the island. Hing Lung Street, stated to have been the most prosperous among them, was mainly populated by Cantonese shopkeepers. Chung Hing, San Hing and Tai San streets, the other main business thoroughfares, also attracted a predominently Cantonese community. By contrast, the Pak She area near the Pak Tai temple was mainly Hoklo and rural. Old people make a distinction between the main streets with their rows of shops, and Pak She where, in the early years of this century, screw pines grew along the beach and each family had its small patch to cultivate sweet potatoes and other crops.

These divisions of the island were based on ties of dialect and kinship, and were strengthened through years and even generations of residence. For instance, one of my informants described the Pak She Hoklos, of whom he was one, as "all cousins and relatives" (1885: 1965). In this kind of situation, the creation of a street and area identity was not difficult. Newcomers were more likely to be relatives from home districts in Kwangtung than complete outsiders; though I have not sufficient evidence to show whether the residents of individual streets, or sections of them, tended to be largely from either Hsin-an, Tung-kuan or Ssu-i before 1899.

Religion was another important element in the creation of street solidarity. There were (and are) major and minor shrines to the earth spirits in the several streets. These shrines were variously described to me. In Tai San Front and Back Streets the main shrine was named a She Tan Kung (*she-t'an-kung*) but it is also stated to have been a *t'u-ti-kung* or earth god. In San Hing Street, the major shrine also had these two names. In Pak She, the shrine was described as a She Tan (*she-t'an*) but residents said that it was not a *t'u-ti* in addition. These attributions are confirmed by the different dates on which the main worship of the year was carried out at the three shrines.[44]

Worship at the street shrines was undoubtedly a strong unifying factor. Besides the main worshipping dates, it was the usual practice for householders to place joss sticks at the shrines twice a month on the 1st and 15th days of the lunar calendar, and to make special offerings on family occasions and in times of trouble when particular attention was always paid to the local gods to get them to assist residents in their difficulties.

At the main worshipping ceremonies the practice and the degree of enthusiasm shown varied from one street to another. Elders say that in their youth, between fifty and sixty years ago, there was scarcely any organized worshipping of the shrines in San Hing Street, where it was casual and individual, "people being left to their own thoughts and actions." At Pak She the position was quite different. Worship was concentrated for several hours on one day, the 18th of the first month. The whole street went by families, taking adults and children, both sexes together, so that the shrine was the scene of great activity for a time. At Tai San Street the celebrations were done in even greater style, perhaps because of being in a prosperous street and in the center of the town.

Here the street activities merged with those of the community at large. Old persons recall that, throughout their lifetime, puppet shows were held every year on the earth god's festival. The arrangements were made by an informal committee of local residents. For lack of room the puppet shows were not held beside the shrine, but at an open space at the busy thoroughfare's western end. The shrine was very well patronized by worshippers, and together with the puppet shows attracted persons from all over the island. Perhaps because of this the committee was able to collect subscriptions outside its own street. As an elder said, "The organizers were Tai San Street people; the good fortune arising from these activities went to the street; but the raising of funds concerned the whole island."

Tai San Street is also noted for another religious event that takes place only once a year, for three days at the time of the Lantern Festival in the first lunar month. A structure known as Lo Tang Pang or "the Mat Shed of the Old Lamp," is put up in the street. An altar table, an incense burner, and a scroll with side couplets are brought with other items from the Hung Shing temple nearby. The scroll is dated 1859–60 and was written by an officer of the Kowloon garrison of the time.[45] These arrangements have been made every year for as long as my informants can remember. In that time, they have always been made by residents of the street, for the street.

Besides the Tai San Street puppet shows, there were other religious occasions that concerned the population of the whole island. The birthdays of the principal gods in the island's temples usually attracted larger numbers of worshippers than normal, including many persons from other places and from the boat population, and were nearly always celebrated with performances of opera or puppet shows.

Perhaps the most important of all local religious occasions, however, was the annual celebration of Ta Chiu, (*ta chiao*) or the Pacification of Departed Spirits, held each year in the fourth moon.[46] Today the Ta Chiu still plays a regular and important part in the social and religious life of Cheung Chau. It goes back beyond the memories of the oldest men (1876, 1884 and others: 1962–71), although its age and motivation are now uncertain. Some elders say it was begun to calm the spirits of those who died from plague, others that it was intended for the souls of persons who had been killed by pirates. Local history is not lacking in instances of either. Its origins are, however, less important than its continuity. Through its unfailing regularity and widespread participation, it has had a binding influence on the otherwise diverse parts of the Cheung Chau community, and together with the other festivals celebrated in street and temple it has added to the many opportunities for local leaders to emerge and practice their financial, executive, and manipulative skills.

Nowadays the Ta Chiu's main external feature is a colorful procession through the streets, in which the street organizations take part. Each provides floats on which small children dressed in striking costumes are cleverly posed with the aid of hidden steel and wire supports. There are also high "bun towers", *pau-shan*, up which the local youths climb to secure lucky "buns" for the year to come, on the conclusion of the religious rites.[47] However, "bun towers" and children on floats appear to be a late development. The oldest residents recall that in their youth, sixty and seventy years ago, the Ta Chiu was essentially a religious occasion without such trappings, although there was, as now, a procession. This was made up by bearers of portable images from all temples on the island, led through the streets by Taoist lay priests, styled *nam mo lo*.[48] It ended at a mat shed specially erected for the occasion. The images were placed in it after their return from the streets, and the priest spent long hours there chanting their responses. The population was required to eat vegetarian food for a period. All persons, male and female, could worship at the mat shed, but only men and boys took part in the procession. It was not until later that small children were paraded round the town; they were first included in the procession no more than forty to forty-five years ago, and for some time their participation was limited to sitting by twos in a wooden float or platform carried by bearers.[49]

The Cheung Chau Temples and Their Affiliations with Local Groups

In the Ta Chiu procession the persons who carried the images from the temples usually came from the communities in their vicinity, because, as in Tai O town, the Cheung Chau temples were associated with different geographical sections and groups of residents. There were four temples in the town areas of the island in 1899. Their names and locations are shown in Table 2.

TABLE 2
CHEUNG CHAU TEMPLES
(Town area)

TEMPLE	LOCATION	AFFILIATION
Pak Tai	Pak She	Pak She and the eastern section of the town: largely, but not exclusively, Wai Chiu people[1]
Tin Hau	Pak She	Boat people and shops and businesses dealing with them
Tin Hau	Chung Hing Street	Chung Hing street residents and boat people
Hung Shing	Tai San Street	Tai San Street residents and boat people

1. One old person (1878: 1971) a Punti woman from San Hing Back Street, typified their attitude when, asked where she usually went to worship, she responded "If there are any problems, I always go to consult the Pak Tai god."

NOTE: There was also a tablet repository, or Yee Chi, (i-ts'u) in San Hing Back Street in the eastern section near Pak She, patronized by the Hoklo (Wai Chiu) community.

Unlike the temples in Tai O, those on Cheung Chau possess few commemorative tablets. The Tin Hau at Pak She is the only temple having one from the 19th century,[50] though it and the Pak Tai temple also have tablets recording subscriptions for major repairs early in this century.[51] This is a pity because inscribed bells and other objects inside the present buildings show that these temples are mostly of 18th century origin;[52] and repair tablets would have had much to tell us about the temple's clientele and the Cheung Chau community of the time.

However, old people and elders have been able to supply data on affiliations at the turn of the century and before. Old residents of Tai San Street have emphasized their special connection with the Hung Shing temple. This was situated at the end of their street, in the area of the charitable or Fong Pin hospital; and they stressed that by long usage the temple managers would come from Tai San Street, and not from other parts of the island. In the same way, elderly residents of Chung Hing Street explained their connection with the Tin Hau temple there, for which they said their street had always provided the managers.

The best instance of these area and group connections is provided by the Pak Tai temple. A private record has been kept of its origins and history in one of the island's leading families.[53] Together with tablets, memorial boards, and other dated objects from the temple, it provides sufficient information to show the close connection the temple has always had with the Wai-Chiu community.

According to this record, a group of Wai Yeung merchants then trading on Cheung Chau paid a special visit to a well-known mountain in their home district in 1777. Their purpose was to request a certain god to receive a sacrifice offered by them, his subjects, so that they might benefit from his favors. They prospered thereafter, attributed this to his blessing, and decided to build a temple in his honor on Cheung Chau. The record relates that this was done with the assistance of local residents belonging to the Wai-Chiu districts, who recommended a Lam Yuk-mo to be principal director of the project. The temple was repaired in 1822, 1838, and 1858. On each occasion one of Lam's descendants was the principal director: his son in 1822, a grandson in 1838, and a great-grandson in 1858. This shows the continuity of the family's fortunes on Cheung Chau and its leadership in local affairs. The record also demonstrates the exclusive group interest of the Wai-Chiu community in the temple for nearly eighty years. In listing the subdirectors for the 1858 repair project, the record states that all these persons were natives of the Wai-chiu districts.

However, practical considerations can bend the intention to maintain solidarity. Another major repair was required in 1904, and on this occasion there were insufficient funds to raise the large sum of money required. The traders of the two districts, the record runs, had to enlist the help of the merchants of the Kuang-chou prefecture living on the island.[54] At least one meeting was called to discuss the problem of how to finance the work. It was decided that $6,000 would be raised and spent on purchasing a steam ferry to carry goods and passengers to and from Hong Kong. After the principal sum had been returned to the contributors, the income from this venture would be used to pay for temple repairs. The ferry was a much-needed and popular service. The repair was effected in this way, and the temple received an annual income from the ferry receipts thereafter.

Besides the temples located in or near the town there were three others in outlying areas: an old Tin Hau temple at Sai Wan in the northwest corner of the island, much patronized by the boat people;[55] another old temple to the Goddess of Mercy at Kwun Yam Wan on the east of the island;[56] and another small Kwun Yam (Kuan Yin) at Nam Tun in the central farming area of the island. These temples with their regular dates for worship and associated activities also provided occasions for social and ritual organization and opportunities to take on and display leadership roles.[57]

Leadership in the Cheung Chau Community

Duties

Through handling the yearly celebration of festivals, the street provided the first opportunities for community service and leadership. It also practiced street leaders in dealing with highly localized situations such as family and business disputes, minor breaches of law and order, and epidemics or natural disasters. Unfortunately for the historian, these activities were seldom recorded in permanent form. Written notice of events would be given and accounts were rendered regularly for the festival celebrations; but they would be ephemera, posted on a convenient wall for all to see and then torn down or destroyed by the weather.

At the next level, the record of the Tung Kwun association is a useful source of information on the activities of district associations on the island and the duties that fell to its leaders, and although compiled in the 1920s it is probably quite representative of the functions carried out at an earlier time. In this association the collection of subscriptions from members for various celebrations and services was a constant duty. A roast pig and other items were sacrificed to Kwan Tai (patron saint of the association: the Chinese god of war) on the 13th day of the 5th month, and at the spring and autumn grave festivals a roast pig, fruit, and cakes were taken to the association's charitable graves and to those of past benefactors. The birthday of Confucius was another occasion for collecting money for dinner and tea parties to celebrate the event.[58] In the 1920s the Double Tenth, the Kuomintang's national day, was also celebrated. Old graves had to be repaired and new ones were required from time to time. Besides securing the funds for their construction, the elders had to negotiate with the authorities and the Wong Wai Tsak Tong for the land and engage a geomancer to site them favorably.

One of the managers' duties had long been to provide for the education of members' children. The account mentions the establishment of a free school by the association in the eleventh year of the Chinese Republic (1922–23). When the school was first formed, an elder recalls, "some stubborn elements" made strong objection for they feared that, after its establishment, the association would have no money left for the spring feast and for the distribution of pork on Kwan Tai's birthday. The elders invited the British district officer to open the school. He must have been advised of the line he should take in his speech and been willing to intervene, because he reportedly told members that it was the intention of those who donated property to the association that the funds should be used to public advantage and not to provide feasts.

The record contains several references to schemes to add to, or improve, the association's property to produce more income for its various activities. It also shows that the loose organization of these associations often led them into difficulties. Here was another field to engross a manager's time and attention. One of them recalled, "In the past there were upright managers, but there were also dishonest persons who appropriated public funds without authority. When [name] was in charge of our association's funds, he reported that he had lost the account books, so that nothing could be audited. It was through my persuasion that he produced 50 dollars to end the matter." He also records how, on the death of a member who had been instrumental in purchasing new property for expanding the association, the managers asked his family for the accounts and title deeds in his possession. The relatives refused to part with them unless a payment was made first. The managers refused, which, he explained, was the reason why no title deeds or accounts were available from the early period of the association's history.

No historical account of the activities of the Cheung Chau Kaifong has come to my notice, so that it is not possible to inject the same detail and liveliness into their reconstruction as in the case of the Tung Kwun district association. Briefly restated, they were communitywide; taking in, at need, defense and security, law and order, watch and ward, educational and charitable work (especially among the destitute, sick, and dying) reception of and liaison with officials, and arrangements for performing regular and irregular protective religious rites and their accompanying entertainment.

All these duties—voluntarily performed without direct remuneration—involved the persons concerned in the expenditure of a great deal of time and money in the course of furthering the work, in making contributions towards programs and projects, and in discussions and entertainment. The effective management of the island rested largely in their hands, and the district government had to rely on them heavily for support, cooperation, and information.

Characteristics

Three important characteristics of local leadership must be noted. First, it was sectionalized in a place in which there were many, often discordant elements. The possibility of strife and noncooperation between dialect groups, was always present;[59] but a successful leader could operate across group lines and reduce the dangers inherent in the situation. Skill in talking and in handling people was developed early in a leader's career.

Second, the personnel of the various organizing groups were all local residents. Inquiries I have made into their history and background show that they were either born on the island or had had many years' residence there.

Third, the wider interests and public service of the few who were leaders contrast with the condition of the many who were led. My interviews with old persons born on Cheung Chau in the years 1875–1900 indicate that complete or near illiteracy was not uncommon among men, and almost entire among women. This low level of education, together with the narrow horizons of their employment in shops or fishing boats, helped to foster a spirit that found the street, and the collection of relatives and friends who made up their neighbors, sufficient for all needs.[60]

The Senior Leaders of 1899: Occupations and Origins

I shall now describe in detail some local leaders. Ideally, I would have wished to describe them in the period of greatest community activity, the thirty years between 1850 and 1880 which saw the establishment of the Po On Study, the Security Bureau, the Fong Pin Hospital, and major repairs to several local temples; but at the time of my inquiries these men were already beyond the memory of the oldest living residents. It has been necessary to pass on to the next generation, to the men who led the Cheung Chau community at the time the island passed under British rule.

A list of the committeemen of Cheung Chau is included in the schedule to the Local Communities Ordinance, No. 11 of 1899.[61] This provides 14 names, presumably of persons considered to be the most prominent and active local residents of the time (see table 3). No indication is given in the papers as to how their names came to be included in the list but it appears from my inquiries some seventy years later that it is accurate.

Two petitions addressed to the Hong Kong government by Cheung Chau leaders at this time were signed by a number of these men and provide contemporary evidence of their high local standing. One petition asked for former Chinese military premises to be used for school purposes, and the other complained about the Wong family and requested that house occupants on the island be allowed to pay crown rent direct to the authorities.[62] Three of the committeemen signed the first petition: seven, including the same three, forwarded the second. This probably makes them the leading committeemen among the 14. In the school petition the three signatories describe themselves as "Elders and shopkeepers in the Island of Cheung Chow, . . . residing and trading there for a great number of years." The other petition does not contain any descriptive material but, as table 3 shows, all seven—indeed all the persons listed in the gazette notification[63]—could be so described.

The seventh person to sign the petition against the Wong Wai Tsak Tong is not on the list of committeemen. He was a Lam Lai, described by elders as a Hoklo fish dealer with much property (business name Liu Shang). When I tracked him down there was some initial confusion with another man of the same name who illustrates the variety of people on the island and the opportunities that existed there for anyone of ability, regardless of origin. This second Lam Lai was of the Tanka or boat people and had been a trawler owner who became wealthy and set himself up in the fish-receiving business (Lai Hing) at Tai San Street.

Several points can be made from the table and the two petitions. First, the committeemen represented the major groups in the local community, with an emphasis on Hoklo and Tung-kuan/Pao-an people. Second, they were practically all shopkeepers,

TABLE 3

THE COMMITTEEMEN OF CHEUNG CHAU IN 1899

NAME	ORIGIN	STREET	OCCUPATION	REMARKS	BUSINESS NAME (where known)
Lo Tsun-pong[1,2]	Hoklo	Pak She	Scaffolder	...	Tung Yee[3]
Man Tat-fu	...	Chung Hing	Fish dealer	Brother of No. 10	
Chu Man-in[2]	Hoklo	San Hing	Fish dealer	...	Kin Shun[3]
Fung Shun[1,2]	Hoklo	San Hing	Fish dealer	Opened other shops	...
Chong Tat-ming	San On	Chung Hing	Boat builder	...	Kwong Tung Fat[3]
Fong Hip-ts'un[1]	Hakka (Wai Chau)	...	Tea house owner	...	...
Ts'o Ts'ing	Tung Kwun	Tai San	Miscellaneous trader and distiller	Large business	Tui Hing[3]
Ts'oi Kai	Tung Kwun	Tai San	Miscellaneous trader and pig slaughterer	Large business	Chung Shun[3]
Lo U-t'ong[2] (?)	Nam Hoi	Tai San	Silk and cloth store proprieter	Opened a wine shop in San Hing Back Street	Kwong Lung Shing[3]
Man Tat-ming	...	Chung Hing	Fish dealer	Brother of No. 2	
Kwan Pak-yau[2]	Hoklo	Pak She	Fisherman	Well-to-do	...
Hung Muk-kwai	Hoklo	San Hing	Fish dealer	...	Hap Tsan[3]
Kwan Lun-hing	...	...	...	...	...
Lam Tai	...	...	Held a regulating post under the Kaifong for over 20 years[4]	...	...

1. Petitioners in the school application.
2. Petitioners in the complaint about the payment of ground rent to the Wong Wai-tsak Tong.
3. Listed among the 39 shops that presented an inscribed board to the Fong Pin Hospital in 1915 (4th year of the Chinese Republic).
4. Lam Tai's name appears as a guarantor in a lease given by the Wong Wai-tsak Tong in January 1904. The lease is printed by wood block with personal details inked in as required. The guarantor was a requirement in each lease and Lam Tai may have done a lot of this work.

NOTE: The romanization of the names is taken from the entry in the HKGG (which also gives the Chinese characters), but the diacritical marks have been removed. I have assumed that Lo U-t'ong above is the same as the Lo Lai Tong of the second petition.

some of them with comparatively large businesses. Third, at least some of these men—and probably more than my sources of information allow—were also involved in district association activity.[64] Fourth, it is interesting that not one of them was from the Wong Wai Tsak Tong, despite its importance as ground landlord with prosperous families resident on the island.[65] Finally, indicative of where the real source of local authority lay in 1899–1905 and earlier, is the fact that 6 of the 7 persons whose names appear in the two petitions were Wai-chiu people; and that 5 of those 6 were Hoklos.

Recruitment

How did such men come to head affairs? Generally speaking, recruitment to leadership positions was by cooption, and one post or duty well-performed led to another. At street level, where there was no formal organization, the leaders emerged because they were able and willing, and known and accepted in a rather narrow community. They acted on their own initiative or had been asked to help by the previous organizers. In the district associations where the leadership was a more formal body than a handful of neighbors, the process of replacement or addition was more deliberate. The management "committees" of the district associations were self-perpetuating. Their leading members sought out new men when one of their number died, became ill, or made himself unpopular. The nomination would be discussed with other leaders, and if acceptable to them would be put forward at the annual gathering of members at the spring dinner held on the Feast of Lanterns on or about the 15th day of the first month. This was the traditional time for settling the year's accounts and confirming the leadership. Unless a power struggle had developed among the heads of the association, it would be unusual for a new name canvassed in advance to be unacceptable.

The Kaifong leadership was managed in much the same way. Here it was apparently usual in the last century for one man to take the chief position and to perform routine duties with the aid of friends and associates selected from among the body of recognized elders. New men would be added to their number at need, in the same manner as for the district associations.

However, it is important to note that though the various levels of public activity were distinct enough and constituted a hierarchical sequence that led from street to Kaifong, the several leadership roles were interchangeable and often performed simultaneously. There was no progression through the hierarchy from street through district to Kaifong, dropping off duties at a lower level in order to assume others at a higher one. A successful leader would find himself discharging duties intermittently, or even simultaneously, at all levels. Advancing years or the pressure of his own business and public duties at the senior level might make delegation or substitution necessary at some stage, in which case the work might be done by assistants or satellites, but in the name of the leader.[66]

In one important area of activity there was an apparent departure from the process whereby from a sea of conflicting pressures, obligations, and miscellaneous considerations, a man emerged as head Kaifong. This was in the selection of religious leaders for a regular festival.[67] As for the head Kaifong position, the choice was made from within the body of recognized leaders; but there the similarity ends. The committeemen would assemble in a chosen temple. They each cast the dividing blocks (*kau pui*)[68] an agreed number of times. The man obtaining the highest number of *sheng*, or favorable responses to his throws, became the director of the subcommittee arranging the festival for that year. Therefore, it was always said that the gods had made their choice of leader. However, it was one made from within a narrow and predetermined group which might not always be the whole body of the Kaifong. Service was voluntary and the number of persons who sought selection by the gods could be drastically reduced if, as sometimes happened, it was considered that the year's prospects were bad and that the performances would be a losing business proposition.[69]

According to elders, a change in the direction of Kaifong affairs occurred about the turn of the century when it was decided that there should be four head Kaifongs instead of one, with each of them doing duty for three months. The situation is not at all clear after this lapse of time, and no written material has become available as yet. However, it seems quite likely that this decentralization of power may have been connected with the complicated negotiations entered into by the whole body of Cheung Chau leaders when the Wai-chiu group sought (or perhaps was obliged to accept) the help of merchants of the Kuang-chou prefecture in repairing the Pak Tai temple in 1904, and that it was symptomatic of the shifts and changes taking place.

I have already noted that 6 out of the 7 leaders who petitioned the Hong Kong government against the Wong Wai Tsak Tong were Wai-chiu people, and it may be that, up till then, as the oldest and largest single group of local residents, they had supplied the leadership of the Kaifong or monopolized control of its affairs. The influx of Cantonese, which by the 1911 census had resulted in their out numbering the Wai-chiu settlers by at least two to one, is the most likely explanation for a requested sharing of power, if such there was at that time.

It is interesting that the Kaifong's growing importance in the community of Cheung Chau, with this shift in its leadership to take in all major speech groups, coincided with the developments noted by Skinner in early 20th century Thailand when such bodies as a Chinese charitable hospital and a Chinese chamber of commerce emerged as "horizontal inter speech group organisations." It is clear that the Cheung Chau Kaifong performed an important unifying role in Cheung Chau in both the 19th and 20th centuries, even when, as in Thailand, the "speech group associations" had been separate and often hostile in the 19th century.[70]

In conclusion, Cheung Chau's capacity to produce good leaders seems always to have impressed outsiders. The praise given by the military officer who supported the Fong Pin scheme in 1877–78 was echoed a generation later by the British district administration which, under changing officers, seems always to have had a lively appreciation of local effort and ability. The reports for 1910–14, for instance, give plentiful evidence of both,[71] and in the years 1919–21 another district officer was even more appreciative than his predecessors. In 1919 he mentioned that "the same excellent public spirit continues to be shown by the Kai Fong ...the town accordingly prospers." In the following year he wrote "I have again to congratulate the Kai Fong on their excellent work in the island's interest." In 1921 he records that the Kaifong "devote much time to education" and had opened a new

Chinese free school during the year. He also expressed his regret in these years at the death of two leading Kaifongs.[72]

Cheung Chau thus presents an example of a small community serving as a market town, manufactory, and home base for a fishing fleet which, in the 19th century and since, has been able to organize itself to meet its own needs, both within the several geographical parts and dialect/district groupings of the settlement, and as a whole. The remarkable degree of success that has attended its efforts has been due to the large number of spirited shopkeepers from the different groups who, in the process of serving their community in a variety of posts and institutions, have built up considerable expertise and have maintained a tradition of public service and self-help over more than a hundred years.

3

THE COMMUNITY OF TAI O

The Town

IN COMPARISON with Cheung Chau, the coastal market center of Tai O on the adjacent island of Lantau was less bustling.[1] Though possessing—for the Hong Kong region—large boat and land populations, it seems to have been at this time in a period of decline, and in consequence attracted criticism from the British district officers who lauded Cheung Chau so frequently. "There is very little public spirit in the place," wrote one of them in 1915.[2] It is clear that Tai O has long suffered from comparison with Cheung Chau, and rather unfairly as their situations were different.

At the end of the nineteenth century the Tai O community consisted of the residents of the two main streets and a boat population. This included those living on junks and other boat people who lived in several hundred wooden huts built on piles in Tai O Creek. The total population recorded at the 1911 Hong Kong census was 2,248 land residents, and something less than the 5,413 floating population given as the figure for the whole of Lantau.[3]

According to old residents, the land population was mainly Cantonese, from the Hsin-an and Tung-kuan districts. It also included a number of persons from northeast Kwangtung employed on the salt pans. The junk families and the people living in the pile huts were Tanka, the boat people of South China. There were, in addition, several hundred villagers, mostly Hakkas, from the four small farming hamlets of Leung Uk, San Tsuen, Wang Hang, and Nam Chung, located on the perimeter of the salt fields where the foothills begin.[4]

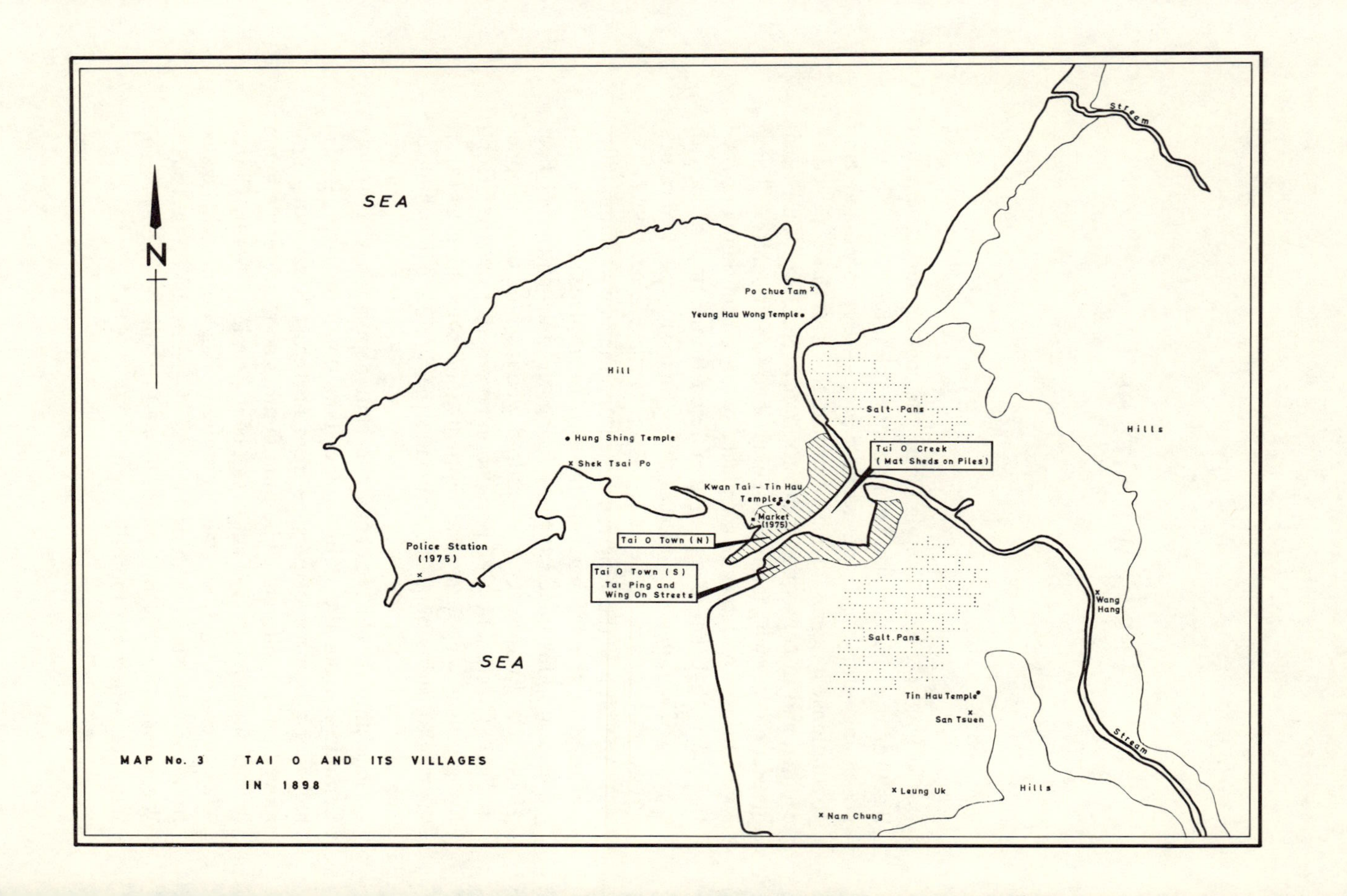

MAP No. 3 TAI O AND ITS VILLAGES IN 1898

Tai O town was not a compact settlement (see map 3). It straggled along a path that in some places became a street, and it was divided into two unequal parts by Tai O Creek. North of the creek, on what amounted to an island, lay the upper portion of the town. Here were located one or two lesser streets with shops and houses, a military yamen for the Tai O guard station and visiting war junks, three of the town's four main temples, and the hamlet of Shek Tsai Po. South of the creek, abutting on the salt pans on the one side and on the inner anchorage on the other, were Tai O's two main streets, Tai Ping and Wing On Streets, the one leading into the other. (Until some ten to fifteen years ago, the main streets were paved with irregularly shaped granite blocks which were not all securely embedded, and in wet weather an unwary person could step on one end and receive a rich shower of mud in the eye.) At the southern end was the hutted settlement of Sha Tin beside the pans, where many of the salt workers lived. The inner creek was a wide shallow expanse of sheltered water that was only a few feet deep at low tide. In it, as a British official wrote in 1904, "Two streets of Quondam boats converted into house boats and standing on piles" took up much of the space.[5]

The houses in the main streets, many of which are still standing today, were built of blue, kiln-made bricks with tiled roofs and painted beam ends, often carved at the ends to resemble dragons, projecting over the frontages of the shops.[6] These houses were doubly owned. The Li Kau Yuen Tong of Sha Wan and other places outside the Hsin-an district was the ground landlord, and the structures erected on the land were the property of the persons who had built them, of their descendents, or of the people to whom they had been sold or mortgaged. Old persons recall (1880: 1962–63; and 1883: 1971) that a man made a "house-to-house land tax collection" on behalf of the Tong, and one of them was able to point out a shop in which he had worked as a boy as one where the collector had stayed. (The land registers show that the Tong owned several house lots in Tai Ping Street; that is, both the buildings and the plots of land on which they stood.) The payments he received were not, in fact, the land tax, but rent owing to the Tong.[7]

Half on land, half on sea, the pile huts in the creek were probably there long before the British took over the New Territories. One of the early administrative reports of the district officer south mentions taking over responsibility from the harbor office for issuing licenses to pile hut dwellers at Tai O Creek when 221 new mat shed permits were issued, at $1 per annum; and a few years after, in 1916, it was stated that there were "still as many as 350" mat sheds there.[8] Besides these sheds, other boat people used old boats drawn up on land and propped up on stones just above high water mark as dwelling places.[9]

Fire was always a hazard to the mat sheds, which were generally made of wood and palm leaves. A fire was noted in the 1916 report and it is no surprise to read of a really big one in 1926 which destroyed 300 mat sheds, though without loss of life since it was high tide. Typhoons, too, were a constant menace to these frail structures, and in 1927, the year after the big fire, the district officer noted that a typhoon had caused great damage to the mat sheds.[10]

The basis of Tai O's prosperity at the end of the 19th century was its fisheries. In addition to local vessels, many others came in for shelter, breaming and repairs, supplies and provisions, and the disposal of their catch. The administrative reports for the early years of British rule show very clearly this dependence on the fisheries. They provide details that emphasize its importance to the town and mark the fluctuations in the yearly catch over a period of years. A fish called the *wong fa* or yellow croaker was of special significance. Orme writes:

> Wong Fa are caught in large quantities during November and December at the mouth of the Canton River near Tai O: they come in with the tide in immense shoals and all the craft from the neighbourhood sally out to catch them.[11]

The catches of this fish alone were sufficient to decide local opinion on whether it had been a good or bad year. The reports reflect this situation, and speak of the success or failure of the *wong fa* season as though it were the whole local fishery. "*Wong fa*...so important to Tai O" (1911), "a record catch of *wong fa* at Tai O —$30,000 worth in 5 days" (1915), and in the 1920s, "business generally was good, the *wong fa* fishing was poor but prices were high," and "a record catch of 600 piculs of *wong fa* was recorded on 20th October" (1926 and 1927).[12]

Even when *wong fa* are not mentioned, the reports are worded to show, above all else, the importance of the fisheries to the town. The 1918 report speaks of bad business, "the worst for twenty years," followed two years later by "at last...a good fishing season" (1920), "an even better fishing season" (1921), "business extremely good...the fishing season was also good" (1922).[13] Two years later it was a different story: "an extremely poor fishing season...Tai O had a bad year," said the 1924 report. "It depends almost entirely on fishing and a severe depression in other industries led to bad business among the shopkeepers and a reduced output of salt."

These reports were compiled by many hands. They describe a situation that must have been no different under Chinese rule, and are therefore invaluable for the insight they give into local conditions at an earlier time.

The fishing industry of Tai O provided a livelihood for a variety of shopkeepers and proprietors of businesses serving the fishermen. Besides shopkeepers selling groceries and miscellaneous goods, there were many others supplying specialized needs, from ship's stores and salt to the manufacture and repair of craft, nets, and gear. The Hong Kong Blue Book for 1906, which probably lists only the larger establishments and not individual workers or small operators, gives 12 boat building yards, 3 rope and sail works, 4 ironworkers, and one oar-making works, besides 4 manufacturers of gold and silver ware, always popular with the floating population.[14]

The second Tai O staple was the manufacture of salt. The proximity of the salt pans was probably one of the circumstances that drew a fishing fleet to the place. At that time, salt was of great importance to the fishing industry, afloat and ashore. It was used by the fishing junks to keep the catch in brine while at sea; and it was used at the various fishing stations like Cheung Chau and Tai O, where fish was dried in large quantities.[15] Orme writes that "the large bulk of the fish trade is in salt-fish, which is exported from Hong Kong in all directions."[16] The demand was great, because salt fish had long been one of the main items in the Chinese diet.[17]

I have not yet found any Chinese record of salt production at Tai O in the late 19th century. However, once again the Hong Kong administrative reports provide figures, with comments, for the years 1910 to 1939.[18] These show the fluctuations in this local industry, whose beginnings can be traced back to the Sung dynasty.[19] Annual production was 30,000 piculs in 1917, dropped to 10,000 in 1929, and to 7,000 in 1931. It rose to 25,000 piculs in 1938. Among the reasons given for the years of decline were: flooding of the pans due to the heavy rain that fell in the summer of 1931; a decrease in the demand in 1928–29 due to famine conditions caused by drought in parts of China; and the cheapness of salt in some years. Good market prices were attributed to economic factors. It is clear from these figures that the manufacture of salt was something of a gamble, subject to many variables.[20]

The fluctuations reported in the local fisheries and in salt production, plus the side effects these had on other trades and businesses in the town led to a mobility that was lacking in the villages. Besides those persons who settled there in different generations, the town's population included many others who came in search of work and left after a few years' residence. Also, Tai O's residents seem to have come largely from outside Tai O rather than from the villages of Lantau.

Many of the town's merchants reportedly came from Nam Tau, the district city of Hsin-an, which was not far from Tai O by sea. The salt pans have always attracted outside capital, and the man who held the pans at the time of the British lease was a wealthy Nam Tau resident.[21] The persons who ran a fisheries business at the pier at Yee O in Tai O Bay also came from there[22] The man who held a British lease for the main breaming beach and foreshore at Tai O was also from Nam Tau.[23] Besides these individual cases, the Block Crown Lease shows that a number of property owners listed in the Tai O schedules gave Nam Tau as their address.

The salt pans in particular helped to bring in outsiders. In Ch'ing times, these included merchants and officials as well as workmen, persons whose names appear on the repair tablet of 1839 in the Tin Hau temple close to the production area.

A change to the Swabue or solar method of salt production

appears to have been made about the turn of the century. This replaced the leaching process which, Lin tells us, was carried out mainly by natives of Lantau Island and was the only method inherited from their remote ancestors.[24] It brought Hoklo salt workers to Tai O, mainly from Po Mei Heung, about three hours' walk from Swabue. One of my informants (1893: 1962) had been a salt worker all his life, as had his father before him, and had joined him at the Tai O pans about 1909. The whole village of Po Mei Heung was said to have been employed for generations in salt production, which would explain why the Tai O salt merchants thought of employing persons from that area.[25]

The Tai O community comprised three other groups that helped form its life and character. These were officials and soldiers, farmers from the surrounding villages who used the town as their market center, and a small religious community in the hills southeast of Tai O.

Tai O had long been a naval and military center. There was a guard station there in 1899, with a yamen that was used as an office by a member of the New Territories Land Court when he went to Tai O to settle titles to private lots in the district.[26] Traces of the curtain wall of the sentry posts, situated behind the Hau Wong temple at Po Chu Tam at the eastern entrance to Tai O Creek were still visible in the 1920s.[27] These posts had existed before 1817 when, according to the Kwangtung gazetteer, additional garrison posts were established at Tai O Hau. Besides the defences at Tai O, there were in 1899 forts at Tung Chung and Fan Lau, the latter long disused.[28] There seems to have been a good deal of local military and naval activity in the 1850s, probably because of the recent establishment of Hong Kong, increased trade and piracy, and poor relations with the British and other foreigners. The first twenty names on the tablet commemorating the repair of the Kwan Tai temple at Tai O in 1852 are those of naval and military officers, with their ranks stated. The command included war junks as well as garrison soldiers.[29]

There was no civil officer stationed at Tai O. It came under the jurisdiction of the subdistrict deputy magistrate who looked after the affairs of Lantau and other places from his yamen in the Kowloon walled city.[30] However, officers of the salt administration were long stationed at Tai O, or made visits there to superintend the production of salt at the pans. The bell at the Tin Hau temple, which is dated 1713, was the gift of persons from Chekiang and elsewhere who were probably serving there in an official capacity, and a repair tablet of 1839 mentions that the terrace beside the temple was built in the Ch'ien Lung period, and was known as the work of a salt official.[31]

The townsfolk included many shopkeepers. Tai O town had been a market for the local villages for a long time, at the least for the three hundred years and more since the arrival in the 16th and 17th centuries of the first ancestors of the oldest clans now settled in the area. However, it did not serve the whole island whose poor internal communications by land and whose long coastline led villages in the eastern and southern parts to use Peng Chau and Cheung Chau which could be reached quite easily by sampan and were much nearer than Tai O. The town was thus the favored market center for only the villages of its northern and western sections.

The Tai O shops provided essential items of domestic economy, and in return the town served as a mart for the villagers' livestock, farm produce, grass, and firewood. As mentioned above, fish was an important item of village production. Many of the Lantau villagers fished from sampans and owned stake nets for offshore fishing.[32] They took their catch to shops in Tai O, or sold direct to fish collecting boats sent by fish dealers from these and other places. But despite its numerous enterprises, many shops, and the volume of business transacted, Tai O was not classified as a market (*hsü*) and had no periodic market schedule within the lifetime or memory of its oldest inhabitants. With its shops and businesses open daily, the town was one of the "coastal market centers" described in chapter one.

The Tai O scene was further diversified by the presence of a small number of Taoist monks and nuns who came from at least two religious houses established in the local hills in the early 1880s. The inscribed lintel above one of the buildings shows that the founder was supported by high officials, a viceroy of Fukien–Chekiang and a literary chancellor of Hupeh, which was probably the reason for the issue of a proclamation by the district magistrate and the commander of the Tai Pang battalion when the houses were first established in 1883. This warned vagrants, soldiers, and villagers grazing cattle to keep away from the area. The text was inscribed on a stone tablet set up inside the place.

Since Tai O was composed of such a mixed population, and since a good catch or a local festival provided incitements to disorder, it is not surprising that the gentlemen of the London Missionary Society took a poor view of the place when they began to pay attention to its spiritual condition shortly after the lease. They found the villagers "poor and uneducated,"[33] and described Tai O itself as "a very needy station, the moral tone of the people is very low, perhaps it is the worst place in the New Territory in regard to the morality of the people."[34] Two years later, the annual report opened: "The town and fishing population of Tai O constitute one of the graver problems that confront the Evangelical Society. The place is a strong-hold of idolatry and is the haunt of the gay and vicious."[35]

The Community

In 1899, Tai O had two bodies that appear to have filled the role of the district associations on Cheung Chau. Like them, they comprised persons from the same districts of Kwangtung, provided premises for meetings, social gatherings, and teaching purposes, and performed sacrifices at certain festivals.

One, known as the Po On Study (Pao-an Shu-shih), is said to have been built, owned, and operated by natives of Tung-kuan district. (The association of Tung-kuan persons on Cheung Chau also gave this name to their body.) A site with the remains of a building may still be seen.[36] The institution probably dates to before 1850, and is perhaps much earlier. According to information provided by the oldest residents, an earlier building had fallen into complete disrepair about 1885. This study is reported to have had two stories, in each of which teachers of Tung-kuan origin taught classes. It was not rebuilt by the Tung-kuan community until twenty years later, when it was again used as a school and meeting place until its final delapidation about 1920.

The other institution, known as the Hip Wo She Hok (Hsieh-ho She-hsüeh), is reported to have been run by a group of persons of Hsin-an origin in 1899.[37] As on Cheung Chau, it was the shopkeepers who were in a position to support and finance these associations. The shops whose proprietors were reported to have played a leading part in the She Hok's affairs at that time included a general grocery, a rope store, two fish dealers, a bambooware shop, and a medicine shop, besides others, illustrating the variety of business undertakings carried on by Hsin-an people at Tai O. Chan Kwong-yue, in whose name the trust was registered in 1905, is said to have been a native of Nam Tau, and the originator of the Hip Wo She Hok. He was probably a Tai O merchant or an outsider with close dealings with the place, but is said to have been long dead by 1899, without living descendents, and his dates of birth and death are not now known.

The Hip Wo She Hok, it is reported, also served as a school in 1899. Though it still stands today, its premises were leased to a salt producing company about 1920 and have not been used for community purposes since then. However, the Lui family, who managed the property for many years, are reported to have applied the rents to the annual worship of Kwan Tai and the Lady Kam Fa on their festival days, and to have arranged for the distribution of pork to subscribing fellow natives on those occasions. This is the sum of local information on this subject.[38]

Besides these two associations, the land registers show that there were five bodies described as *she* in 1905. Each owned one shop, except where more are shown in brackets in table 4. The houses which they owned were all located in Tai Ping or Wing On Streets.[39]

TABLE 4

SHE AT TAI O

NAME OF SHE	ADDRESS	LOT NOS.
Kwong On She	Tai Ping Street	133
Sun Yik She (2)	" "	134–35
Wing Fuk She (2)	" "	210–11
Fuk Luk She	" "	263
Sik Tsz She	Wing On Street	275

As in the case of the Po On Study and the Hip Wo She Hok, there has been difficulty in getting exact information about these bodies,[40] though it is fairly clear that they were important to the life of the place in 1899 and before. From what old persons can remember, they performed religious and social functions within the streets in which their property was situated. The religious function is prominent, as they appear to have been connected with various small shrines to the earth gods situated in the main streets. The shops they owned had presumably been subscribed for at an earlier time, and the rents were probably applied to religious purposes, including opera and puppet shows, and to support various welfare activities.

One old resident (1883: 1963) recalled that they numbered thirty to forty persons each, from what he called "lower class people," and carried on such traditional activities as Chinese boxing, lion dancing and religious observances. He thought that their membership was probably cross-dialect and not separatist, their purpose being a social and religious one. However, he had not been a member and I have not been able to find anyone who was, or would admit to it.

The recollections of another informant (1963), who was born in a large village near Hai-p'ing, Kwangtung, in 1877, may give a clue to their motivation and activities in 19th century Tai O. He recalls numerous small *she* within each of the several divisions or *pao* of his village. The *she* were linked to a number of families in each geographical subunit of the several *pao*, and elected a manager every year. Their activities were largely religious. Their main function in his youth was the organization of ceremonies at the lunar new year when pork, provided from the fields owned by each *she*, was distributed among male members, a ceremony which, he said, was quite distinct from the distribution of pork in the subbranch of his clan at the same time of the year.

C.K. Yang provides useful comparative material on this subject. He links the gods of earth and grain within the *she*. He cites the *she* of Fo Shan, Kwangtung, which he styles "neighbourhood units." Their organization was based on the common worship of these two gods by the inhabitants, and they served, in addition, for the wider social purposes I have presumed for Tai O.[41]

One of my informants (1892; 1963–71) has recalled details of a religious practice at street level that is of great interest, and may descend from the *she*. When he lived in Wing On Street with a relative who operated a shop there in 1915–18, a wooden board bearing the characters *feng-hsiang-shen*, meaning offerings of incense to a deity, was passed daily from house to house. The circulation was continuous, and proceeded diagonally to each house and shop in turn, from one end of the street to the other. Wing On Street merged into Tai Ping Street, the other main thoroughfare of the town, and in 1915–18 the board circulated in both. The board was kept moving at all times, even during the lunar new year and the earth god's festival.

The origins of this practice are unknown, but other old residents consider it as predating the lease of the New Torritories. It may be, in earlier times, that the *she* were each responsible for carrying out the practice in their own sections of these streets, and that after their decline it was reduced to one board circulating in both streets, without being tied to any one altar. The practice of circulating such boards is reported from other places in the region.[42]

The Tai O land registers contain another *she*; the "Association to Respect Characters." Old persons say that the rents from the property registered in its name were used to pay a man who went round the town, collecting and burning all discarded paper with characters written on it. This was out of respect for the written word, which should not be trampled underfoot. The organizer is reported to have been a man from Tai Ping Street. Schofield recalls that the practice was still being continued in the 1920s.[43] It is recorded from other parts of China.[44]

As on Cheung Chau, perhaps the most important institution at Tai O at this time was the Kaifong. It directed public business and, as usual, was composed of the leading shopkeepers. Schofield recalls, with reference to the 1920s, that the Kaifong ran a sampan ferry across the creek—it still does—a stone pier at Shek Tsai Po, and an electric light plant. When he visited Tai O, the committee or its chairman would come to the police station to see him about all kinds of public business "with requests or complaints, or because I sent for them to enquire into some local problem."[45] The Kaifong was of great assistance to the district officer and to the Chinese district authorities before him. As in the Cheung Chau cases cited in the last chapter, the connection was important enough for the district officer south to mention with regret the death of the "chief elder of Tai O" in his administrative report for 1926.[46]

Like other Kaifongs of the region, the Tai O committee employed night watchmen. Wing On and Tai Ping Streets were shut off at night by the insertion of wooden bars into gateways at the ends of the streets. According to old residents, the watch patrolled, beating the time with bamboo rods and brass gongs.

This introduces another interesting parallel with Cheung Chau, and gives an insight into town management before 1899. In Wing On Street, in the period 1915–18, the shopkeepers paid their subscriptions to a man styled a *Tei Po* (*ti-pao*). He is described as "a person not receiving any pay for the post, considered reliable and held in general respect." In these years its holder was a man from one of the town's leading shopkeeping families. My informants stressed that one had to have leisure to be a *Tei Po*, because he had to transact public business and settle disputes. The *Tei Po* was not elected, and was connected with the Kaifong who probably decided on nominations to the post.[47] On Cheung Chau a similar officer, styled locally *Po Cheung Kung* (*pao-chang-kung*) was appointed by the Kaifong. There, this post had been held by only two men in forty years of my informants' lifetime, and the last died without replacement before the Japanese occupation. Emphasis was laid on his knowledge of places and people and of his assisting the Kaifong with elections and counts of households. These two early twentieth century posts are presumably linked with the pre-British practice of having a functionary in localities to aid the district administration with reports and information.[48]

In all, Tai O, despite its age and size, turned out to be a disappointing place in which to trace the detail of community organizations and practices in the late 19th century. However, the historical material on community cooperation that follows, taken from temple inscriptions of an earlier time, compensates in some measure for these deficiencies.

Community Cooperation in Temple Repairs

Tai O has four main temples. They are important to any study of the Tai O community because, through the survival of commemorative tablets and other dated material, they provide evidence for the interaction and cooperation of the land and sea populations. They are a symbol of unity as well as of diversity. The Kaifong had its community office in the side hall of one of them, reflecting joint importance to the town.[49] The four temples were dedicated to Kwan Tai, the God of War; Hung Shing, the God of the Southern Sea; Yeung Hau Wong, a loyal minister of the Sung dynasty; and Tin Hau, the Queen of Heaven.

Each of these temples had its own, well-defined area of concern (see map 3). On the north side of the creek, the Kwan Tai temple took in the town from the present market eastwards to the Hau Wong temple and former garrison posts at Po Chue Tam. The Hung Shing temple at Shek Tsai Po covered the hamlet of that name and the straggling area between the market and the present police station. South of the creek the Tin Hau temple at San Tsuen took in the most densely populated and prosperous part of the town, the Wing On and Tai Ping Streets. Finally, the Hau Wong temple at Po Chue Tam, although not exclusively concerned with the boat people, represented at the turn of the century, the special interests of the leading families of the 100 and more fishing boats of the *sok kwu* (*so ku*) or trawler group.[50]

The present Kaifong elders have told me that the managers for religious celebrations and theatrical performances at the other three temples were always found among leading persons living or doing business in each temple's special area. When major repairs were under consideration, the managers would look to other parts of Tai O town and community for financial help, but in no case would the directors include outsiders.

There are altogether ten dated inscriptions on slatelike tablets that record the repair of the temple structures from time to time. They span the period 1802–1930. In the Hau Wong temple there is a tablet of 1877. There are three tablets dated 1835, 1852, and 1903 in the combined Kwan Tai–Tin Hau temple. The Tin Hau temple at San Tsuen contains tablets of 1839 and 1895. The Hung Shing temple at Shek Tsai Po has the most tablets, including the earliest, dated 1802, 1841, 1875, and 1930. There had been older tablets in the temples—some of the surviving ones mention earlier repairs to the temple buildings that would also have been commemorated in this way—but they have been lost or destroyed.

The temples also contain cast-iron bells, all inscribed with the names of the donors and the dates of presentation.[51] Though earlier than the surviving tablets, it is fairly certain that the bells still do not provide a true indication of when the temples were founded. Direct, and inferred, information from the tablets and inscriptions indicates that the Kwan Tai and Hung Shing temples were probably constructed in the Ming dynasty. The Tin Hau temple reportedly dates from the Shun Chih reign (1644–62). The Hau Wong temple may also have a Ming beginning, or an earlier one, but there is no information available.

The most important contribution the tablets and other dated items in the temples make is not settling the matter of founding dates, but providing good evidence for the continuous and uniform cooperation between land and floating people in the repair of the local temples. There can be no question about this as the pattern is common to all temples through a time span of 130 years.

This situation modifies the outcast status so often attributed to the boat people. Together with the generally peaceful co-existence that I have earlier reported from many places in the Hong Kong region in the late 19th century, it shows that relationships between the two groups, though they remained distinct and showed a degree of economic exploitation, were more normalized in practice than the literature allows.[52]

The four tablets in the Hung Shing temple give a very clear picture of the joint responsibility assumed by each part of the Tai O community when repairs to this temple had to be made. The 1802 tablet shows the equal participation of land and sea people in the work, and described as "local gentry, boat people, and merchants" (*shen-chin ch'i-lao shang hsi-shih ch'uan-chih hu-hsiang cho-ting k'ai-pu*). The list of donors to the repair is a long one. The 1841 tablet mentions a meeting at the temple of land residents and members of the floating population (*yao-chi shui-lu chung-hsin sui-miao kung-i*), and lists separately the contributors from each group and their respective donations. There were 115 contributors from the land group, and 114 from the sea. However, the latter gave nearly twice the amount contributed by the land people: 321.304 taels, compared with 168.69 taels. In 1875, an equal responsibility was assumed, according to the tablet, but it does not mention the total amounts. The tablet for the last repair, in 1930, mentions a meeting at which, as usual, land and sea residents were represented, and again the sum needed for the repair was collected from both parties.

The Kwan Tai-Tin Hau temple in the market place has two mid-19th century repair tablets, one dated in 1835 (Tin Hau) and the other dated 1852 (Kwan Tai). As in the case of the Hung Shing temple, the respective parts played by land and sea residents are noted in the introductory passages describing these occasions and in the lists of donors. The Tin Hau tablet lists many individual land contributions, mostly from shops, and others from what it styles "boats of this port" (*pen-ao ch'uan*), but without giving totals. The Kwan Tai tablet mentions that "officials, merchants, scholars, elders, visiting gentry, land and sea residents, fishermen and woodcutters were all conscious of the powerful and effective spirit of Kwan Tai and unanimously agreed to unite to rebuild his temple" (*ha-ao keng-chi wang-lai kuan-yuan shang-ku shui-lu shi-shue yue-chiao jen tang*). The first twenty names on this tablet are those of officers of the military and naval forces of Hsin-an. Unfortunately, though it lists the total expenses under several heads, including the cost of constructing a guest hall, it does not specify the source of contributions. At the 1903 repair, the total sum expended was 2,627 taels. Of this sum 1,475 taels were given by residents of the "local streets, the four villages and other ports" (*chieh-fang ssu-hsiang ko-fou*).[53] A further 1,152 taels came from three types of fishing boat, listed as *ku-ch'uan*, *wang-t'ing* and *tiao-t'ing*.

The other two temples provide similar information. The Hau Wong tablet of 1877 shows that the large sum of 2,103 taels of silver was raised and spent on the repair works. It is a misfortune that the tablet does not show the sums provided by the various groups among the many contributors. The tablet confines itself to stating that the funds were secured from "local kaifongs, fishing boats, villages, and outside ports" (*chieh-shang wang-ch'uan ko-hsiang ko-fou*). However it does show that whatever the major part of its clientele in normal times, contributions were made by all sections of the Tai O community and by the boat people's outside contacts when a major repair was necessary.

The last of these temples, the Tin Hau temple at San Tsuen also shows land-sea cooperation. The cost of the 1839 repair was

566.527 taels of which 138.7 taels came from the *t'o-ch'uan* or trawler section of the floating population. Another entry on the 1839 tablet gives it a special interest. This shows that the officials, managers, and workmen employed on the salt pans had taken part in its repair, then and in the past. On that occasion four persons, one of them an official (styled here *hsin chien*), gave three silver coins, and 20 others gave copper cash. The tablet also states that a terrace or raised area in front of the temple was built in the Ch'ien Lung period, and was named after an official from the salt administration who, presumably, had either paid for the work or suggested the idea. The 1896 repair tablet from this temple does not list total amounts or individual or group contributions, but it does contain one useful reminder:

> On this stone tablet appear the names of many but not all the donors. At this late date it has been like groping in the dark for pearls. Some are bound to be missed. Forgetting a few names is perhaps inevitable, but if there has been any omission it is not intentional and should be pardoned.

To summarize, the information secured from the four temples is proof of the joint participation of the land and sea people in temple repairs for over a century. It demonstrates mutual confidence in these matters. This is the more remarkable in that the arrangements on these occasions—even, perhaps, at the Hau Wong temple—had to be made by the land people, whose leaders were literate, used to handling business and money matters, and had contacts among the builders and craftsmen who could carry out the work. The repair tablets give the impression that the directors were always land people, and mostly shopkeepers, since the names listed under this head are nearly always those of shops, not individuals. However, the land directors must have always had to consult with the leaders of the boat population, who had to be in agreement with the proposals.[54] Moreover, the boat people's subscriptions can only have come through the hands of their own leaders, who would have had to present separate accounts and answer any questions on the subject coming from their own community. There were probably disputes and even accusations from time to time, but the process of consultation, leading to continued contributions, seems to have been firmly established, probably from a period before the tablet of 1802, the earliest now available to show this pattern of cooperation.

The accounts of Tai O and Cheung Chau concern two communities that appear similar in many respects. Their land and sea populations were large for the Hong Kong region, and were similar in size. They were each a home base for a fishing fleet and, as marketing and servicing centers, attracted boats from other areas. Each was a market center for a considerable number of villages in its vicinity. Each was considerably larger than the regular, periodic markets held at Yuen Long, Shek Wu Hui, Sha Tau Kok and Tai Po and was on a daily marketing schedule and not, like them, a three-day one. Tai O was also a salt producing center. Both had a garrison—Tai O a fairly large one—and Cheung Chau also had a customs station. Many of the shopkeepers, who represented the sinews of these two communities, came from the same districts of Kwangtung, particularly from other parts of Hsin-an and from Tung-kuan. Besides, the two places were only ten miles apart.

Yet in 1899 the two communities were different in many ways. Cheung Chau had flourishing district associations, while Tai O's two bodies of Hsin-an and Tung-kuan natives were declining with the premises of one of them already in ruins. Tai O had numerous, well-endowed, and interesting *she*, but these probably existed in little more than name at the time of the lease; and though, in comparison, the Cheung Chau street communities were not so formally organized for religious and social purposes, a spirit and energy was present that resulted in the emergence of street associations by the 1930s.

It is in this matter of community spirit and life force that the difference between the two places is so marked. This was so, it would seem, in 1899. It was remarked by the early British district officers in their annual reports on the events in the district, and it was still evident to me as late as 1957–62.

The reasons for this do not lie in any essential difference in the nature or capacity of their inhabitants, but is to be explained in the different economic fortunes of the two places. These led

Cheung Chau on an upward spiral of expansion and prosperity, modest enough but sufficient to keep the community full of hope and its leaders brimming with ideas for the improvement of their private and public weal. Tai O had no such good fortune. Located at the mouth of the Pearl River Delta, its harbor was affected by sediment carried in by the sea. The harbor was silting up in 1899, and, as is stated by all old residents, the process had probably begun, and produced an ill effect, many years before.

4

Shek Pik

A Multilineage Settlement of Cantonese Farmers

I have a particular link with Shek Pik and its inhabitants, for between 1957 and 1960 I was responsible for removing the villagers to allow the construction of the Shek Pik Reservoir.

Shek Pik, though for all its history a remote valley on an offshore island, is a long-settled and interesting spot. Its beaches were inhabited in the pre-Han period, and were the site of an important archaeological excavation in 1937.[1] Closer to the period of this study, it was, in my opinion, in some way connected with the last wanderings of the defeated Sung court and army in the years 1276–80 and after.[2] It was probably inhabited by Yao aborigines at that time and later,[3] and the first Chinese peasants probably entered the valley between the end of the Southern Sung dynasty and the middle of the Ming.

The Settlement

The Shek Pik valley located directly under Lantau Peak (3,030 feet), is two miles long and half a mile broad. Before the construction of the reservoir it was intersected by a fast-flowing mountain stream, fed along its length by short tributaries issuing from the hills behind and on either side.[4] The valley was a patchwork of thousands of small paddy fields, rising gently from sea level behind the estuary to a height of fifty feet in front of Shek Pik village and encroaching in terraced steps onto the foothills on either side.[4] On the western side, in particular, many fields, each with its rubble retaining wall, had been cut long ago from the steep hill sides. Behind the village, and already deserted by

1899, were tens of acres of what had once been terraced fields rising by gradations to a height of 600 feet. There were ten acres at Tung Wan, a basin branching eastwards from the foot of the main valley; and another fifteen at Shek Lam Chau, an isolated fertile area half a mile further along the coast and only accessible by hill path or sampan. Tai Long Wan, the bay adjoining Shek Pik on the west, had also been farmed before 1899.

In 1899 the Shek Pik population centered on the village of Shek Pik Wai in the upper valley and the smaller village of Fan Pui nearer the shore. The Wai was encircled by a substantial rubble wall with a main gateway facing west. There was no wall around Fan Pui. There was also a small group of houses at Hang Tsai, near Fan Pui but connected with the main village. There were a few agricultural structures in the outlying valleys tilled by Shek Pik and Fan Pui people, used at planting and harvest times, and some temporary structures behind the main beach, used by villagers during the shrimping season for making and storing shrimp paste.

The two main villages had the customary grove of large trees behind them, which provided *feng shui* protection for their inhabitants. A British district officer recalls that in 1920 the trees behind Shek Pik Wai were exceptionally thick and completely overshadowed the village.[5]

The hillsides were thickly studded with the graves and urns of departed ancestors, especially those of the earliest generations at Shek Pik. Many graves, untended for generations as descendants or whole families died out, had gradually merged with the hillside, and their memorial tablets had been lost or were so weathered they were no longer readable. Others had been lifted and removed to more favorable locations on the advice of geomancers.

The first reliable population figures for the two villages is given in the 1911 colony census.[6] The larger had then a recorded resident population of 363 persons, and the smaller had 59 inhabitants. These figures compare with the 202 and 59 persons respectively, who removed from the two villages in 1959–60. The elders say that the population had been more numerous in the 19th century, and have often affirmed that there were "999 males," their way of emphasizing large numbers, in the upper village in their grandparents' lifetime and before.

"An Ecological Succession of Clans"

Chinese settlement at Shek Pik is more varied, and probably longer, than may be supposed from the history of the long-settled lineages living there in 1957–60. C.K. Yang has already stated this hypothesis for another old multilineage Kwangtung village in his study of Nanching near Canton. He wrote of "an ecological succession of clans in the community," but without elaboration. I provide this detail for Shek Pik, so far as is possible with available sources (see table 5).

Section A was compiled by inquiries among the extant families. This produced genealogies of varying length and detail for the Tsui, Chi and the two Fung lineages. A successful search for ancestors' graves with tablets giving genealogical data, checked with the lineage heads, provided information on the Cheung, Wong and Chan lineages; though in each case their older men had at first said that they knew little of their family's origin and length of stay at Shek Pik. The result of these searchings and questionings showed that these seven lineages had each contained many families and had been resident at Shek Pik from between 7 to 15 generations.

However, in the course of my inquiries it became clear that many more lineages had been living in the valley within the memory of the older men and their recollection of what they had been told as boys by their fathers and grandfathers. They were able to recall that survivors of the Mau, Kong, Chung and Ng lineages lived in the village when they were young. This is confirmed by entries in the schedules of ownership drawn up at the land settlement, and by other evidence. Length of residence is mostly uncertain, but in two cases it is likely to be long. The Tsui elders understood from their parents' generation that the Maus and Kongs had preceded them at Shek Pik. The Chan founding ancestor's grave—he arrived about the middle of the 17th century—lists his wife as a Mau; and a Kong is one of the six donors of an altar table dated 1804 in the Hau Wong temple.

Section C. provides information on another group comprising three more lineages of Wong, Yue and Hung, all said to have been settled at Shek Pik for some time before the lease. The Wong story came from one of the still numerous Wong lineage,

TABLE 5

CHINESE SETTLEMENT AT SHEK PIK

LINEAGE	DIALECT	DISTRICT OF ORIGIN	NO. OF GENERATIONS AT SHEK PIK
A. Living in the valley at the time of their removal for the construction of the Shek Pik reservoir			
Tsui	Punti	Tung-kuan	15th in 1960
Chi	Punti	Hsin-an	12th in 1960
Chan	Punti	Hsin-an	11th in 1960
Wong	Punti	Hsin-an	10th in 1960
Fung (Fan Pui)	Punti	Hsin-an	12th in 1960
Fung (Shek Pik)	Punti	Hsin-an	9th in 1960
Cheung	Punti	Tung-kuan	7th in 1960
B. No longer at Shek Pik by the 1950s, but recalled as having been there in their youth by the village elders; confirmed by entries in the Block Crown Lease			
Kong	Punti	...	perhaps before the Tsuis
Mau	Punti	...	perhaps before the Tsuis
Chung	Punti	Tung-kuan	6 generations on Lantau; first four spent at Shek Pik
Ng	...	...	...
C. Lineages that have changed their *hsing* (surname). There were descendants of the first two living at Shek Pik in the 1950s, and a surviving concubine of the third. The village elders are positive on the change of name.			
Yue, now Tsui	...	...	perhaps long settlement
Wong (汪), now (黃)	...	...	perhaps long settlement
Hung, now Fung	...	...	perhaps long settlement

NOTE: Outside owners have been carefully excluded from this account. They have been identified in consultations with the village elders, and may be described as persons from other villages not residing at Shek Pik though owning fields and even houses there.

who stated, without proof, as his ancestral tablets had been lost in a prewar house collapse in the old village, that he was of a different name and ancestor from the rest. His story is given some credibility by the altar table of 1804 mentioned above, which lists a donor of this name. It seems that, at some time in the 19th century, for reasons now unknown, this man's fore-bears had changed their name with the agreement of the other Wongs.

Surviving members of the Yue lineage entered the Tsui lineage about the time of the lease. According to the Tsui elders this was "because being few in number they wanted more relations in the village, and we were agreeable."[7] Many of the fields in an adjoining bay are said to have belonged to this lineage, but the owners are already shown as Tsuis in the registers drawn up at the land settlement in 1904. However, the memory remains, and both the Tsuis and the descendants of the Yues agree to it. The Yue lineage is said to have owned much land behind Shek Pik Wai, which points to early settlement.

The third case of a change in *hsing* concerns a family called Hung who became Fungs of Shek Pik. The concubine of the last male survivor (1860–1942) said that he had often told her that his lineage had over sixty male descendants worshipping at the tombs on the grave festivals when he was a boy. The change of name has been confirmed to me on several occasions by different elders.[8]

This recital, which deals only with the more recent past, uncovers elements in the village situation that are not apparent from a routine inquiry. It hints at a shifting situation in which families and individuals came and went over the years, and their fortunes rose and fell, with an effect upon the community that is perhaps more dramatic than in a one lineage village. In such circumstances, the demands made upon the village population for organization and leadership were correspondingly greater.

Ownership of Land at Shek Pik

At the time of the British land settlement in 1904, it appears that about 124 acres was in private ownership, most of it in the hands of villagers. This land was held by the village lineages and others as shown in Table 6.

Besides this acreage, there was another 50 acres that had gone out of cultivation by 1899.[9] The field boundaries were clearly visible and they had been surveyed and given lot numbers like the rest. They are therefore included in the registers of the Block Crown Lease. However, most of the fields in this category, described as fallow or waste, were not claimed by villagers at the land settlement.[10]

The total built-over area registered in private ownership in

TABLE 6

LAND OWNERSHIP AT SHEK PIK, 1904

NAME	AGRICULTURAL	BUILDING	TOTAL (in acres)
Tsui	23.56	0.90	24.46
Chi	20.29	0.59	20.88
Fung (SP)	17.96	0.70	18.66
Chan	16.63	0.66	17.29
Fung (FP)	9.43	0.42	9.85
Cheung	7.85	0.25	8.10
Wong	4.73	0.18	4.91
Mau	2.41	0.05	2.46
Ng	2.32	0.10	2.42
Chung	0.59	0.03	0.62
Temples[1]	1.77	0.10	1.87
Outsiders[2]	12.53	0.01	12.54
Total	120.07	3.99	124.06

1. These were the Yeung Hau Wong and Hung Shing temples owned by the villagers.
2. Mainly by a family from another village, a local religious house and a land-owning *t'ang* of Tai O shopkeepers (Sui Sheng T'ang).

SOURCE: Based on BCL registers for demarcation districts nos. 312, 315, 318, 319, 321, 323.

1904 was around 4 acres. At 0.01 acres (436 square feet) to the usual village house at this period, this means there were then about 400 structures in the valley. From the total building land registered for each lineage in 1904 (see above), ownership can be established as follows:

Tsui	90 houses and structures*
Fung (Shek Pik)	70 " "
Chan	66 " "
Chi	59 " "
Fung (Fan Pui)	42 " "
Cheung	25 " "
Wong	18 " "
Ng	10 " "
Mau	5 " "
Chung	3 " "
Total	388

*This is a maximum, since some structures occupied more than 0.01 acre.

There were, in addition, 37 unclaimed houses in the old village, mostly registered as being in ruins, and 38 lots with huts on them, nearly half of them unclaimed and in ruins.

This land was held in individual ownership by the village families and not collectively by the various lineages. Table 7 shows the spread of ownership in the main lineages.

As can be seen, the holdings were generally small, especially in the larger lineages such as the Tsuis, Chans, and Shek Pik Fungs. There is little doubt that they had been smaller, since the area had experienced depopulation through disease since about 1850, and some of the persons listed may have benefited from the holdings of close relatives, such as fathers' brothers, dying without living male issue.

Ten of the 213 personal entries recorded above are listed as owning houses but no land. There is no way of knowing how many villagers owned neither. For this reason, a survey of land farmed by households, taking in owned and rented areas, together with an indication of household size, would be more informative than the entries given above. I have not the means to provide this information on the economic family.

It is clear, both from the small size of many holdings and from the information available in a rent and property book relating to fields in the Shek Pik valley purchased in the 19th century by a lineage from the adjoining village of Yi O near Tai O, that renting, from other villagers and from clan and temple holdings as well as from the outsider landowners noted in table 1, was quite common.

The entries in the rent book cover the period of continuing depopulation. They show that renting continued and that the rents were falling gradually, presumably in line with this worsening situation. Between 1902 and 1921 the average rent for twenty-two lots of fields fell from 1.75 *shih* per *tou chung* to 1.43, with indications that rents had also been declining in the twenty years before.

Before 1899 all or most of the land at Shek Pik had been owned by the Li Kau Yuen Tong of Sha Wan, an outside gentry family that had held Lantau since Sung times. However, their ownership was vested in the subsoil, and was recognized by payment of ground rent twice a year. For all practical purposes, the villagers

TABLE 7

Land Holdings by Personal Entries 1904

Main Lineage	No. of Entries	Entries Above 3 Acres	2–3 Acres	1.50–1.99 Acres	1–1.49 Acres	.50–.99 Acre	.25–.49 Acre	Rest	Highest Agric. Holding	With Its Bldg Entry	Shared Entries
Chan	33	...	1	...	6	5	7	14	2.66	.04	4
Cheung	21	...	...	...	1	4	5	11	1.47	.02	1
Chi	27	...	3	...	3	11	2	8	2.74	.03	2
Fung SP	37	1	...	1	4	7	4	20	3.94	.06	2
" FP	18	...	1	...	3	3	2	9	2.28	.06	1
Mau	4	...	...	...	...	3	...	1	.92	.02	...
Ng	7	...	...	...	...	2	1	4	.79	.03	...
Tsui	55	...	...	...	4	10	12	29	1.34	.03	8
Wong	11	...	1	...	...	2	2	6	2.15	.01	...
Total	213	1	6	1	21	47	35	102	...	...	18

Notes: Lineage trust holdings are excluded from the table (7 entries).

There appear to have been more undivided holdings before registration, since some of the individual holdings within lineages are exactly (and suspiciously) alike, and may indicate divisions created for, and arising out of, the land settlement.

See Hayes 1962: note 10 for a statement of holdings in 1958.

Source: Based on BCL registers for demarcation districts nos. 312, 315, 318, 319, 321, 323.

who were their tenants acted as though they owned the fields, transferring and mortgaging them at will.

From the aspects of organization and leadership, the essential points in the local situation were the virtual—after 1899 actual—ownership of land by the peasant cultivators, and the fact that all were smallholders and, with some variations, in a like social and economic condition. The first bred an independence of mind that the second required, if leaders were to come forth in the absence of gentry members or of outside direction from gentry or shopkeepers in the local market centers.

Lineage and Village Institutions at Shek Pik

At lineage level, there had been modest halls for ancestor worship in some lineages, but none were registered as such at the land settlement of 1904, perhaps because they had already fallen down in the decay that accompanied the depopulation noted above.[12] There were also *tso* organizations, tied to halls where these existed. These may be described as small family trusts, intended to ensure the continuance of sacrifices to the founding or other important ancestors of the clan. The *tso* property, usually agricultural land, was either rotated among clansmen, who would be made responsible for the year's sacrifices, or was rented out to produce a small income to meet ritual expenses. Land held in this way did not amount to very much at Shek Pik. According to the Block Crown Lease a Tsui *tso* owned 0.02 acres building and 1.08 agricultural; three Cheung *tso* owned 0.39 agricultural in all; a Fung *tso* of Fan Pui owned 0.92 agricultural and a Fung *tso* of Shek Pik 0.27 agricultural. There were several other smaller holdings.

Below lineage level there were in some families fields that had been earmarked to provide an income for ritual needs. These were usually set aside in a division of property between sons and looked after by rotation among them. The proceeds were devoted entirely or in part to meet worshipping expenses. At Shek Pik they were commonly called *hsiang yu tien*, and in the larger families of the region *cheng ch'ang tien*.[13] Such land was jealously guarded. It was usual in local deeds of sale and mortgage to make a point of stating that the land being sold was not used to provide ancestral sacrifices or educational subsidies for clansmen.

These lineage and family institutions were supported by genealogical records. At Shek Pik the surviving accounts from the Tsui, Fung and Chi lineages contained information on family origins, and gave lines of descent and the names of descendants in clan or branch. They listed the locations of graves and one of them provided guidance on practices for worshipping at the two grave-worshipping festivals in spring and autumn.

At village level, there was the public property usually to be found in the multilineage settlements of this region. At Shek Pik, this comprised a school with kitchen and teacher's quarters attached, two temples, and some shrines. Some agricultural land was attached to these properties to produce an income that would support them and their activities.[14] There was, too, a village orchard, used not to produce fruit for sharing and eating but to provide village funds after auction, crop by crop. All this property was generally referred to as belonging to Ah Kung, that is, to the founders of the village, and thus was commonly owned by their descendants.

Besides property held in common, there was the village itself. This was a personification of the whole community and constituted an entity that was as much a reality for its inhabitants as were the various institutions established at lineage and village level. It had to be represented in its dealings with the outside world, and sometimes protected against it. Village duties included preparations against harm from other villages and outsiders and from the supernatural. It should be noted that protection against the spirit world and the influences of place was put on a more regular footing at Shek Pik and most local villages than protection against human harm, and perhaps did more to create and retain a sense of community than any other single factor.[15]

Some reference should also be made to the less formal institutions of the local village. There is a well known Cantonese saying "the dancing lion drives away plague."[16] This refers to the village lion dancers, a kind of youth club under a "master." This club played an important part in every ceremony to ward off disease or pacify evil spirits, going in procession round the various localities together with the priests and elders. These groups usually kept their equipment and did their training in the village temples. They were generally regarded as a village institution, whose personnel were available to assist the elders at regular festivals and special events.[17] They were found in Cantonese and Hakka villages alike, at Shek Pik and elsewhere.[18]

Within the village community and outside it, there was also scope for leadership in the economic field, as in the performance of the essential middleman duties in the sale and mortgage of land and the organization of money loan societies; to name but two types of activity open to villagers.

Lineage Leaders and Their Duties

At Shek Pik and the adjoining villages, authority within the lineage rested with the lineage elder, *tsu chang*, and the elders of its three or four branches, known locally as *fang chang*. Together, these men led and regularized the internal affairs of each lineage.

Inside the lineage, these leaders were the embodiment of tradition, charged by custom with ensuring that the multifarious aspects of family and lineage life, especially ritual ones, were carried out in accordance with old practice. They were responsible for overseeing important domestic arrangements such as the adoption of children, the taking in of husbands for widows or girls (known locally as *chiu long yap she*), the division of family property, and mediation in any disputes and disturbances that might arise within the lineage.[19]

These men did not only operate within their own lineages. They contributed to the management of village affairs whenever necessary and ensured compliance with village decisions. Also, their concern with behavior inside the lineage made them ultimately responsible to the village and to the civil authorities for the conduct of all lineage members.[20] They had, besides, a prescribed part to play in the business of other lineages inside the village. On those occasions where another lineage recorded a decision on family and property matters in writing they acted as witnesses; in effect becoming its guarantors and arbitrators in case of need.

An early example of division of property which has survived

from Shek Pik shows this practice at work. It took place within the Chi lineage which was already well established in the village. A genealogy from one of the branches of the family shows that it had been settled at Shek Pik and the adjoining village of Shui Hau for five generations when the division was made in 1789.

A deed of partition concerns twenty *tou chung* of land and other property divided among five sons, one of them already deceased. It was drawn in quintuplicate, and witnessed by two persons stated to be branch heads (*fang chang*) and two others from different lineages stated to be village elders (*chi lao*). Besides the latter, the document stated that the apportionment took place "in the presence of the elder of our lineage, branch heads and relatives."

A petition, undated but apparently written two years later, was addressed to the "village elders and to the heads of our lineage" (*hsiang-lao tsu-chang*). The writer was the adopted son of one of the brothers who had shared in the division of property. He was trying to recover half of his father's fields, given to relatives when he left the village but still not returned to him. The result of the petition is unknown.

It appears from my experiences as a district officer for Shek Pik that the same pattern of documentation and action in these and other family transactions was being followed one hundred and fifty years later, in the years after the reoccupation of Hong Kong in 1945. A document recording the taking of a husband into a woman's family on her remarriage, dated February 1946, was signed by the heads of that lineage, the village headman and two elders from another lineage. An adoption paper of 1959 was also signed by the village head in addition to the lineage chief, the head of branch and fellow clansmen. There was, besides, a paper of the same year concerning the giving away of a girl as a future daughter-in-law, but the taking-in document is missing.[21]

This is a dangerously small number of documents[22] on which to make this statement of lineage leaders' involvement in the family affairs of other lineages. I would not bring it forward had not the Shek Pik elders and those of adjoining villages repeatedly affirmed that it was customary to draw up these papers on all such occasions and for them to be witnessed in this way, thereby opening the prospect that more of these documents may come to light to prove the point.

The role of outsiders in such essentially domestic business is important. It is clearly purposive, and was known to all concerned. The petitioner in the 1789 case pointed out that the division of property on which he based his appeal originated with the same village elders and lineage leaders to whom his petition was addressed, and he appealed to them to uphold justice. It would therefore appear that the standard procedures had been designed for just such eventualities. Where the settlement of family matters involved other lineages and village leaders, it provided sound preparation for the handling of village affairs in the same way that participation in street affairs prepared townspeople for leadership functions in the Kaifong of the coastal market centres.

Village Leaders

The problems of leadership and control were probably always greater in multi than single lineage villages because authority was dispersed among the several lineages. At Shek Pik they were rendered more difficult still because the various lineages were intermingled and did not have their own sections of the village as at Nanching and elsewhere.[23]

In these circumstances, it appears that the authority necessary to control the different parts of the village community had to come from, and be exercised through, the several lineages who made up the settlement. The present elders agreed that a form of participation in decision making has been essential to good management and has been the foundation of village rule since their boyhood.

Various Chinese terms were in common use for the English description "elder" in the 19th century and before. The three descriptions (*fu lao*, *chi lao* or *chi min*) can be found in 18th and 19th-century papers and memorial tablets for the region. They can also be seen, sometimes in combinations of two or all three together, in Chinese petitions from the villages to the Hong Kong magistracy in the 1840s.[24] It is interesting that eldership was elaborated in this way, though the precise meaning and delineation of these terms is not yet known to me. It may be significant, too, that their use occurs in the context of the village rather than the lineage.

An interlineage council of elders, such as Yang found at Nanching, Kwangtung,[25] was the source of village authority at Shek Pik and many other local multilineage settlements.[26] This organization is affirmed by Lockhart who mentions the "village council" composed of "representatives of the clans inhabiting the villages" and its part in dealing with "theft, disputes about land, domestic squabbles and cases of debt."[27]

The participation of the lineages in village government is thus established, and elders from all lineages in multilineage villages could expect to play some part in deciding matters of importance. However, their individual influence depended upon their lineage's numerical strength and their own caliber. In multilineage villages like those of South Lantau, the lineages were seldom equal in numbers. At Shek Pik the Tsuis were the oldest and most numerous lineage and have long played an important part in village life. At Tong Fuk, as the oldest settlers and through their claimed connection with the powerful Tangs of Kam Tin, the Tang family have assumed the leadership during the time I have known them and, it is reported, long before. In the Pui O group, the Cheungs led the field. At Nanching, Yang reported that such an imbalance was reflected in the smaller representation of the lesser lineages in the village council.[28] Unfortunately, I have no historical information on this point from Lantau.

Nonetheless, where members of the strongest lineages played a leading part in village affairs, there is no suggestion that the other lineages were not consulted, or that their elders did not take part in the process of decision making. Influential village leaders could not always answer for or control persons outside their own lineage; so they, too, needed the sanctions provided by their fellow members of the village council. They had also to cock an ear for expressions of dissent from local power groups or weighty individuals.[29]

Under British rule it appears to have been the practice for one of the elders to adopt (to the general satisfaction) or be placed in (with the agreement of all who mattered) a leading position in village affairs and to become thereby its headman. The elder who acted as headman was known as the *hsiang-chang* or "village head."[30] He was a kind of *primus inter pares* among the elders who, among his other duties, would take care of the official business of the village.

In multilineage villages such as those existing on Lantau, the headman did not have to come from any one lineage. This is shown clearly at Shek Pik, where six persons had held the office of village chief in the twenty years before 1941. They had come from four of the seven lineages then resident in the village. At Shek Pik, the longest in office had held the post for less than ten years. Most had served for two or three because, as the elders told me, "they had their own affairs to see to, and being headman was a troublesome job for which one got paid nothing."[31] Thus there were no set periods or terms of office, nor, under the circumstances, could there be. The support of the other elders and the concurrence of the village at large were vital to continued tenure.

Berkowitz describes the type of leadership setting and practice still to be found in many villages of the Hong Kong Region as "consensual politics."[32] The village representative, formerly headman, "had the job of creating concensus in his village in regard to both external and internal problems. This concensus served as a fundamental basis of community solidarity and thus played a role in the maintenance of tranquility and order. Persuasion and influence, not power, dictated his everyday affairs." Though writing of the 1960s, his assessment accurately reflects the position at a much earlier time.[33]

The position of headman presents a problem that I have not yet been able to resolve: whether the headman of the Hong Kong region was a native institution or one deriving from the requirements of foreign rule from the 1840s on. There is a confusion between elders, tepo, and headmen in the Hong Kong region from the start of British rule caused by the appointment of elders to the position of tepo in early Hong Kong, after the Chinese style. These men were at first styled "Paouchang and Paoukea" (*pao-chang* and *pao-chia* in standard romanization) but soon after were always called Tepo.[34] Under this title, they were invariably considered as headmen by British administrators and magistrates, and regarded as the chief person of a village to whom information, instructions, and complaints could be addressed by people and government alike.[35]

In Hong Kong this officer was clearly the village headman; but in Chinese territory the tepo was a person nominated by the elders of a village and sanctioned by the district magistrate to act as a semiofficial functionary.[36] Werner, writing, one supposes, of the north, mentions both tepo and the equivalent of headman. The tepo came under the "village elder," *hsiang-lao* or *hsiang-chang*, and was obviously a useful functionary rather than the embodiment of his own or village authority.[37]

In the south, the position may have varied, which would have been scarcely surprising. Baker's informants at Sheung Shui said that before 1899 there was a lineage leader *primus inter pares* styled *hsiang-chin*, equating to village head;[38] but Yang does not mention a headman in his account of Nanching, despite the existence of the "interlineage council" common in the Shek Pik area. (This was perhaps due to the creation of *pao*, *chia*, and *hsiang* by the Nationalist Government in 1932 which may have replaced the headman or tepo of earlier times).[39] Kulp, too, writing before these changes took place, does not mention a headman for Phoenix Village in north-east Kwangtung.[40] This uncertainty remains until more information comes to hand.

The Duties of Village Leaders

Village affairs at Shek Pik came under a wide variety of heads which, for convenience, we may style religious and secular. On the religious side they took in a number of functions, among which the most important was probably the organization of periodic Ta Chiu rites to protect the village. These had to be arranged and financed for the seven day period of the celebrations. This involved collecting subscriptions, hiring priests, contracting for the erection of a mat shed theater for the rites and the accompanying puppet or opera performance, and making arrangements for young men to act, in rotation and without payment, as watchmen to protect livestock and other property left in unlocked houses.[41] Subscriptions were laid down by long usage, and were levied in kind on a sliding scale for adults, children, animals, and poultry. These Ta Chiu took place every two and a half years at Shek Pik.

There were also the entreating and thanksgiving ceremonies in the 1st and 12th moons and the celebration of the birthdays of the principal gods of the two village temples to arrange, events in which it was usual for the entire community to take part. Opera or puppet performances were commonly held on the latter occasions. More routine ritual protection involved the supervision of the daily succession of families who in turn lighted joss sticks and swept shrines at five places within the village perimeter.[42] This range of duties for what, in the 19th century, was a population numbering five hundred to a thousand persons or more, emphasizes the importance attached to protection against the supernatural.

On the secular side, there were village rules to enforce in an agricultural community interested in the safety of crops and livestock, the timber and firewood in private or village plantations of hillside trees,[43] the produce of the village orchard,[44] and, especially, the protection of the graves and burial urns of ancestors.[45] Tenancy and cultivation rights were also included.[46] Family, lineage, and village interests were involved in this rural charter and the headman and elders would be brought into it at need to confirm, elaborate, and, it must be supposed, innovate.

These rules could be written or unwritten, generally the latter. At Shek Pik they had not been put in writing, but were well known and carried fixed penalties for various misdemeanors, categorized by old custom.[47] Offenders were reported and summoned before the headman and elders or arrested and confined if this was necessary and feasible. Younger men could serve as constables for this duty.[48]

The initiation and carrying out of local public works, like the construction and repair of dams (*p'o t'ou*) to improve or safeguard irrigation and the maintenance of existing systems by cutting grass on verges and clearing out stones and earth from the earth and rock channels (*shui tsun*) in normal use were also a village or—more usually—group activity that required initiative and supervision.[49] On Lantau the determinent of involvement was the dam: there were four in the Shek Pik Valley and three at Pui O. In the areas served by each dam and channel system, responsibility for supervising work was usually shouldered by persons with the biggest holdings, since they had most to lose by neglect. The construction and repair of paths and bridges was another task in this general category.[50]

The overseeing and maintenance of the two Shek Pik temples and the village school, together with the hiring of teachers and appointment of temple keepers, as well as seeing that both received the usual fees of office, were also important matters that fell to the village leaders.[51]

As already mentioned, the headman and elders in the village council were quite closely involved in the major business of the village lineages, not through interference but at request, in order to strengthen the validity of decisions and to assist later in case of dispute.

There was also the handling of relations with outsiders coming into the area. At Shek Pik in the last century these included Hoklos using the local waters and beaches in their seasonal fishing incursions, Tanka boat people, and visiting charcoal burners who carried on their work on the hills above the South Lantau villages. All were likely to interfere with village rights on hill and shore, and to give occasional trouble.

There were also relations, all potentially unpleasant, to handle with other villages and the government, although I have little or no information on these subjects for Lantau from the late Ch'ing.

Finally there were full-scale attacks by outsiders bent on plunder and devastation to be warded off. Fleets of pirates were common in the region and at one time posed a major threat to security throughout the delta.[52]

All told, this represented a formidable burden of work for persons who were not paid to perform the duties. It follows that if they were to be undertaken with a maximum of efficiency, helpers were required.

Village Helpers

Beneath the headman and the elders were managers of various trusts and agents for particular duties. These jobs could be performed by other villagers or by one or other of the leadership group, since it was quite common for a capable man to engross duties, and plural office holding was more often the rule than the exception in rural and market life.[53]

Unlike the elders or the headman who continued in office for as long as they had the inclination or gave satisfaction, village helpers usually had fixed and short terms determined by the tasks in hand. Duties were entrusted to them for a year at a time in the case of, say, management of the village ferry, orchard, or forestry lot; for the period of a major festival; or for the time required for a certain task, subject always, if money was involved, to a public accounting for their stewardships. At Shek Pik the presentation of the accounts was usually done by public notice posted on the walls of the Hau Wong temple which served as the village office.[54] A manager could be, and often was, reappointed for another or later term of office, but this was always conditional upon a satisfactory acquittal.[55]

Such men came to their posts by the nomination and agreement of the elders with the silent acquiescence of the village. Usually, only men with property would be allowed to hold posts involving the management of fields and property, and such duties were supposedly rotated. Books carrying lists of names were said to exist, though I never managed to see one. These provisions were not always followed. Not everyone wanted to have the job, and not all candidates were acceptable. For those who were and did, the consent of the elders was probably the deciding factor, and they would be instrumental in seeing that the right man's name was suggested.[56]

Headmen might also have an assistant. It appears that the Shek Pik headman had one in the early years of this century. He was a kind of constable *cum* runner who would summon elders and villagers when required and generally help out in many ways.

The Village in an Emergency

External threats severely tested the resources of village leadership. The elders in council decided what steps to take in any emergency, and they were responsible for seeing that their section of the village played its part. Troubled times produced occasions for joint action.

Shek Pik Lo Wai, as its name suggests, was walled. An extensive rubble wall encircled the village, and there were several internal towers guarding the entrances. These had probably all been erected during the troubled times of late Ch'ien Lung, but none of the elders could say with certainty. Whenever constructed, they represented a major undertaking for the village, requiring much prior discussion and organization. An additional protected place, styled "fort," (*p'ao t'ai*) had been built by the villagers, perhaps about the same time and for similar reasons. This refuge was situated on the hillside away from the two villages, and was intended for use when the settlements were unsafe. It is mentioned as a place name in land documents, and is recalled by the elders as a spot where they played as boys, when tending cows.[57]

No documentation of these events is available for Shek Pik, but a clan genealogy from Pui O gives an account of similar action taken there in that period. The genealogy of the Cheung clan of Pui O records:

> In the 53rd and 54th years of Ch'ien Lung (1788–90), a Tung-kuan man, Tam Ah-che, became a sea robber. He robbed and killed, burned houses, in great measure, took away the men as slaves and women also. The local officials and soldiers would not dare to face these robbers.

The Cheung clan and other villagers later took measures in their own defence. The village council held a meeting and decided to turn the settlement into a fortress to guard against the pirates. This involved construction of a walled enclosure, built of stone, and replacing the existing wooden gateway by a stone structure. As the positioning of the wall and its main gate was of great importance, for geomantic reasons as well as military considerations, a message was sent to Shing Mun to invite a Cheung Lam-to, presumably a noted geomancer, to advise on the siting and on auspicious days for carrying out the work. The record ends:

> Work began on the 13th day of the 8th moon of the 8th year of Chia Ch'ing, and the gate was fixed on the 16th day. All the village men and women cooperated in the work, which took a month to complete.[58]

Representation in crisis was taken seriously. The elders at Tung Chung and Tai O considered it their responsibility to go on board Western naval ships with presents after the vessels had made attacks on warjunks and pirates at those places in the 1850s.[59] In Deep Bay in 1864 two village headmen, armed with visiting cards, called upon a joint Anglo-Chinese naval force before its action against local pirates.[60] The object in each case was to protect themselves and their communities against misunderstandings and retaliations.

Leaders and Facilitators in the Village Economy

I turn finally to initiatives at village level in the economic field, as I have some material from Lantau on land transactions and money loan associations. Land dealings and credit were important subjects in traditional Chinese rural society. They are areas of activity where the requirement for leaders and fixers is immediately obvious. Moreover, all the evidence from the Lantau villages points to the considerable volume of such transactions in everyday life.

This section explores the extent to which villagers managed such matters or were content to let specialists—their own people or outsiders—take over.[61]

The Middlemen in Land Transactions

In land transactions, it was the usual practice for a middleman to bring a seller and buyer together and, following a successful negotiation, to arrange for a deed of sale to be drawn up in the customary form, signed, and witnessed.[62] This work would be best handled by persons of some age, experience, and finesse—the qualities required of a successful elder or village leader.

The surviving land papers from Shek Pik and Pui O provide information on this subject over a period of approximately sixty years between the 1830s and 1890s. The results are not quite as I had expected.

In 29 deeds where middlemen were employed in transactions

at Shek Pik, 19 of them were of the same name as the seller. In local circumstances this means that they were his relatives. In several cases they are specifically stated to be his nephews and in another, an uncle. In one case the middleman was of the same name as the purchaser. Only in the remaining 9 was he not related to either side in the transaction. Moreover, with the exception of one man who handled two negotiations, all the middlemen in the 29 cases are different.

In eleven deeds whose details were copied into a Pui O clan account book, there was no middleman stated for either the single sale or for five of the ten mortgages that made up the rest of the book. (One of the five mortgagors stated specifically that he made a personal approach to the mortgagee.) The middlemen for the other five deeds are all relatives of the mortgagor: "my father's cousin," "a relative living next to us," "a distant uncle," "my clan brother"; and all were different persons.

I conclude, somewhat tentatively, that, in the second half of the 19th century, no professional middlemen had emerged in the South Lantau villages as specialist negotiators to whom all villagers turned in their need; and that neither the elders nor the village headman had used their position to become land brokers, at least not overtly. It seems that performing the task of a middleman was considered to be a family duty, and one for relatives, even younger men like the nephews mentioned above, to perform. However, more evidence is needed. I am, in fact, surprised at the result, knowing how these things work today, when many village representatives and rural committee chairmen take an active part in land deals.

In other respects the result of this inquiry is pertinent to my thesis of peasant abilities. Though raising doubts as to the existence of specialist middlemen in these villages, the material does provide a further demonstration of the general capacity of the Hsin-an peasantry for managing the many and varied aspects of their daily life.

Money Loan Associations and Their Leaders

Another field for economic leadership was opened by the same need for money that prompted sales and mortgages. These transactions seem often to have originated—in Thomas C. Smith's phrase—"in poverty rather than enterprise."[63] It is no accident that the Shek Pik collection includes papers on the activities of three small money loan associations; and on the financial dealings of a lineage trust which increased its capital by loaning money to villagers.[64] These various papers are dated between 1879 and 1895.[65]

The money loan papers show that:

1. The number of members in the associations was small (16, 13 and 12), although Shek Pik village was comparatively large.
2. Membership was not restricted to one lineage, or even to members of the village. In the thirteen-member association 11 members came from 5 different lineages of Shek Pik, and the remaining 2 members were outsiders. This suggests that the groups were formed on the basis of acquaintance and a mutual and contemporaneous need for money.
3. Participation was sustained. The two men whose names occur most often in the papers were engaged in various money-raising activities through most of the sixteen year period.
4. Land and house deeds were sometimes used to guarantee payments of the periodic installments which all members of the association agreed to make upon entry.

The papers on the activities of the lineage trust, the Chi Wing Shing Tong, show two kinds of arrangement: money loans made on payment of interest and loans made on the security of mortgages of land to the Tong.

These papers clearly represent only a portion of the many similar transactions that must have been taking place almost daily in the area: that is, if one includes the time required for planning, visits, meetings, discussions, and agreements. Certain skills were obviously required, including the ability to talk and interest others, a head for figures and the facility to keep written accounts. The latter were important assets when, as the papers show, silver, silver dollars, and copper cash were all used together, with land used as security at need, and interest had continually to be calculated and entered in the books.

Unfortunately, whilst giving these indications, the deeds provide very little information on leadership in either the loan associations or the Tong. The only organizer named on the papers belonged to the Chi lineage and his activities covered a minimum period of twelve years, 5th to 16th years of Kuang Hsü. Another unnamed organizer is mentioned in a deed executed by this Chi in Kuang Hsü 5. He had then to hand over two houses in mortgage to the organizer of the 16-member association in which he had taken the first payment in 1879.

However, even this single transaction brings out an interesting point. Chi could not sign the deed but finger-printed it instead. A Chan of Shek Pik wrote it. This implies that the ability to write was not a prerequisite for being the organizer of an association, despite complexities arising from the mixed money media and from sometimes having property to manage. Writers were perhaps easier to find than organizers.

The only certainties about the loan field and its leaders that can be deduced from these few but interesting papers is that money transactions were continuous and often complicated events;[66] that village men were involved in their management; and that illiteracy was no bar to being an organizer if other qualities required in this complex arena of money, chance, and human relationships were otherwise demonstrable.

In short, the evidence, slight though it is, again strengthens the general case for peasant self-sufficiency in local management.

Summary

To conclude, village authority at Shek Pik and similar places was represented by a body of elders from the various lineages and by a headman coming from among their number. The latter acted in accordance with the general consensus and had to be careful not to go beyond it. Any assistants operating in public affairs or regular stewardship of public property came under the same authority, and all village functionaries were, as one of the responsibilities of management, expected to post statements of account for all to see.

Besides the community business described above, the village

leadership was continuously involved in both making and testing customary law. Village rules covered a wide range of ordinary activities; and it was also usual to bring leaders of the village and of other lineages into important family business of the kind normally settled in writing, such as divisions of property, adoptions, and the taking in of husbands.

Besides routine secular duties, the management of religious rites was one of the most important, continuous tasks for village leaders in this period, and a crisis arising out of disturbed spirits was one of the most serious ever likely to face them.

There were other opportunities for leadership in the village economy; as in the formation and direction of loan organizations and money societies, and performing the role of middleman in the sale and mortgaging of private land. Information available from the Shek Pik area indicates that there was probably much activity of this kind, and that ordinary villagers were performing these duties in the 19th century.

Lineage and village leaders therefore got plenty of practice in man management and in handling a wide range of public affairs. It is important also to note that they seem to have operated entirely without direction or interference from outside. This made the rural communities of the area self-reliant places, the extent and efficiency of whose internal organization were largely determined by the capability or incapacity of their own leaders.

Kulp said of another Kwangtung village at a later time, "It enjoys local autonomy so long as it pays its taxes and commits no crime."[67] This seems to me also to have applied to the Shek Pik villages of the Hong Kong region in the 19th century.[68]

5

Pui O

A Linked Group of Hakka and Punti Farming Villages

The Villages and the Pattern of Settlement

THERE ARE TEN VILLAGES in the Pui O group.[1] Lo Wai, San Tsuen, Law Uk and Ham Tin are at Pui O, a wide, shallow valley running back from the sea and lying behind a long beach. Four others are situated in scattered locations in the Shap Long Peninsula which extends south from Pui O. These comprise Shap Long itself, Tai Long with Lung Mei, and Mong Tung Wan. Two more small villages lie along the coast to the west of Pui O—Shan Shek Wan and upper Cheung Sha. (See map 4.)

The population in 1899 was well under one thousand. The village totals recorded separately in the 1911 census report come to 513 persons,[2] but for some reason this generally comprehensive and useful paper does not list all the villages in the group. Five of the ten are omitted—Ham Tin, Tai Long with Lung Mei, upper Cheung Sha and Mong Tung Wan—although they are all shown on the survey sheets and registers of the Block Crown Leases and are certain to have been in existence at the time of the survey. Even adding the likely populations of these four settlements in 1911, the group could not have numbered much more than 850 persons at that time.

The interest of the Pui O group villages lies in the diversity of settlement within an area of no more than a few square miles,[3] and within so small a population. In 1899 there were twelve lineages (*tsu*) living in the villages of the group, six Hakka and six Punti, distributed as shown in Tables 8 and 9.

The tables show that the major lineages in each dialect group have been living together in the same area since their arrival in

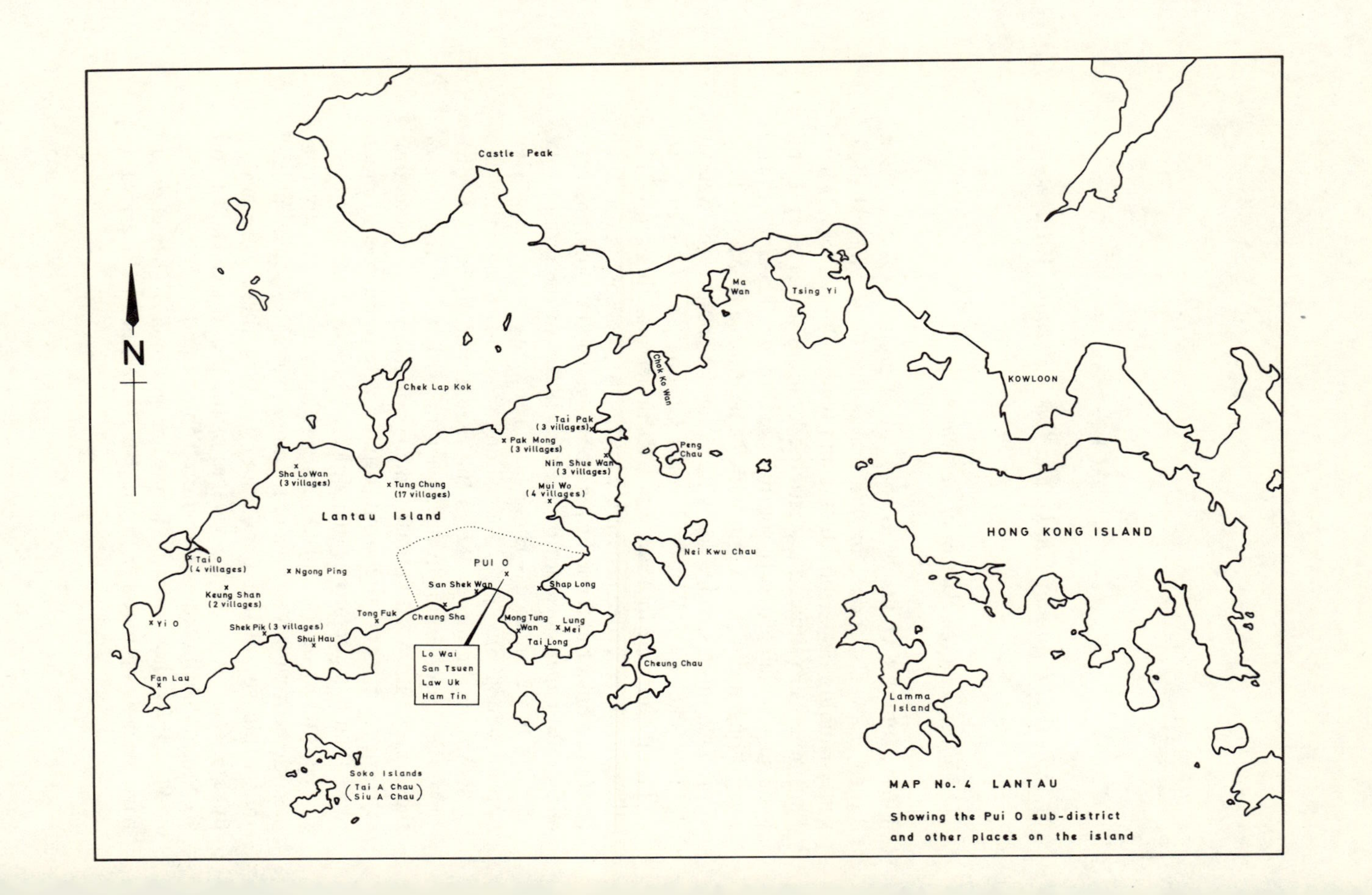

MAP No. 4 LANTAU

Showing the Pui O sub-district and other places on the island

TABLE 8

HAKKA AND PUNTI SETTLEMENT IN THE PUI O VILLAGES

VILLAGE	POPULATION IN 1911	HAKKA	PUNTI
Lo Wai	165	Cheung, Wan	Law, Chan, Fan
San Tsuen	132	Ho, Tsang	Wong (earlier)
Law Uk	37	Mo	Law, Fung, Tse
Ham Tin	omitted, but say 100	Cheung	Chan
Shap Long	95	Cheung	. . .
Tai Long	omitted, but say 100	Cheung, Ho	Chan
Lung Mei	omitted, but say 50	Cheung	. . .
Mong Tung Wan	omitted, but say 40	. . .	Fan
Shan Shek Wan	46	Mo	. . .
Upper Cheung Sha	omitted, but say 40	Lau, Tsang, Cheung	. . .
Total	513 but say 850	6 clans	6 clans

NOTE: Based on BCL registers for demarcation districts nos. 316, 329, 331–35, 337–42.

TABLE 9

LENGTH OF SETTLEMENT IN THE PUI O VILLAGES

LINEAGE	HOME DISTRICT	NO. OF GENERATIONS AT PUI O	SOURCE
Cheung	Kim Hau, South Fukien	12	Genealogy
Ho	Sha Wan; Chia-ying-chou	11	Genealogy
Wan	Luk Tei Tong, Mui Wo; Lantau	8–10	Oral tradition (record lost)
Law	Luk Yeuk Tsuen, Sai Heung; Hsin-an	10–11	Oral tradition (record lost)
Chan	Sha Tseng; Hsin-an	8–10	Spirit tablet
Mo	Pak Mong Fa; Hui-yang	9	Genealogy
Tsang	Pak Kap; Hui-chou	11–12	Oral tradition
Lau	Yim Tin near Nam Tau; Hsin-an	5–8 (claim to be first at Cheung Sha)	Oral tradition
Fan	Nam Tau; Hsin-an	4–5	Oral tradition
Tse	Nam Tau; Hsin-an	6	Oral tradition, and ancestor's grave (repaired 1893)
Fung	Nam Tong near Sham Chun; Hsin-an	5	Oral tradition
Wong	unknown	an estimated 6–7 when left in 1890s	Oral tradition, Cheung account book and *tsu p'u* listings

the 18th century, and that Hakka and Punti have long settled together in the four villages of Lo Wai, Law Uk, Ham Tin and Tai Long. In every case except that of the Lau clan of Upper Cheung Sha, the families in the outlying villages of the group all settled first in one or other of the three central Pui O villages of Lo Wai, San Tsuen and Law Uk, and branched out from there at a later date.

Land Ownership

At Pui O, the village families held most of their land under the Li Kau Yuen Tong of Sha Wan. Its ownership rights were swept away at the British land settlement, and the fields registered in the names of the villagers who had held surface rights prior to that time.

TABLE 10

OWNERSHIP OF LAND AT PUI O BY LOCAL LINEAGES, 1904

LINEAGE	DIALECT GROUP (Hakka or Punti)	AGRICULTURAL LAND	BUILDING LAND[1]	TOTAL (in acres)
Cheung	H	93.30	2.33	95.63
Ho	H	41.91	1.78	43.69
Law	P	18.89	0.42	19.31
Chan	P	14.18	0.32	14.50
Mo	H	9.00	0.32	9.32
Tsang	H	6.59	0.10	6.69
Wan	H	5.18	0.18	5.36
Lau	H	2.67	0.06	2.73
Fan	P	2.49	0.16	2.65
Tse	P	1.23	0.02	1.25
Fung	P	0.01	0.05	0.06

SOURCE: Based on BCL registers as in Table 8.

1. Since the usual village house site measured 0.01 acre the maximum number of dwellings can be ascertained by removing the decimal points.

The Hakka predominance in the subdistrict shows up very clearly in table 10. The Hakka Cheungs then held 93.30 acres, almost half the agricultural land within the boundaries; whilst together the Hakka clans held 158.85 acres and the Punti ones only 37.77 acres.

Table 10 also reflects the advantages obviously possessed by the early settlers, who were mostly Hakka. Taking building and agricultural land together, the seven arrivals before 1800—all but two of them Hakka—owned 194.50 acres. The four coming after that time—three of them Punti—held only 6.69 acres.

Table 10 includes land registered in the names of individuals and of the various family trusts known locally as *t'ang* and *tz'u*. The Cheung held 11.73 of their 98.30 acres in this way (12 percent); the Hos held 2.70 acres in trusts out of 41.91 (6.6 percent); the Laws 1.45 acres out of 18.89 (7.6 percent). Trust holdings in the smaller clans were insignificant or nonexistent, with the exception of the Mos who held 2.71 of their 9 acres (30 percent) in trust, the largest percentage figure for the whole group.

Table 11 conveys in a general way the spread of ownership among the individual villagers of the Pui O group. It does not include trust holdings. The entries are contained within a spectrum ranging from minimum holdings of a very small part of one acre to the largest of just on six acres. Among them, 118 (45 percent) are less than half an acre in size; another 118 (45 percent) range from a half to two acres; leaving a further 20 (10 percent) above that figure. (Households with insufficient land might obtain extra fields from clan holdings, or by renting from villagers with surplus land or from outside owners, one of which was a shop from Cheung Chau [Fong Yi Hop].)

There is, unfortunately, no way of tabling land farmed by households, as opposed to land owned by name, though this would be far more meaningful, especially if household sizes could be established. Regrettably, I did not make a special study of these arrangements, here or elsewhere, at a time when it would have still been possible to learn something of value. Such evidence as I have points to large households and much cooperation in farm work, before and after the Lease. (A "household" is here defined as a number of persons eating together and sharing farm work as a unit, though usually living in separate houses, i.e. the economic family.)

Among examples are the following. A woman born at Shek Pik in 1866 and married to a villager of Law Uk, Pui O, recalled that there were three tables eating together when she entered her husband's family in 1887, which implies an undivided establishment. A note on another family in this clan states that a household of six brothers did not divide until the last was married. My best informant at Pui O, born in 1886, said that his father's property (he died in 1913) was not divided until thirteen years later—by which time both he and his brother had sons—and then because of strife between their wives. The old mother arranged the division. The Block Crown Lease registers show cases in which land is jointly registered in two, four, or more names, but the circumstances of such registration are unknown, though it could imply that these persons ate and worked together. Also, many of the holdings registered in individual ownership at that time could still have been worked jointly.[4]

The Cheung Clan: A Peasant Lineage

The largest of the local lineages was the Cheung clan. The tables show that it was also the longest settled in the subdistrict. It was represented in six of the ten villages of the group and held half the private land. It was easily the most numerous of the families settled in the area, probably numbering half the local population.

A closer look at this lineage will show the extent of its internal organization, and the degree of sophistication that could mark what was yet but a very modest lineage by South China standards.[5]

The Block Crown Leases show that, besides its ancestral halls, the Cheungs possessed five *tz'u* and twelve *t'ang* trusts all registered as owning land in 1904.[6] Five more *t'ang* organizations can be traced in old papers in their possession. This is a large number for a peasant lineage of this size, and is not matched by any other on Lantau Island.

The Cheungs had apparently been long in the ascendant, outpacing the other old clans. As early as 1772–73 a Chan transferred 70 *tou chung*—nearly twelve acres—to a Cheung. The deed of sale by chance survived.[7] Other papers in a clan account book show that the process of land accumulation from other clans was going on in the late 19th century, with transactions also going on within the lineage.

The Cheung lineage seems to have been a very fertile one. The contents of its genealogies indicate the great numerical increase that took place after its arrival on Lantau, and the wave of human energy that it released on the countryside.[8] Local public works in the area, notably the reported retraining of a stream for *feng shui* protection as well as land production, and the reclamation of part of an estuary with a protective bund hundreds of yards long, reflected this situation.

The lineage produced quality as well as quantity. Two of its members, at least, amassed enough wealth to purchase degrees in mid-Ch'ing.[9] Three persons from the Ham Tin and Lo Wai branches were the largest individual landowners in the sub-district, registered with 5.99, 3.39, and 3.24 acres respectively, with two other Cheungs among the few persons holding land over 3 acres. (See table 11.)

It is regrettable that so little should be known of past leaders of this lineage. It is only possible now to write of one of their number from the late 19th century, though he may serve to show the type of man to be met with at an earlier time.

Cheung Kwong-chuen (1850–1916), who belonged to one of the Ham Tin families, was a farmer who went into business locally on his own account. He opened a shop in a small house situated below the main village of the Pui O group and secured goods from the nearby fishing port and market center of Cheung Chau. His customers were not only villagers, but included boat people from the creek and outside anchorage which were more frequented in his time than nowadays. Kwong-chuen was a usurer as well as a shopkeeper. As usual, his loans were made for interest at high rates or in return for mortgages of land. Copies of the deeds relating to ten of his mortgages, undertaken on his own behalf or as a *t'ang* manager, have survived in an old account book. One of them, relating to the year 1898, shows that he was capable of lending in one single transaction what was then, to a farmer, the considerable sum of $120—the equivalent of 90 ounces of silver. As happened more often than not in deals of the kind, this land, consisting of an acre and a quarter of good paddy fields, was acquired by him seven years later when its owner was unable to repay principal and interest.[10]

Cheung was prominent in local affairs. In the words of an old villager who remembers him well, (1886: 1962) "He managed everything there was to manage." Besides playing a leading part in lineage affairs, including control of various trusts, he was

TABLE 11

AGRICULTURAL HOLDINGS BY PERSONAL ENTRIES, 1904

Lineage	No. of Entries	Entries Above 3 Acres	2–3 Acres	1.50–1.99 Acres	1–1.49 Acres	50–.99 Acre	.25–.49 Acre	Rest	Largest Holding[1]
Cheung of Lo Wai/ Ham Tin	65	3	4	6	4	12	12	24	5.99
Cheung of Tai Long/ Lung Mi	10	...	1	1	4	2	...	2	2.13
Cheung of Shap Long	33	1	1	5	2	5	6	13	3.16
Cheung of Cheung Sha	5	1	...	...	...	3	...	1	3.20
Ho of San Wai (San Tsun)	67	1	1	2	12	7	8	36	3.01
Ho of Tai Long	6	...	1	...	3	2	...	...	2.61
Chan of Tai Long, Shap Long, Wang Tong Tsai	20	1	1	...	4	2	1	11	3.79
Mo of Shan Shek Wan	12	...	...	1	1	5	4	1	1.61
Tsang of Cheung Sha	5	...	1	2	1	...	1	...	2.12
Lau of Cheung Sha	1	...	1	...	...	...	...	...	2.67
Fan of Mong Tung Wan	4	...	...	...	1	2	...	1	1.21
Wan of Lo Wai	13	...	...	...	2	3	2	6	1.36
Tse of Lo Wai	1	...	...	...	1	...	...	...	1.23
Fung of Lo Wai	2	...	...	...	...	...	...	2	0.01
Law (Loa) of Lo Wai	21	...	2	1	5	7	2	4	2.84
Total	265	7	13	18	40	50	36	101	

SOURCE: Based on BCL registers as in Table 8.

1. Building holdings of largest landowners in each lineage: .15, .03, .06, .03, .04, .10, .05, .04, .03, .06, .07, .02, .02, .03, .01 respectively.

Holdings are entered on the registers in single or joint ownership. Lineage trust holdings are excluded from the table.

active in village management. Villagers from the subdistrict and, by report, some from outside it took their disputes to him for settlement. He helped to arrange various public services, including a regular ferry to the local market center. He also took the lead in managing the affairs of the local temples and in repairing them when this became necessary.

Such personages as Kwong-chuen gave the Cheung lineage status in the Pui O subdistrict and outside it. Locally, Cheungs were prominent among contributors to the repair of the Pui O temples. The cast iron bell of the Tin Hau temple, dated 1799, was given by a leading elder of the time, and the names of Cheungs head the donors of inscribed boards presented at the major repairs carried out in 1839 and 1914. The lineage's graves are many, often substantial, well constructed, and widely distributed over the island.

However, the Cheungs must be seen in their proper context. Despite its prominence, the lineage was essentially peasant. Its members were not landlords, but held their land in the main from the Li Kau Yuen Tong; they tilled the fields and mended their dykes and irrigation channels; they fished the local waters by stakenet and sampan; took wives from and sent daughters to other peasant lineages in neighboring settlements; sought lowly employment abroad; and generally maintained a thoroughgoing, highly localized peasant existence. Such activities and characteristics are confirmed by the contents of the genealogies and account book, and by the recollections of old men.

In common with others of its kind, then, the Cheung lineage had many ordinary members who were possessed of considerable capacities for organization and self-management. From time to time it also produced a few elites; but these, despite their higher talents, remained peasant by their location, activity and outlook, and family and marriage ties, as exemplified by Cheung Kwong-chuen's career and situation.

The Institutions of the Pui O Villages

The exact position as regards village leadership and institutions around 1899 is rather blurred; and not only by events such as the long decline in population and prosperity from about 1850 on or by the passage of time with its removal of reliable witnesses. The strong lineage ties within the subdistrict and the predominence of the major representative of the local elite of the time (Cheung Kwong-chuen) who, until his death in 1916, seems to have managed most things in his own lineage and in the group, also add to the difficulties of unraveling the true position.

However, it would appear that village institutions included, in the multilineage settlements, the informal council of elders, the headmen of villages—both well in the background with persons like Cheung Kwong-chuen around—and the managers of various village bodies. The latter were of two kinds: one connected with the religious protection of the settlement, the other with the provision of other communal needs.

In the first category, we find from the Block Crown Leases that two of the villages of the subdistrict held property in the name of the settlement. There was a Pui O Tsung and a San Tsuen Tsung. The description "Tsung," meaning "public," indicates their communal character.[11] Referring to the San Tsuen trust, my most reliable informant (1886: 1964) has said that its purpose was to ensure the worship of the earth gods of the village, and so protect its inhabitants from harm. A small revenue was obtained from renting out the fields and was applied by the Tsung manager to worshipping purposes. Otherwise, the year's rites were secured by rotating the fields among villagers who would then be responsible for their performance. The manager of the trust would present his accounts on or about the 20th of the first lunar month, at the earth gods' festival. These Tsung were considered to be very old institutions, dating back to the foundation of the villages.[12]

In the second category, we find bodies such as the Hap Hing Tong of Lo Wai. This held no land, though it is shown in the registers as owning a well. Elders recall that at the time of the lease it owned and operated a large public row boat, used to take villagers and their produce and purchases to and from Cheung Chau and elsewhere. The Tong still exists today and is generally regarded as the community organization of this multiclan village. It owns furniture and crockery loaned out for major social occasions, finances the village unicorn dancers, and arranges the celebrations at main festivals such as letting off the fire balloon (*hung meng teng*) at midautumn. It could authorize tree felling or arrange other means of raising money to make purchases or meet a deficit. With the exception of the temples and the thanksgiving rites mentioned in my discussion of the institutions of the Pui O group below, which were all intersettlement in character, no other village institution is recorded.

Village Groupings on Lantau and Their Relevance for Local Leadership

In the 1950s the Hong Kong government wished to extend the rural committee system to all parts of the New Territories. This scheme is explained in an annual report which states:

> In a partial return to the traditional organisation found here in 1899, groups of villages have been encouraged since 1946 to organise themselves into areas, usually centering on a market town, and to elect a rural committee.[13]

To the writer's knowledge there were difficulties on Lantau Island. Scattered along its length and breadth, by the shore and in the hills, the island's village communities were linked in some places and separate in others. The Pui O group of villages was chosen to be the nucleus of one of the four rural committees planned for Lantau, but its membership fell short of the wider grouping desired by the British authorities and had to be extended. This took time to arrange because of former independences and certain mutual coolnesses, and it was another ten years before the South Lantau Rural Committee was inaugurated.

This regrouping into the four areas required by the British district administration in the 1950s, the innovation it represented, and the adjustments it required, all highlight the unorganized state of the Lantau community before that time.

The purpose of this section is to describe the rural groupings as they were then, essentially the same as in the late Ch'ing; to show that they appear to have been of local origin and do not equate with governmental systems of control, liaison, or tax collection; and, through examining what they did and did not do, to show that their activity was usually confined to giving mutual support in danger and to sharing rites of protection against disease and the supernatural. The shared institutions and rituals of the Pui O group are a typical example of the kind. There was no higher-level organization uniting the grouped villages.

The patchwork of alliances that made up the social and political organization of the island in the late 19th century is set out in table 12 and map 1. The information upon which it is based has been obtained during a long period of intermittent consultation with local elders across the island.

This grouping depends, in the main, on geographical location. The linked villages of the largest group, Tung Chung, are all situated in the one valley and the slopes leading from it to the surrounding hills. This explanation applies to the Mui Wo, Shek Pik, and Tai O groups also. Others are explained by being situated next to each other, like the Pak Mong, Tai Pak, and Sha Lo Wan linkages.

However, these attributions do not cover all. The Pui O group took in villages that could have existed in smaller linkages had they not been joined by lineage ties. There are also unlinked villages to account for. Some of those remaining by themselves can be explained by geographical isolation. In other cases it would seem that numbers, as well as location, helped to determine whether villages stayed single or became associated with others. The unlinked settlements are usually larger villages in self-contained and generally isolated geographical locations.[14]

It is notable that marketing links were also very varied: "on" to Tai O; "off" to the nearby islands of Peng Chau and Cheung Chau, and, from the north side of the island, "off" to the opposite mainland at Castle Peak. According to old residents, there was also considerable marketing to delta ports like Shek Ki before 1899 from the South Lantau villages, due partly to fishing and charcoal burning, whose products were in demand in those more populated areas. Marketing was not a vital factor in determining or enforcing linkage.

There was no obvious consistency in determining these matters, and there were clearly other reasons that hindered or precluded

TABLE 12

VILLAGE GROUPING ON LANTAU IN 1899

Group or Village	No. of Villages	Land Population of Group (based on 1911 census)	Temples	Market Centers
Tung Chung	17	1,275 including Cho Lo Kok	3	Tai O and Yuen Long
Sha Lo Wan	3	About 350	1	Tai O and Yuen Long
Tai O Villages	4	286	2	Tai O
Shek Pik	3	422	2	Tai O and Cheung Chau
Keung Shan	2	About 200	...	Tai O
Pui O	10	About 850	3	Cheung Chau
Mui Wo	4	284	1	Cheung Chau
Pak Mong	3	220	...	Cheung Chau and Yuen Long
Tai Pak	3	About 200	1	Peng Chau
Nim Shue Wan	3	About 200	1	Peng Chau
Chuk Ko Wan and other hamlets of NE Lantau	...	About 100	...	Peng Chau
Shui Hau	1	214	...	Tai O and Cheung Chau
Tong Fuk	1	198	2	Tai O and Cheung Chau
Yi O	1	About 250	1	Tai O
Fan Lau (Shek Sun)	1	About 200	1	Tai O

association. These could be of a varied kind, such as those arising from animosities or quarrels in the course of settlement and family history.

However rationalized, this is a surprisingly decentralized situation in a region where villages tend to become linked. At the time of the lease of the New Territories the terms *yüeh* and *hsiang* were in common use for a subdistrict or group of associated villages, especially around Kowloon. There could be found the Nine Yüeh of Sai Kung, the Six Yüeh of Sha Tin and the Four Yüeh of Tsuen Wan as well as the linkages of Kowloon itself.[15]

Besides the *yüeh*, there were a number of associated villages under the term *hsiang*. Some examples of these can be found in the *Gazetteer of Place Names in Hong Kong, Kowloon and the New Territories*, published in 1960. They include the Pat Heung of Shek Kong, the Sap Pak Heung of Yuen Long, and the Sap Sz Heung of north Sai Kung.[16] Another large traditional grouping is the *hsiang* of the Lam Tsuen valley near Taipo, otherwise known as the Ch'i Yüeh.[17]

The looser Lantau situation is reflected in the frequent use of terms for single settlements and the general absence of those for groupings. The individual village in the Hong Kong region is usually styled *ts'un*, and this term appears to have been in use for centuries, judging by the entries in the Hsin-an gazetteer.[18] On Lantau it is to be found in many village names, local genealogies, and grave tablets, and generally in old spoken usage. The term *hsiang* is also used for individual villages, though less frequently, and appears in this sense in three local instances.[19]

Terms used to describe higher linkages, of the type noted above, such as *yüeh* and *hsiang* (in its associated sense), and another styled *tung*, are scarcely to be found on the island. A very old resident of Pui O (1887:1960–62) applied the term *yüeh* to his own group of villages, but this is as yet uncorroborated. The Cheung family record (1927) has Pui O *hsiang* as the area unit, copying from an earlier version. Tai O, with its villages—since the term could not be used for the town alone—is also styled a *hsiang* on a bell of 1713 in the Tin Hau temple at San Tsuen, one of its four small associated settlements. The old Pui O man quoted above stated, again without my being able to substantiate it, that *tung* was used to describe the adjacent Mui Wo group of villages.[20] I have found no other instances.

Official sources, Chinese and English, are of little help in determining the existence of grouped villages and subdistricts. The district gazetteer and similar geographical works do not deal with the island's internal arrangements. The only piece of information comes from British papers, though they provide only inconclusive and rather puzzling information. A map lodged in the Hong Kong Land Registry in 1899, seemingly prepared in connection with the Local Communities Ordinance, divides Lantau into three areas.[21] The lists of committee men for Lantau gazetted under the same ordinance are also three in number,[22] but though the areas from which they come match the map divisions, the lists omit half the villages, including some of the largest and oldest settlements.[23] Moreover, no local information is now available as to whether the divisions were established ones or an internal British arrangement.[24]

Real or not, it does not seem that these divisions had any official application. Lantau does not appear to have had any administrative or fiscal subdivisions under the Ch'ing. For general purposes of government in the early 19th century, the whole island, together with Hong Kong Island and some mainland areas, came under the deputy magistrate at Kowloon who was responsible for 492 villages,[25] much more than the Lantau total. Lantau was certainly included in the fiscal divisions for the county since these are mentioned on tax receipts and official registrations of sales and mortgages of land, but, as for administration, only as part of a much wider area.[26]

In the light of the foregoing—that is to say the small and varied size of groups, the existence of single unlinked settlements, and the official administrative and fiscal arrangements described above—it appears most likely that those groupings that did emerge were due to local and not official initiative; for it is difficult to believe that administrative direction would have been so haphazard.

What then motivated them and led to their continuance? What they did *not* do is of equal importance in understanding their position as what they did.[27] In the first place, the groupings were never intended to replace the village nor to preempt village authority. The villages of the groups were still under the control of their elders and would act on all things, including group interests and cooperation, as they saw fit. Without their support the group meant nothing. Its absence subtracted nothing from village authority, though it may have been an occasional addition to village strength.

Secondly, the groups were not the beginnings of an attempt to create a territorial exclusiveness in rural life. The village families did not confine themselves to taking wives from within the group, even if, as at Pui O and Tung Chung, there was a sufficient number of villages and a large enough population to make this possible. The family marriages to the third generation of the present elders, and the information on earlier unions provided by surviving genealogies, illustrate a much wider marriage field, off the island as well as on. Also, it could and did happen that the Lantau lineages might belong to several groupings, either from the outset, or when segmentation occurred at a later time.[28]

Dead as well as alive, the family weakened the cohesion of the geographical grouping. Like wives, grave sites were continually being sought across intervillage boundaries. Many inspections and inquiries show that graves were quite frequently sited outside the single village or linked village areas to which their occupants had belonged. Occasionally, too, one comes across the large grave of a rich outsider sited far from his native village or even county. The geomancers who decided these matters were often itinerant and not natives of the district. Intent only upon finding a good site, they left to their clients the complications that might ensue if they advised on a grave in another village area.[29] Graves led to territorial "invasions" once or twice a year, when families from another village or group visited them at the Ching Ming and Chung Yeung festivals. Crisscrossing of boundaries occurred frequently on Lantau at such times, with family groups going in all directions to seek out their ancestral graves.

Other intrusions took place for religious purposes. An interesting case is reported from Pui O. The Tsang lineage of Luk Tei Tong in the neighboring Mui Wo group of villages still visits several shrines in the Pui O valley every year in the first lunar month. In the course of two centuries' residence in the district they have never lived at Pui O, but these shrines to the earth god are linked with a first, or early, ancestor who operated a stake net there. He established the shrines to promote the fishing and to protect him on his journeys to and from his home.

Finally, groupings did not prevent outsiders from buying fields and houses in member settlements. Such purchases by persons from other villages were as common as the opportunities for doing so, which arose out of economic crisis and the inability or unwillingness of agnates to buy the property up for sale. The purchaser might find it more prudent to rent to villagers than attempt to put in a tenant of his own, but there was no ban, and such events contributed to the weakening of territorial solidarity.

To summarize, the Lantau village groupings did not subordinate the village to the group; no loss of authority was involved at village level. Nor did the group seek to influence local practices by promoting exclusiveness where none existed. It did not prevent intermarriage with families in other groups, the selection of burial sites outside the group boundaries, the undertaking of economic or religious activity in other subdistricts, and the purchase of land by outsiders. Instead, all the evidence points away from any kind of regulation or interference with local family, village, and economic practice to other, more constructive purposes. The true and limited purpose of these groupings was to provide mutual assistance for villages in times of trouble; in fact, to give protection against men and against spirits.

Protection against men was important in all its gradations, from mutual interest in the punishment of petty offenders to the full-scale summoning of a community for defense against pirates and bandits. In the latter connection, mutual aid was a big consideration on a place like Lantau where the villages were separate and divided by a difficult terrain that hindered communications between friends but helped enemies. Although there were garrisons of Green Banner troops at Tung Chung and Tai O, posts at Cheung Chau, Peng Chau, and other places nearby, and after 1887 a Chinese Imperial Maritime Customs station on Cheung Chau with a customs' cruiser or two within call, these offered little immediate protection—only the promise of belated retribution, not always forthcoming. The village communities had to be self-reliant in defense and to preempt the help of other villages if they could.[30]

In the more routine matters of rural life, the group could afford some assistance to individuals. It could act as the largest unit of local custom, operating its own set of rules, or helping to enforce the rules of individual villages. Once agreed, the rules of the group applied in all villages. This is shown in the Tung Chung case which required offenders against the rules of the united *hsiang* to be paraded through all 17 villages. In another local instance the Mui Wo community was also accustomed to following its own local rules, as I found as district officer in 1957, when local custom in the event of animals grazing on other persons' private property was cited to me. This case had been aggravated by pursuit of the offending cow which was in calf and its subsequent death by hemorrhage caused during the chase. Such rules may have differed little from one place or group to another; but their importance lies in their being recognized as local custom with local application.

Protection against spirits was equally important in these settlements and, to local minds, required far more frequently than precautionary measures against human attacks. The protection of the gods was enlisted through joint or shared religious activities throughout the year, and the accompanying entertainment was intended as much for gods as men.[31] The performance of the periodic protective rites common in the Hong Kong region known as Ta Chiu was a major interest in the linked villages before 1899. Before and after the end of the century Ta Chiu ceremonies took place at Tai O, Tung Chung, Sha Lo Wan, Tong Fuk, Shek Pik, and Mui Wo, but in all but one case they had ceased before the Pacific War. The Mui Wo ceremony outlived the rest, but the one held there a few years after the war was the last. Thus ended what was probably a long tradition in the history of these village communities.

I come now to the crux of the matter of association. The varied nature of the group relationship described above shows that these were not formal alliances of the *yüeh* type, but chance linkages whose ties varied greatly from one group to another.

In places like Tung Chung, Mui Wo, and Pui O, the linkage was apparently a confederation of equals, probably because of the numbers involved. Other groups comprised a large village with minor satellities. Such dependent status could arise through later settlement, smaller numbers, tenant relationship to landowners or perpetual lease holders from the large village, and patronage of the shops, schools, and other facilities of the larger settlement. The Sha Lo Wan group falls into this category. The Shek Pik group was partly of this kind and partly linked by lineage ties. Pui O was in a category of its own because of the greater importance of lineage ties, which placed the main clan in six, and some other clans in several, of the ten villages of the group, and concentrated lineage rituals in the founding settlement. The Tai O villages, again, were somewhat different because of their closer ties with the market center through proximity, small size, and participation in the economic activities of the place, notably salt-making.[32]

This variety in the nature of the Lantau rural groupings, from genuine confederations to others groups in which minor villages had satellite status, strengthened or mitigated as the case might be by lineage ties, helps to emphasize their lack of organization. Though some villages might have a recognized meeting place in a local temple,[33] none were sufficiently institutionalized to have built a *kung so* or public office. Moreover, there is neither indication nor remembrance of any general institution for combining all, or even part, of them on an island or sector basis.[34]

No one, it seems, took the initiative to link the groups on an island basis or one incorporating several of them together. One could ask whether a market town was not capable of taking this initiative, and it is, I think, a fair question. However, the answer would be negative for Lantau. There was not one market center for the island in the late Ch'ing, but many. The economic associations of its village communities led in all directions. There was thus no opportunity for political leadership based on, and enforced by, the economic domination of town over country. And whilst the town had more and better schools[35] and some prosperous shopkeepers, what small evidence of leadership is available for the times shows that persons with a name and influence beyond their village or their group were villagers and not townsmen.[36]

Another valid question when considering potential or actual area leadership is whether the wealthy absentee literatus landlord might not have filled the gap. This, it seems, was never the case in the later 19th century. The most local communities could expect was a contribution to temple repairs, and usually less than was provided by some other subscribers.[37]

My conclusion is that, by the late 19th century, there was an inchoate and confused intervillage situation on Lantau. Villages were grouped or single, the former in linkages that appear to have been self-forming and had no connection with either the administrative or fiscal divisions of the Hsin-an magistracy. There was no network of groups that covered all the settlements, nor any institution serving this purpose. This situation matched the government's civil and military dispositions, which included Lantau in wider areas of responsibility. The district administration accepted and used the existing groupings and power structure without requiring anything more formal or hierarchical to be put in their place. Nor, apparently, did local people see the need to form their own higher institutions.

The Institutions of the Pui O Group

Against this background, it will come as no surprise to find that, as a group, the Pui O villages had few common institutions. There was no formal body of elders to deal with matters of mutual interest nor a common *kung so*, only a number of indications that the villagers were, in their own estimation, a group of people linked by more than the lineage ties that bound many of them from different settlements together.

The most regular sign of group solidarity was the performance twice yearly of rites known locally as *tso-shen* and *huan-shen*. These were held in front of the shrine to the earth gods (*pai-kung*) at Lo Wai. They took place on the 5th day of the second month and the 22nd day of the twelfth month of the lunar calendar when, in accordance with old custom, villagers gathered to worship at the shrine, followed by the distribution of pork.[38]

The notices were sent out from Lo Wai to all the villages in the group, and on each occasion the arrangements were made by several men of the Lo Wai and San Tsuen clans acting by rotation. Families wishing to join in the occasion paid their subscriptions and sent representatives to Lo Wai to worship the gods and to collect their share of the ritual pork. Before the Pacific War, the elders say, these ceremonies were supported by all the villages of the Pui O group, but attendance has fallen off in recent years though the practice is still observed.[39]

Other evidence for group solidarity may be found in the local temples. The elders state that the Tin Hau temple at Pui O belonged to all the villages of the group. Their proprietary interest in it, and the wide support given in times of need, is shown by a memorial board presented when the temple last received a major repair in 1916.[40] It contains 26 names; among them 11 Cheungs, 7 Hos, 3 Laws, 2 Fans, a Chan, a Tse, a Chau (place of origin unknown), and a Chu who was a leading merchant on Cheung Chau, the market town where the Pui O villagers did most of their buying and selling. An earlier board, dated in 1839, contains the names of 6 Cheungs, 5 Hos, 3 Chans, and 1 Law.[41] The bell, the oldest dated object in the temple, dated 1799, was presented by a Cheung.[42]

A second temple at Pui O provides additional evidence of group solidarity. This is a larger and older building, now in ruins, dedicated to the Hung Shing god. The building has a bell dated in the K'ang Hsi reign (1705–06) and was last given major repairs in the Chia Ch'ing and Kuang Hsü periods (1800–1801 and 1875–76 respectively). Though by report much patronized in times past by the boat people, who came in large numbers to it on the Hung Shing festival in the second lunar month, it was a village temple. It was managed by local people in the same way as the Tin Hau temple described above and pertained to all settlements and not to one particular village. This seems to be substantiated by the names of subscribers, who came from the Pui O villages as well as from the boat population, on the memorial tablet recording the Kuang Hsü repair, and by the appointment of a villager of the group as temple keeper.

The joint ownership of these temples is also witnessed by the arrangements for paying the temple keepers. In accordance with local custom, they could expect to collect a certain amount of rice from families in all the villages of the group, unhusked at the first crop and husked at the second harvest.

There are, otherwise, no other joint functions or indications of group solidarity to be brought forward.[43] All other organizations and activities in the Pui O group were conducted at village or clan level. Nor was there any linkage with adjacent or other groups on the island to indicate solidarity on any higher level of association.

Pui O demonstrates the lack of a strong group organization among and between the village communities of Lantau Island in the late Ch'ing, with the corollary that the peasant lineages were thrown back on their own management resources, each in its own locality. Assuming, for present purposes, a reasonable economic situation, it is clear that the ensuing stability or instability of village life depended largely upon the quality of this low-level rural leadership.

6

Ngau Tau Kok Village

A Newer, Specialist Settlement of Hakkas

Ngau Tau Kok was a village of stonecutters and cultivators which was formerly located on the seashore on the north-eastern arm of Hong Kong harbour.[1] It was one of a group of four adjacent villages, known locally as "The Four Hills,"[2] whose inhabitants, mostly stonecutters, exploited the rich granite formations in the area until they were used up in the early decades of this century. The villagers were Hakkas, a people who are traditionally connected with stone quarrying in South China.

The Four Hills

The Four Hills were a part of the New Territories leased to Britain by China in 1898. The quarries were known to the Hong Kong government and were soon recognized as a valuable acquisition to the colony. An official report of 1912 states:

> The New Territories are very rich in granite which appears chiefly in the form of granite boulders on the hillsides. By far the most important quarries are those which stretch Eastward along the North of Kowloon Bay as far as Lyeemun. They extend over about 100 acres and are leased to contractors for an average annual Crown Rent of $15,000: from these is supplied most of the granite now used in Hong Kong.[3]

The quarries of the Four Hills had been working long before the British occupation of the New Territories. As early as 1810 the stonemasons of East Kowloon were persuaded by one of the Tang family of Kam Tin to cut stones for the construction of a fort at Kowloon at low wages as a gesture of assistance against the pirates, who were then particularly troublesome in local waters.[4]

It is clear from various accounts, and from the histories of the families cleared from Ngau Tau Kok village in 1966,[5] that the use of the area for stone quarrying by individuals living and working at sites opened all over the hillsides of the Four Hills preceded the establishment of this and possibly the other villages of the group. A good description of the area in earlier days is given by Rev. George Smith, later Bishop of Victoria, who visited it from Hong Kong Island in December 1844. He records that his party

> first landed at a stone quarry, where the Chinese workmen were induced to leave their labour, and, without any difficulty or delay, about twenty natives were assembled round us, and formed a little congregation of attentive hearers.... We proceeded over a space of two miles, which was covered at almost every level and habitable spot by native huts of rude construction, but with substantial outer walls to repel the inroads of pirates and freebooters.[6]

This seems to have been true for much of the second half of the century, judging by facts that emerged in the course of settling claims to land in the Four Hills district just after the lease of the New Territories. Some interesting papers were produced by a man who claimed to have purchased a large area of land from the Hsin-an magistrate in 1892; nothing less than "the whole area of foreshore between Li U Mun and Ngau Tau Kok, with an apparent frontage of above 2 miles."[7] Inquiries were made through the British consul general at Canton, and the viceroy relayed the acting magistrate's report on the claim to the Hong Kong government.[8] After confirming the man's status as owner, the magistrate went on to make some observations about the recent history of part of the area. These show the condition of the place and the character of the persons who lived and worked there.

It appears that for ten years the French had been permitted to quarry stone there for the Roman Catholic cathedral in Canton, apparently ending in 1885, when the Tsungli Yamen instructed the viceroy to have the quarry closed. This was easier said than done. According to the magistrate's report, "since there was profit to be made, certain disorderly ruffians proceed to quarry stone there, and cases of strife and dispute continually arose, and there were complicated proceedings at law for many years. Repeated orders were received...to close the quarry, and trial was threatened in case of disobedience" (which by implication continually occurred). Afterwards, more reputable persons applied to quarry there, and were refused, "this being found not in accordance with a former decision fixing a limit of time for such operation."

The land case that occasioned the presentation of this material was apparently confined to the marine frontage, and the magistrate said he had no means of knowing whether there was "any undue encroachment upon the hill country."

This hill land was variously used for farming and quarrying in the 19th century, and there was at least one large landowner. A Li family, place of residence unknown, mortgaged 130 Chinese acres (*mou*) to some Yaus of the nearby farming village of Tseng Lan Shue[9] in 1807–1808 and sold it to them in 1860. The family sold 80 Chinese acres of taxable hill land at Ngau Tau Kok to one of its members in 1861, and a smaller area was given on perpetual lease to one of the present Ngau Tau Kok village families in 1877.[10]

It appears that there were many such small holdings of land for houses and cultivation, mostly in connection with the quarries. Three other deeds in the Hong Kong Land Registry, dated 1878, 1888, and 1892 and registered by one purchaser in 1900 relate to land on the shore "suitable for storing, shipping and landing stones;" to a stone quarry with 2 mat shed houses and vegetable plots, (including the right to use a cart path and wharf belonging to the quarry); and to a row of five tile-roofed houses. These were all situated at Sai Cho Wan, one of the Four Hills. These properties had belonged to persons of the same name as the purchaser, and had come down from a father or earlier generations.[11] Some of them were probably similar to a group of nine houses compensated on Stonecutters' Island in the 1860s, when the Hong Kong Government removed the inhabitants, and then described as "one large establishment for Stone Cutters, with a yard and Blacksmiths' sheds enclosed by a gateway."[12] Even so, much of the hill land at the Four Hills was clearly unleased and was therefore under the magistrate's charge and disposal.

The Hsin-an magistrate's interest in the Four Hills was mainly financial, since, apart from the land tax, the quarries were a regular source of income for the district government. The monthly fees from quarrymen at the Four Hills came to over 120 taels at the end of the 19th century, according to the statement of revenue for the whole of the Hsin-an district attached to Lockhart's report.[13]

It appears that this revenue was not secured without official intervention from time to time. The affairs of the Four Hills frequently caused trouble for the authorities. In the early 1890s successive magistrates visited the place personally, and one of them reported that he had "called the people of the Four Hills together again and again and examined them." These visits resulted from continual disputes.[14]

Quarrymen with troublesome dispositions were not unknown to Hong Kong. It was rough work, and the calling seems to have attracted persons who were tough and quarrelsome. An early British report of 1844 states:

> The stone cutters have been working here for many years before our arrival. The majority of the men are unprincipled. They cannot be considered as domesticated, and are in the habit of coming and going according to the state of the trade.[15]

It was not until later that families long working individual quarries began to move into a settlement with others of their kind.

The Village of Ngau Tau Kok

By 1899 the village of Ngau Tau Kok, a settled, compact community with closely grouped houses fronting onto the single main street, was still a fairly recent development.[16] Discussions with the elders of the families who classified themselves as "old Ngau Tau Kok" have produced the following table which shows this beyond any doubt. It has been compiled from family records, the information known to old persons, grave tablets, and the like.

LINEAGE	HOME DISTRICT	APPROXIMATE DATE OF ARRIVAL
Liu	Ng Wah	1850–60[17]
San	Tam Shui (Wai Yeung)	1850–60
Yim	Tam Shui (Wai Yeung)	before 1865
Li	Wai Yeung	1860–70
Law	Tam Shui (Wai Yeung)	about 1870
Chung	...	1860?
Ko	Tam Shui (Wai Yeung)	1875–80
Wu	Wai Yeung	1870
Mau	Wai Chau	1890

It is likely that there were other families, but these had either died out or left the village before 1966, and were not available for interview.

Although Ngau Tau Kok village was lately settled and multilineage, some lineages having a dozen families but most less, it was from the start a closely-knit community and quite unlike farming villages of similarly mixed settlement. Ngau Tau Kok quickly acquired its multilineage population, whereas villages such as Shek Pik and Pui O got their lineages in the course of generations, if not centuries. The way in which new settlers were obtained was also quite different, and created from among persons of different names a tightly knit group with common geographical origins and narrow interests. One sees here no trace of the traditional rural reluctance to grant ownership, and even tenancy, of land and buildings together to newcomers (so as to create rights of belonging) that can be cited time after time in the experiences of families seeking to enter the old villages of the region—and still noted in contemporary Hong Kong by Aijmer.[18]

The rapid buildup of families from many lineages can be traced to the existence of the stone quarries of East Kowloon and the continuing demand for stone for building purposes, which brought a steady stream of persons to the area, some with their families. The homogeneity of the village can be explained by the tradition that restricted stonecutting to Hakkas; and to their practice, shared with many other Chinese callings, of recruiting their clansmen and fellow natives to new and promising enterprises.

Hakkas have long been connected with stonecutting. Lockhart lists their chief pursuits as agriculture and quarrying.[19] Orme mentions the main stone quarries of the New Territories in his report, and adds, "The quarrymen are nearly all Hakkas from Kweishin, who settle at the quarries until they have made some money and then return home."[20] Other writers have commented on the Hakka specialization in this calling.[21]

Specialization in employment often leads to selective recruitment, as mentioned above. The Hakka stonecutters of East Kowloon obtained their labor from their home districts in Kwangtung, and not from the Hakka villages of Kowloon and the New Territories. Conversations with many old persons in Ngau Tau Kok established this beyond any doubt. Seven of the nine lineages still living in the village in 1966 came from the Wai Yeung (formerly Kwei Shin) district of Hui-chou prefecture in Kwangtung. The old people recall how, in the first and second generation of settlement in East Kowloon, the newcomers had come in response to an invitation or suggestion from a clan member or a native villager already employed there. There were incentives to becoming a stonecutter, for although the work was hard, the pay was good.[22]

The stonecutters were not the only skilled workers required at the quarries. Stone polishers were also employed, and these too were Hakkas and fellow clansmen. I was told that the two trades were specialist, and not interchangeable. Blacksmiths, another well-known Hakka calling, were also needed at the quarries, as tools had constantly to be sharpened and replaced.

Some of the families at Ngau Tau Kok entered an allied occupation, that of construction and building, in which Hakkas were also to be found in large numbers. Two of the nine lineages mentioned ancestors resident at Ngau Tau Kok in the late 19th century, who as individual workers went far and wide in the pursuit of this employment. One of them was said to have belonged to a group of village men who went around the region on building work. Places like Macau and Lantau were mentioned as being on their itinerary.

Women were also recruited from the home districts. Many of the wives and unmarried daughters of the stonecutters worked at the quarries, breaking aggregate and carrying baskets of stone onto the waiting junks. The wife might be as expert as her husband in the technical aspects of quarrying. In one case, a widowed mother-in-law, competent in acquired skills and character, entered into partnership to open a new quarry. In the smaller quarries, wives might cook for the family and the hired labor, for whom food was included in the daily wage. The wives and daughters of the village families were also engaged in some cultivation to provide vegetables and sweet potatoes, as well as foodstuffs for pigs.[23]

Women were brought more often into Ngau Tau Kok as wives and child brides (*hsin-pao-tzu*) than directly for labor. Sixty years ago, it was common for girl children to become child brides, and a good number of the surviving elderly women in the settlement to whom I spoke had come into Ngau Tau Kok in this way.

This taking of only Hakka wives in an area where crossdialect marriages were quite common[24] is explained by Ngau Tau Kok's continuing connections with its home area in China. This, in turn, was based on the requirements of a specialist settlement. Cantonese women were unaccustomed to work in the quarries, might not relish this employment, and, I was told, might not be equal to the physical labor.

These factors explain why Ngau Tau Kok began, and for as long as it stayed a village of stonecutters, remained a homogeneous Hakka settlement of persons coming mainly from the same home areas in Kwangtung. There was a vital economic need to keep in close touch with the source of labor and of future wives. Its inhabitants' links with their native place remained stronger than in many farming villages, Hakka and Punti alike. There was not a single ancestral hall in the village—a sure sign, in an otherwise prosperous settlement that could afford to build them, that links with the home villages were close and kept up.

The quarries began to fail not long after the extension of British rule and the village families had to look elsewhere for their livelihood. Many of the men went outside to work, and family budgets were supplemented by selling vegetables in the urban parts of Kowloon. Grass and firewood were also sold as opportunity offered. Some families left the village, but most of them stayed because they owned the houses in which they lived.

As often happens in Chinese villages, the decline of the quarries was blamed on the destruction of the local *feng shui* by the action of one of the quarrymen in cutting into a rock called the Cow's Head—a natural feature from which the village took its name—interfering with its vital spirit and causing it to die, with grave consequences for the rest of the inhabitants. This is the explanation for the failure of the quarries given, and believed in, by the older village residents.[25]

The Institutions of the Four Hills

The Four Hills are of special interest because of their meeting house and the use made of it both by the Hsin-an magistrate and, after 1899, the Hong Kong government.

The Chinese district government was intent on securing its revenue and on keeping the peace. As stated above, one of the late 19th century magistrates went several times in person to the Four Hills to sort out problems of this nature. The magistracy also arranged for a noted *feng shui* spot, undoubtedly the rock referred to above, to be protected against quarrying in order to avoid the arguments that would occur whenever it was rumored that someone wished to cut stone there. In the course of these magisterial visits a proclamation was issued in 1893, which laid down a control system.

This interesting proclamation, entitled "in the matter of establishing certain rules and issuing a notice for general information. . . ," was to be posted "at the stone hill" at Sai Cho Wan.[26] It does not appear that there had previously been such a comprehensive regulation governing the affairs of the quarry district, despite the disputes mentioned elsewhere in the papers and the known turbulence of the quarrymen. The proclamation, which is available only in English translation, mentions deputies, constables, and the headmen of the Four Hills with their "stone hill meeting house." The last named were the leading quarry masters of the area.

It is, unfortunately, not clear from the surviving papers when the Four Hills meeting house was established, and I have been unable to obtain definite information locally. It appears, however, that it may have been in existence before the magistrate's proclamation and that he simply made use of it for his own purposes.

The leading feature of the new control system was that the headmen of the Four Hills were to collect all revenue owing to government direct from those persons loading stones onto boats. Six-tenths of this money was to go to the district government, and the remaining four-tenths to the Stone Hill meeting house. The first portion was to pay "the deputies in the office"—this probably refers to the petty officials kept on site by the magistrate —and the salary of the headmen of the Four Hills. The remaining four-tenths was to be used by the meeting house "to meet yearly expenses of joss meetings and free schools."

The proclamation contains the usual warnings about misbehavior and abuse. The headmen had to personally inspect the accounts and levy the taxes according to the rules. They were not to "favour and work mischief, reporting little where there is much, or misappropriate or embezzle," for which they would be called to account. The inspectors—presumably the deputies are meant—and the managers of the Stone Hill meeting house "shall combine their strength and manage their affairs with real earnestness. If there be a nest of mischief, and it is found out, they will be punished and degraded and will not be pardoned." For their part, the boatmen coming to the hills to buy stone were informed that they "shall obey the notice, and deal in ready money. The taxes must be fully paid before they are allowed to clear."

It is instructive that the Hong Kong government adopted this system in its entirety after the lease. Crown rent was fixed for each of the Four Hills, and the headman of each area was to be "personally responsible for the payment of the Crown Rent of the group which he represents," issuing permits to the quarry masters as required. The latter were to pay a royalty of 14 per cent on the value of all stone cut in their quarries. The mode of measuring the stone and estimating its value was to be settled by the quarrymen's guild of "the Four Stone Hills," or in case of any dispute arising, by the Hong Kong official charged with the protection of Chinese, the registrar general. The headmen were to "apply all surplus monies remaining in their hands after paying the Crown Rent to such lawful purposes as the Guild may, with the approval of the Registrar General, direct." These extracts are taken from Rules for Granite Quarries from Lyemun to Ngau Tau Kok in Kowloon Bay, made on 14 June 1904.[27] In case of nonpayment by the quarry masters, the headmen could call upon the support of the registrar general, the police and the courts.

Another institution stood behind the headmen and their meeting house in the maintenance of good order and the avoidance of disputes, before and after the changeover to British rule. This was the guild of masons in Hong Kong. It was only one of 25 or more controlled by the head guild in Canton, to which, says Clementi who prepared a report on guilds for the Hong Kong government in 1903,[28] all important matters in this calling were referred for decision.

The guild in Hong Kong was divided into two sections: the guild of master masons (Tung Chia Hsing) known as the Weng Shing Tong (Yung Sheng T'ang): and the guild of artisan masons (Hsi Chia Hsing).[29] The former is reported as having about 120 members, and the latter between 2,000 and 3,000, with members coming from Canton when there was pressure of work. The larger guild was subdivided into name and district groups. The rules of the two main guilds are minute in their stipulations as to how the trade should be conducted by masters and men. Had they been followed at all times there would have been little trouble at the Four Hills or elsewhere. The rules of the artisan masons, which are dated 2 September 1889, contain strict regulations governing the feeding of employees by masters; wages and sickness benefits are also covered.

The four headmen of the Four Hills were considerable personages in the area, their prestige augmented, no doubt, by the "face" and authority given to them by both the Chinese and British governments. Old residents have told me that they had their own constables after 1899, and probably before. Each headman had six attendants: four for his sedan chair, one flag bearer, and a rifleman. The man who carried the banner, white with a blue edging, also beat a gong to announce the headman's arrival. These persons accompanied them on their inspections of the piers and quarries and made a show in their white uniforms; they were also present on ritual occasions.

In addition to the management of the quarries, the headmen had local responsibilities exercised through the Four Hills meeting house. Old persons clearly recall the various activities of the meeting house at the beginning of the century. There was, in fact, no separate structure. As often happens in the Hong Kong region, the "public office" (*Kung so*), as it was called, was in the Tin Hau temple at Sai Cho Wan. According to local report, this was the temple associated with the Four Hills. It had been subscribed for, and built, by local residents at an earlier time.[30] The headmen also managed its affairs.

The duties of the Four Hills meeting house were mentioned briefly in the Hsin-an magistrate's proclamation as the arranging of "joss meetings and free schools." Old residents confirm that a school was for long established in one of the side rooms of the temple; and, under British as under Chinese rule, the organization of religious festivals and of the accompanying opera and puppet performances was an important part of the year's proceedings. The settlement of business and family disputes is also reported.

The existence and activities of the Four Hills community office does not seem to have prevented the people of its four member villages from establishing their own institutions. At Ngau Tau Kok there was a village school in the early years of this century, and perhaps before, constructed on a site (lot 766) held by managers acting on behalf of the whole community. The Ngau Tau Kok villagers also maintained a separate identity from the other three settlements of the Four Hills through a religious celebration performed in the seventh moon. From at least the early days of this century this was confined to the residents of Ngau Tau Kok village and was organized by its own leaders. For one day and two nights there were religious ceremonies and accompanying entertainment by a puppet troupe for village people. This practice was identified with one of the local shrines near the village. This shrine has been removed twice in the last twelve years for redevelopment, but if the date on its stone tablet is to be trusted (1821) it seems that local stone cutters may have organized these celebrations during most of the 19th century;

that is, even before the establishment of Ngau Tau Kok village. Because of its geographical location it became identified with this particular village and the rites have continued every year up to the present.

Similar community activities were also to be found in each of the other three main villages of the Four Hills: Lyemun, Cha Kwo Ling and Sai Cho Wan. But in the days of the Four Hills' prosperity, which was probably before each village became fully established as an individual, compact settlement in the later 19th century, the community affairs of the subdistrict must have been handled mainly by the public office, headed by the leading quarry masters of the place. This assumption is, however, speculation, since the documents that would convert surmise into certainty have yet to be found.

Summary

This description of a specialist settlement of Hakka stone-cutters, within a larger group engaged in identical activities, shows the capacity of quarry masters and artisans for organizing and maintaining an important local institution, the Four Hills meeting house. This was used both in the management of rural affairs and in assisting the magistrate to secure government's revenue and to keep the peace; being aided in these latter duties by the authorities when and as required.

The chapter also describes the character of the Hakka settlement of Ngau Tau Kok, one of the Four Hills, and shows how its engagement in a specialist occupation led to differences in buildup and maintenance that distinguish it from the farming villages of the region, whether of Puntis or other Hakkas. However, neither the differences nor the existence of the Four Hills meeting house had an inhibiting effect upon the village structure. Ngau Tau Kok had a separate and lively existence under its own leaders, despite the presence of a strong community office in the subdistrict.

7

KOWLOON CITY AND KOWLOON STREET

The Community Institutions of a Yamen, Market, and Rural Subdistrict

The Kowloon Subdistrict

KOWLOON was a farming district when the British took possession of Hong Kong Island in 1841. It then consisted of a central agricultural plain with the walled city of Kowloon in its midst, lying together with its commercial suburb, Kowloon Street, under the shadow of the Lion Rock. Rough, hilly areas with rocky outcrops interspersed with stretches of farmland extended the plain to the south, east, and west, and to the north the Kowloon foothills cut off the area from the hinterland.[1]

Away from the city and its suburbs, the subdistrict was dotted with farming villages. A total of eighty-two villages and hamlets is recorded for New Kowloon by the early 1920s, some of which probably dated from after 1899.[2] There had originally been ten others in Old British Kowloon, afterwards augmented by new settlements begun after 1860.[3]

Detailed information for all the settlements is not available, as the various colony census reports give patchy and varied covering at village level. However, it is clear that many of them were small, with populations of under a hundred persons at the end of the 19th century, and that very few of them would have exceeded five hundred persons.[4] A second marketing center, Sham Shui Po, growing in importance as the century drew to a close, completed the subdistrict.[5]

The villages comprised single and multilineage villages, large and small, with lineages settled at various times since the Sung dynasty. There were Punti and Hakka villages, and settlements in which both groups lived together. The largest and oldest farming villages of the central plain were all Cantonese, but the extremities were settled mainly by Hakkas. Four of the five Cheung Sha Wan villages in west Kowloon were Hakka, and the stonecutters' villages of east Kowloon were Hakka to a man. There are no returns giving numbers in the different speech groups for all the villages, and only an indication can be provided. A population of 7,306 persons for the Kowloon City census district is given in the 1911 census, of which 3,070 were Punti and 4,044 Hakka, with 192 Hoklos.[6]

Kowloon City was the main feature of the area (see map 5). Under the title of Kuan-fu Shih it had long been an official center;[7] but its wall was a late creation as shown by Stewart Lockhart's report which gives the following account of its history and appearance:

> ...Kowloon is situated about a quarter of a mile from the sea shore. It is enclosed by a stone wall built in 1847, forming as nearly as possible a parallellogram, measuring 700 feet by 400 feet, and enclosing an area of 6½ acres. The wall is built of granite ashlar facing, is 15 feet in width at the top, and averages in height 13 feet. The wall has six watch towers, at present occupied as family dwellings, and two gateways, with doors made of wood and lined with iron sheeting. The parapet wall is built of granite, and has 119 embrasures. It is approached by four flights of stone steps.... The city contained civil officials and a military garrison.... The garrison amounts to 544; the civil population to 200.... The civil population...lives there simply because it is dependent on the military. It does not engage in trade, there being no shops of any kind within the city.[8]

As Lockhart stated, there were no shops within the city wall, and all the commercial and manufacturing trades of Kowloon were carried out in its suburbs, known locally as Kowloon Street. This served as the principal market for the whole subdistrict.[9] Its many shops stretched along each side of the path that led from a stone pier to the south gate of the city. A few short side streets completed the little town.[10]

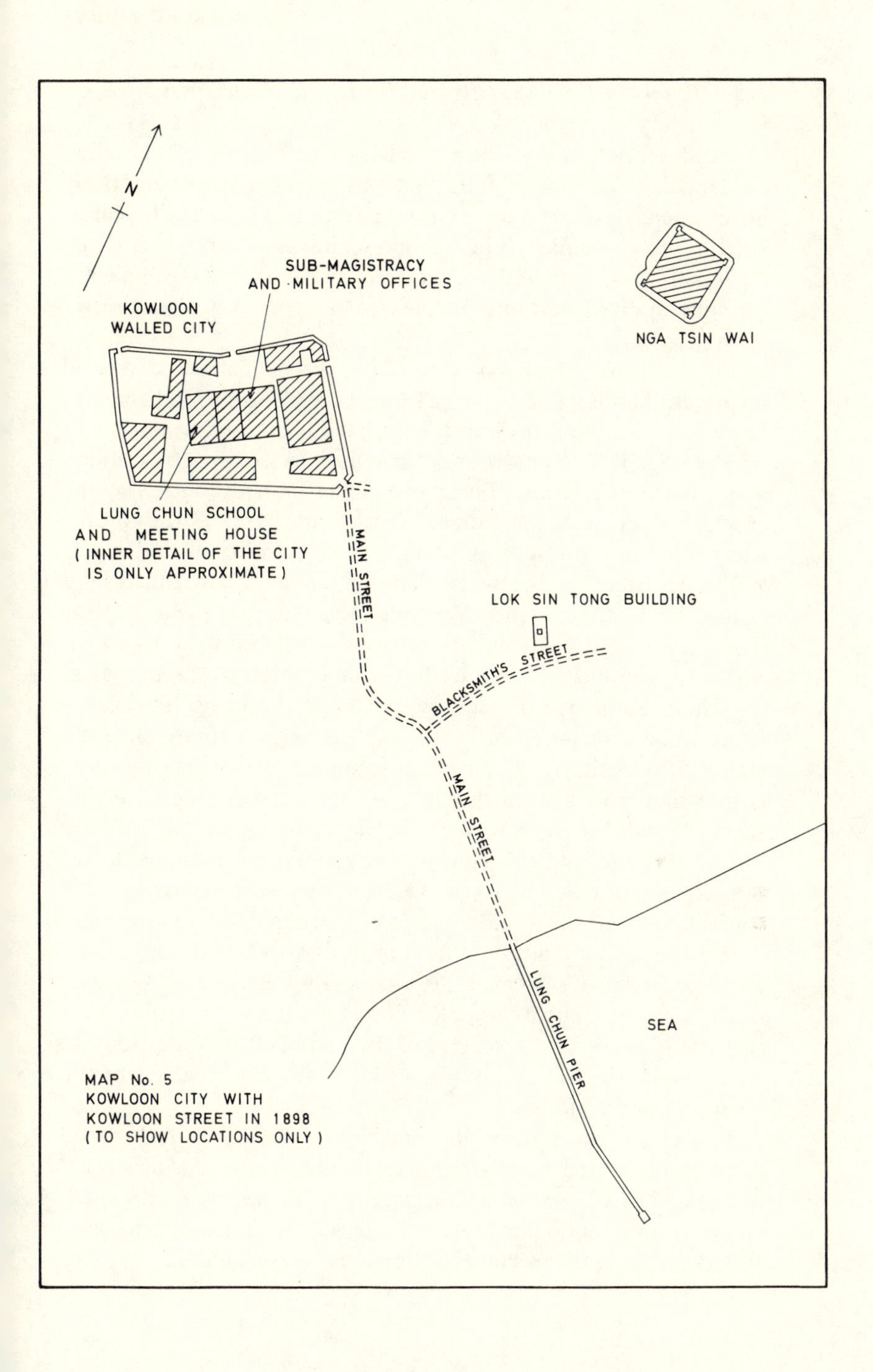

MAP No. 5
KOWLOON CITY WITH
KOWLOON STREET IN 1898
(TO SHOW LOCATIONS ONLY)

Land Tenure in Kowloon City and the Kowloon Subdistrict

A differentiation must be made between land inside the walled city and land outside it. The first was considered to be entirely government property under Chinese rule, and became thereafter British crown land.[11] The second comprised land in private ownership, together with stretches of hill land as yet unopened for cultivation or building purposes, which again passed directly to the crown.[12]

The land on which Kowloon Street was constructed was all in private hands. The principal owners of land around the city before the Lease of 1898 appear to have been the Ng lineage of nearby Nga Tsin Wai, "the walled village in front of the yamen" as its name proclaims. Their first ancestor had come into the area at the close of the Sung dynasty, and by 1898 the lineage was settled in a number of villages in the vicinity of the city.

The registers of the British land settlement show much land remaining in their ownership, but other sources make it clear that they had previously owned more, especially in Kowloon Street. A number of sale deeds for land there were entered at the Hong Kong Land Registry just after the lease. The deeds relate to land disposed of by the Ngs at various times since the eighteenth century.[13] Their advantage over the British registers is that they give historical depth to the ownership detail of the survey schedules.[14]

The Ngs had sold this land or had given it on perpetual lease; but, in either case, had reserved for themselves payments to cover taxes for the building or agricultural land in question. These amounts are always stated in the leases and deeds of sale, and are cited as a responsibility that a new purchaser must continue to meet. The reason for inserting these provisions was that the Ng lineage (or several of its members) was the party in whose name the ownership was listed in the land registry of the Hsin-an magistrate.[15]

Away from the walled city and its commercial suburb much of the land in the subdistrict was in the hands of village cultivators. These were of two categories. There were the small village proprietors belonging to lineages long settled in the area[16] and there were later comers. Some of these held land under individual title or under clan ownership, and others were the perpetual lessees of landlords large and small who had leased it to them at different times, often generations before.

The pre-1898 position is still unclear in detail, but the available evidence seems to indicate that besides the Ngs of Nga Tsin Wai and other local landlords giving perpetual leases, the Tang lineage of Kam Tin still held some land in Kowloon. Indeed, at an earlier time they may have held all or much of the ground there, although, as absentee landlords, they had let and sold it for centuries before 1899 and squabbled over it among themselves.[17] Like the Ngs they had preserved their rights to ownership by making a charge to cover the land tax.

All these arrangements were upset by the New Territories Land Court, which made a strong differentiation between landlord and tenant, usually in favor of the latter. The Court almost without exception transferred the Ngs', Tangs', and others' Kowloon properties held on perpetual lease or annual payments to the lessees, omitting practically all trace of their former ownership from the new land registers.[18]

The Institutions of Kowloon City and Kowloon Street

Kowloon City (as the seat of an official) and Kowloon Street (as a market center) both predated the British occupation of Hong Kong Island in 1841. The villages of the surrounding area, though of varying age, had also been established long before then. However, besides the Kaifong of Kowloon Street, the only two institutions of note that the British found there at the end of the 19th century both dated from after 1841.[19] One of these was a free school and meeting house, completed in 1847. The other was a charitable foundation operated by the local merchants and village elites, established in 1879–80.

The first of these, the Lung Chun Yi Hok (Lung-ching I-hsüeh), or Dragon Ford Charitable School, was located inside the city. A memorial tablet commemorating its construction was composed by Wang Ming-ting, the district magistrate of Hsin-an, and is dated in the autumn of 1847.[20] The building is still standing, though in a delapidated condition. It is a fine, large structure in the traditional style, and consists of an entrance hall with two inner halls separated by courtyards. Its construction and decoration are of the kind found in the large ancestral halls of the major clans of the Hong Kong region. It is built of blue baked bricks on a granite foundation with granite lintels and frames to the main entrance. It has many pillars of painted wood, set on granite pedestals, carved and painted eave boards, fine stucco work on the exterior walls, and the usual curved and decorated tiled roof with pottery tile ends.

It is not clear from the tablet whether the school owed its origin to the initiative of the local elites, or to that of the Kowloon deputy magistrate and his colleagues. They figure prominently in the text, which makes no mention of local effort or support. However, it is significant that the tablet states that the stone was inscribed by two directors named Tsang and Ng, and others, which suggests to me local participation in the financing of the building project.

By the end of the century, and probably before,[21] the Lung Chun school was being used for more than scholastic purposes. Old residents of Kowloon villages near the city have told me (1884, 1885, 1890: 1960–68) that it was a meeting place used by the local officials, leading merchants, and elites of the surrounding area to discuss public business, and not only the affairs of the school. This is confirmed by an entry in the report on the work of the New Territories Land Court for 1900 by H.H.J. Gompertz, who stated that he had made Kowloon City the first base of operations and "by courtesy of the Trustees . . . obtained as an office the building used before the Convention as a general Meeting House and School room within the Walled City."[22]

A few years later, at the time of signing the Block Crown Lease for Survey District No. 1, in which the school was situated, the names of the trustees are given in the schedules of ownership of property there.[23] I have only been able to identify one of them from other sources. This man, Ng Shue-fan, was a leading member of the Ng lineage of Nga Tsin Wai, Kowloon.

The second of the Kowloon institutions, the Lok Shin Tong (Lo Shan T'ang) or Hall of Willing Charity was, as its name suggests, a benevolent institution intended to relieve suffering in the Kowloon area. Like the Lung Chun School it was serviced by the merchants and village elites of Kowloon Street and the surrounding districts, and, as we shall see, also owed something to official initiatives for its foundation.[24]

The Tong's large assembly house was located in one of the offshoots of Kowloon Street.[25] It was built on land said to have been donated by the Ng clan of Nga Tsin Wai. Like the Lung Chun School it was a fine structure using traditional materials, though being later it was more influenced by Western style. The building was stripped of historical relics during the Japanese occupation, when, to quote from a record compiled by one of its former directors, "people scattered and no one looked after it, and all the wooden fittings were taken by rascals, to the great loss of the Tong." Fortunately, the writer had used these memorial and presentation boards before the war to compile a record of the institution, and his account, together with the recollections of old residents, makes it possible to be reasonably certain about its origins.

The oldest board, presented at the inauguration of the Tong in 1880, had four large characters that may be translated "Recall with compassion sickness and suffering." These establish the main objectives and intentions of the founders. The board also carried the names of twelve persons. Eleven of these are described as *chang chien jen* or organizers, and the twelfth is listed as the building supervisor for the project (*tu kung*). These men are listed variously, some as natives of Shantung, Chekiang, and Tientsin. They were probably officials of the Kowloon yamen and garrison, as it is unlikely that merchants from these far-off places would be found in Kowloon at the time. Other names carried no indication of their native place, but since few of them can be identified by old residents as being members of the local village lineages, they may also have been outsiders, perhaps engaged in business locally. Nevertheless, it is likely that there was a big local contribution to the building costs, as in the case of the Lung Chun School. Other memorial boards dating from the last decade of the century offer like sentiments and came from official and other donors.

The Tong also received the support of the local officers in their official capacity. A deed dated 12 March 1899, just before the British occupation of the city, provides a certificate of the title for the Tong's five trustees in respect of a shop in Kowloon Street. This shop was seized after a stabbing to death on the premises, which were being used as an opium shop, and was handed over to the Tong by the assistant magistrate of Hsin-an stationed at Kowloon, "to help in its charitable acts."[26]

The recollections of old persons, and the evidence of a surviving grave provided by the Tong for victims of the great plague of 1894 on the hillsides not far from Kowloon, confirm that the organization was fulfilling the purposes for which it had been formed. Then and later, it was providing herbal treatment and Chinese medicine, coffins for burial of paupers and persons without relatives, and was giving disaster relief, including food, bedding and clothing, all without charge. It was also educating poor children.

It appears that the village elites from the districts surrounding Kowloon, whose fellow villagers used Kowloon as their market center, were invited to take part in the management of the Tong from its early days. Village tradition is strong on this point. Old men in the main Sai Kung villages have stated (1877, 1879, 1885, 1886: 1960–64) that village elites stayed there overnight when they went to Kowloon on business if their homes were too far from Kowloon to return the same day.

Local tradition and the biographies of several late 19th century village leaders support the connection. One of them, Chan Tak-hang (c. 1830–92), of Cheung Kwan O in Junk Bay not far from Kowloon, came from a village that had been founded in the 18th century by members of two clans whose main settlements were at Nga Tsin Wai and elsewhere in Kowloon. According to a descendent, he was a merchant who had, among other enterprises, a general store in Kowloon Street and a cargo junk that took local granite to Canton. He had prospered, bought himself a literary degree, (*Kuo-hsüeh-sheng*) busied himself in good works, and built a guest house in his village that is still standing today. Some of the stone footpaths and piers of the area are said to have resulted from his benevolent generosity. He was a director of the Lok Shin Tong, and is claimed as having being a founding member in 1880. His son followed him on the board. His portrait, showing him in his official robes, still hangs in the guest house.[27]

Membership in the Tong is also attributed to other leading men from various places in Sai Kung. The names of men from Sha Tin and Tsuen Wan, that is, from the other *yüeh* areas traditionally associated with the Kowloon subdistrict, have also been given to me in this connection.

The Kowloon villagers provided their quota. As is to be expected, the Ngs of Nga Tsin Wai were prominent among the Tong's leaders. Two of them in particular are recalled by old residents. Ng Shue-fan (1848–1906) "a thin man with a small beard," was a teacher in the clan's large school that served the families of the surrounding area. He had failed the district examinations several times, but later purchased a degree. He was also the clan accountant. Another was Ng Shue-tong, also a scholar by purchase,[28] said to have received a commendation from the Ch'ing government for aiding in the defence of Kowloon city against rebels in the 1850s.[29]

However, not all the local leaders were men of this sort. One of the persons mentioned by my informants was Li Ping-ngam of Sheung Sha Po, described as "an honest farmer who, on coming back from a meeting in the Yee Hok in Kowloon city, would take off his shoes and go back to work in the fields."

Allowing for the participation of these village leaders, it is likely that the Tong's leadership came mainly from the merchants of Kowloon Street, who would have been the most reliable source of the funds that were continuously required to carry on its good works. Five trustees are named in the certificate of title mentioned above but none of them appear to have been villagers from the long-settled lineages of the area, and they may be presumed to have been shopkeepers. Emphasis on recruitment from merchants seems to have continued into British times.

A third important local institution was the Kaifong of Kowloon Street. A Kaifong organization was needed in every small town and market village to carry out certain basic functions that were not provided by the district administration and yet were vital to the health, safety, and good order of the shopkeepers and other inhabitants of the place. In Kowloon it is likely that the Kaifong existed before the establishment of the Lok Shin Tong in 1880, and before the completion of the Lung Chun school and the coming together of its trustees in 1847.

Circumstantial evidence for the early existence of the Kaifong can be found in a tablet commemorating the repair of the Hau Wong, the most important among the local temples, in 1821–22.[30] On that occasion the eight principal directors were all shops; proof of the existence of the shopkeepers of Kowloon Street and their interest in the good management of the local temple. Other evidence of the existence of local leaders and the close relations between them and the military and civil officers of Kowloon City is the association of their names in the tablets, memorial boards, and other inscribed objects that have survived in temples in and around the city.[31] The earliest known of these records, which existed before the war but is now lost, was a tablet by a broken bridge near the Kowloon City rifle range, dated 1828.[32] It listed an officer of the Tai Pang battalion (which provided the troops stationed at Kowloon) and shops owning passage boats as leading contributors to the construction project.

By providing a nucleus of responsible and better-off citizens who could make the necessary financial contributions—both capital and recurrent—and supply the leadership and experience in public business essential to the continuance of the two new bodies, the Kaifong made possible both the Lung Chun School and the Lok Sin Tong. Without its support, and its contacts with leading men from the surrounding districts, official initiatives would have meant little.[33]

To conclude, the village memory that connects rural leaders so strongly with the Lok Sin Tong also emphasizes their liaison and consultative functions with the Kowloon officials. This points more to the role of the men than to that of the institution. There were insufficient men of means and talent to provide separate staffing, and I believe that in the late 19th century the personnel of the Kaifong, the Lok Sin Tong and the trustees of the Long Chun School, like their finances, tended to coalesce. It was, too, as we have seen, usual practice in the market towns for the local leaders to play several roles simultaneously in the institutions of the place.

Since first writing the above, lists of trustees for the Tong and School in 1899 and 1904 respectively have come to my notice and may appear to disprove this for that short period, in that they give different trustees for each institution. However, it helps to sustain my contention that one of the persons listed for the *School* is remembered locally for his long connection with the Tong.

Civil and Military Liaison with Local Communities

Kowloon City was the seat of a deputy magistrate with administrative responsibility over a wide area that, in 1819, had included 492 villages.[34] I have therefore chosen this section to discuss the relationship between local leadership and the district government. In the absence of material showing this liaison at work, I have been obliged to do this in terms of its institutionalization.

It is well known that the Chinese district administration relied on local elites to assist it in the performance of its duties.[35] Within the area of their influence, they performed a facilitating role that benefitted officials and people alike. The civil officials of the district government and the military and naval officers of the local command required influential contacts in the rural areas to assist them in the collection of taxes, the prevention of serious crime, and the avoidance of local unrest. They required reliable intermediaries who could report on the local situation, and, when necessary, explain government measures to the population. They would also have welcomed information on the wrongdoings of the runners and clerks of the yamen, so frequently the subject of adverse reports, and the misdemeanors of soldiers and ratings.[36]

On their side the people needed a means of approach to the officials. This was very necessary at a period when the senior staff of the *hsien* government was located at only four places in the district and comprised few officers, led by literati who were far removed from the everyday life of the common people by their education, mode of living, behavior, and the pomp and circumstance with which they were generally surrounded.[37] The magistrate himself would be an outsider, usually not familiar with the local dialects and, without the local elites, possessing no contacts in the county.[38]

However, the literature has tended to deal with the two ends of the officials-literati spectrum: government control of localities through the gentry (and other elites); and the philanthropic public work of the gentry in their home areas.[39] What may be termed the middle area, liaison and consultation between the two in the routine business of district management—and especially the institutionalization of this interaction—is not so well covered, perhaps because it is taken for granted. In this section I shall deal with the subject at subcounty level, and show that, in the Hong Kong region, liaison was achieved through use of the military as well as the civil authorities. However, I can only take the elucidation so far as my sources permit. These are stronger for examining the means for interaction rather than the occasions for it.

I have been told by a magistrate who served at the end of the Ch'ing period that there were usually four councils or *chü* in each county. These operated in the east, north, west, and south sections. Each *chü* had a paid staff of clerks, recorders, messengers, and the like. There were normally twelve counselors to each *chü*, chosen from among the gentry or elites of the area served by the *chü*, with no fixed term of office. They had civil jurisdiction only, though they also dealt with petty thefts, and the amount of work they handled depended on their public spirit and energy.

There was a central *chü* in each county, situated in the county seat, but this, according to my informant, Kam Cham-lun (1878–1962) who served as a *chou* and then as a *fu* magistrate in Hupeh for some years before the revolution of 1911, was more like a club. Styled a *pin hsing kuan* it was a meeting place and boarding house for the gentry of the district. It had no jurisdiction, since disputes not settled by the *chü* went directly to the magistrate. This central body was, if the magistrate desired, a convenient means of approach to the leading men of the whole county.

In Hsin-an county, these four councils are by no means proved by the sources at my disposal. I have yet seen evidence for only one of them, that for the eastern section of the county. Information on this council, and for the eastern section, comes from Lockhart's report. The New Territory lay in what he styled the "Tung Lo or Eastern Section" which, he wrote, "is practically that portion of the district of San On contained in the map attached to the Convention."[40] This had a council which he styled "the Tung Ping Kuk or Council of Peace for the Eastern Section.... It has its council chamber at the market town of Sham Chun which is regarded as the centre of the Eastern Section."[41]

The Tung Ping Kuk is mentioned in other Hong Kong government papers. During the British occupation of Sham Chun in 1899[42] certain persons had been authorized to build a pier. This concession cut into the rights of the Kuk and led its leaders to petition the district magistrate of Hsin-an. They stated that all craft which moored at the wharf at Tong Chu Wan in Lo Wu Village had always paid dues to the Tung Ping Kuk, but that recent events had led to a diversion of vessels to a new pier "with the result that the Kuk will have no funds to meet expenses." Commenting on this imbroglio, a British official reported to his seniors that "The Tung Ping Kuk... was a society of the gentry of the District... accustomed to collect tolls from boats anchoring at Tong Chu Wan...."[43] Its existence and through it that of Lockhart's Eastern Section are thereby confirmed.

Below the Tung Lo and its council there appear to have been groupings called *tung*. It is clear from Lockhart's wording that they were intermediate bodies located in the hierarchy of political units between the village and the *lo*. Each *tung* in the eastern section had its council, and sent nominees or representatives to the Tung Ping Kuk, the council for the *lo*.

It seems fairly clear that these *tung* did exist. There is another reference to *tung* in the colonial office papers of the time. In making proposals for the future government of the newly leased territory, the officer administering the government of Hong Kong in 1898, Major General Wilsone Black, advised that "We should govern somewhat in the present Chinese system i.e. the Village elders to rule the villages which grouped according to tipo limits, form a Tung having a council composed of representatives from the village Elders." Each Tung, he continued, would in the future send a representative to the council of the new British resident. All minor offenses were to be dealt with by the elders, with the right of appeal to the Tung and further to the resident.[44]

Nevertheless, my inquiries in the mainland and island areas of the Old Southern District produced no information about these and similar institutions.[45] This shows that the Tung Lo, the

Tung Ping Kuk and any other *tung* and *chü* in Hsin-an county either had gone from the living memory of ordinary persons or were not operative in these parts of the *hsien*. For reasons that follow I consider the latter the more likely. However, this questioning did uncover other institutions that appear to have served the same purposes as the councils of the *tung* and the Tung Lo.

Old persons in the Sai Kung, Clear Water Bay and Kowloon villages all referred to the meeting house in the Lung Chun Yee Hok in the Kowloon walled city and the Lok Shin Tong of Kowloon Street as providing channels of communication between the leading men of their districts and the Kowloon civil and military officers. Before turning to the question of liaison in places where there were no such bodies, I wish here to say something more about these institutions, their personnel, and the bearing this has on aspects of local consultation and liaison in the late Ch'ing.

As I have already shown, the members of these Kowloon institutions were not graduates, though some of them had purchased degrees. It seems—which is altogether in character—that realism prevailed in organizing local representation. The magistrate's main interest was in gaining help from the influential men of the district, with or without degrees. This situation may follow the practice in other parts of China. The *chou* magistrate mentioned above told me that in his and other districts the councils of the poorer regions were augmented by prominent nonliterati. The normal requirement of scholar membership, if such there was, was waived in order to secure the presence of persons who carried weight in their localities. Applied to the *tung* and higher councils of the Hong Kong region, this brought in the merchants and nongraduate elders of the Kowloon area; and in places where no councils or special consultative institutions existed, as on the islands of the Southern District, it enabled the officials to deal with whatever local leaders there were in existence.

Such men may be described as *hsiang-shih* or *shen-shih*, terms still applied in the Hong Kong region today. With reference to the 18th century, Jonathan Spence has assessed them very accurately in *Ch'ing-shih wen-t'i*:

> It was a term that two busy local officials could not dispense with but also could not define exactly; it referred to local

> people of influence whose opinions needed to be recorded. But these people did not of themselves form a class, they were not the gentry and not scholar-officials. They were the local elite.[46]

There were, as I have indicated in this thesis, many such persons in poorer districts like Hsin-an. The possession of degrees by purchase by some of their number does not, in my view, remove them from the group.[47]

Consultation and Liaison in Outlying Areas: The Military

An investigation of the practice of consultation and liaison in some of the islands and coastal settlements of Hsin-an may help to show how the district administration controlled places of this kind and liaised with communities along the long stretch of the Kwangtung coastline.

As stated, my many discussions with old local people in the islands have uncovered no trace of a council of leading residents, or any hint of attendance at one elsewhere. Nor, in the main centers of population, have I discovered any institutions like the Lung Chun School and Meeting House or the Lok Sin Tong of Kowloon that served as focal points for the surrounding areas. Cheung Chau and Tai O were both relatively large centers of population and possessed district association premises and some large temples; but there is no remembrance that any of them had served as a meeting house used regularly by officials and the local elite, or had attached to themselves this reputation in the way recalled for Kowloon.

It would appear, then, that *tung*, *chü*, and special institutions were either not feasible or not required in coastal and offshore communities. Instead, a second method of contact and control may have to be considered, namely that exercised through the local forts and garrison posts and their attendant naval forces.

In this respect, the islands were well served, for there were posts and personnel everywhere. The main garrison on Lantau until 1899 was at Tung Chung Fort, and there were garrison posts and a small military yamen at Tai O. There had been another garrison at the Fan Lau Fort in the early part of the century but it had been long abandoned by 1899.[48] Most of the inner islands had their garrison posts also, including those at Cheung Chau, Peng Chau, and Lamma which had small numbers of men under junior officers. Ships of war were attached to the larger garrisons and visited others from time to time.[49]

Informal contacts as well as continuous liaison for official purposes seem to have taken place in these localities. An old resident who lived in a village beside the Tung Chung fort said that the elders made visits there, and it is clear that the leaders of the Cheung Chau and Tai O communities were in close contact with the local garrison commanders. Liaison was close enough in most places for it to have been the usual practice to ask the military and naval officers to help worthy causes. Colonel Lai Chun-bin's interest and help in the Fong Pin hospital scheme on Cheung Chau has been noted above, while surviving tablets commemorating the periodic repair of the many temples of the area show that military officers contributed frequently to the cost. Their names always head the long lists of donors, presumably for reasons of "face" as they were never the leading contributors in amounts given. It was also common for military and naval personnel to present memorial boards on these occasions.[50] In contrast, there are hardly any subscriptions or presentation items from civil officers.

One major factor in facilitating this liaison was the local birth of many of the officers.[51] They were often Kwangtung men, unlike their civilian counterparts, many of whom were outsiders. Those stationed in Kowloon and the islands came from the Tai Pang battalion whose headquarters were at the town of that name in northeast Hsin-an, the seat of another assistant magistrate. Such men already had local interests or soon developed them. One of the Kowloon officers of 1899 was described as "a small military mandarin in charge of the island of Peng Chau. His elder brother had a large business at No. 37 Hing Lung Street [Hong Kong] and he himself has long been resident in Hong Kong."[52] A Kowloon genealogy from one of the smaller villages Chü of Tai Hom, records that one of its members (1808–67) was an officer of the local garrison. The biography of one senior officer, Cheung Yuk-tong, a Hui-chou man long stationed in

Kowloon in the 1850s and 1860s, can be found in the bulletin of the Hui-chou fellow countrymen's association of present day Hong Kong.[53] Cheung was seemingly very closely associated with the local communities, and examples of his calligraphy can still be seen on several temples in Hong Kong, Kowloon, and Macau and in a fine temple scroll on Cheung Chau.

This informal, regular, local contact was extended to the officials in land stations and cruisers of the Canton customs after the establishment of the posts at Fu Tau Chau and Cheung Chau in 1868 and, later, of the Imperial Maritime Customs stations at Ma Wan and Cheung Chau after 1887.

This scattering of troops and war vessels across the local waters and coastal settlements was not unique to this part of Hsin-an. The *Kuang-tung T'u-shuo* of 1864–65, quoted above for that particular *hsien*, lists the posts and garrisons for the whole of Kwangtung and provides full details of the ranks of officers and the number of men supposed to be stationed at each.[54]

I take the view that, in addition to whatever military and police purposes were intended, liaison was another reason for posting troops so profusely across the region. This role is apparently confirmed by a contemporary European writer, a former British consul in China, who wrote:

> Colonels, majors, captains, lieutenants, sergeants and corporals were, and no doubt still are, each in command of greater or smaller bodies of men, stationed in the cities, towns, and markets and cooperating with the civilian *hiens*, assistant magistrates, and other small fry, down to the village headman.[55]

There can be no doubt that, in the virtual absence of civil officers from many parts of the district, the military forces played a very important part in liaison with the ordinary local population in this region in the late Ch'ing, and that this was probably so along many other parts of the Kwangtung coast. If this is so, it would explain why the civilian authorities were so interested in trying to ensure that the military and naval personnel did their duty without oppressing local inhabitants.[56]

There is sufficient information from the area to indicate that the military and naval forces did not always behave well. By report (1876: 1963, 1885: 1965) soldiers in the posts at Peng Chau and Cheung Chau made money by selling breaming and market "rights." Cruiser crews were as interested in selling opium as in arresting dealers.[57] Guard boats on the Delta "squeezed" fishing boats.[58] Some members of the Kowloon City garrison were as interested in selling tea and cakes as in their duty.[59] These are only a few of the irregularities recorded or remembered from this region. However, they are but warts on the image of what was probably on the whole a successful liaison.

To conclude, while the local forces' military effectiveness in preventing robbery, piracy, and clan wars may be open to considerable doubt,[60] their dispersion and the local liaison that ensued, whether by chance or design, benefitted the civil authorities. On the basis of this local evidence, I suggest that insufficient weight has been given in recent scholarship to the liaison role of the military and naval forces of the late Ch'ing empire. It is scarcely mentioned by Hsiao,[61] and the usual picture, reported recently by William S.T. Waung,[62] gives a misleading because insufficient picture of the situation, at least for Kwangtung.

However, the obvious weaknesses of both the civil and military authorities at county and subdistrict level help to emphasize Ramon Myers' observation, from his study of Ch'ing Taiwan, that formal control worked effectively at local level because officials used informal organizations to check potential troubles before they became dangerous.[63] This, in turn, points up the great importance of these informal elements in strengthening government's authority and guaranteeing a general compliance by the populace in normal times.

8

Summary and Discussion

Organization and Leadership in Six Locations

GENERALLY SPEAKING, the organizational and leadership situation in the six areas described above was characterized by fragmentation: into lineage and village units in the rural areas, and into street and dialect groupings in the coastal market centers. By their convenient small size and cohesive nature, these bodies both enabled and encouraged self-direction.

This tendency towards independence was greatly assisted by the loose control of land under gentry landlords who were largely absentee. It was usual for land to be divided into surface and subsurface rights, whereby the tenants shared in the ownership and, in the case of houses and shops, owned the superstructures. Moreover, the absence of landlord gentry from management—the prevailing and most characteristic feature of these areas—positively required these communities of peasants and shopkeepers to be self-directing.

Looking at the situation in more detail, we find on the rural side a strong, self-contained lineage development at Shek Pik and Pui O. Though generally small in numbers, the village lineages possessed a distinctive social and ritual life, carried on through many generations of settlement. Each clan usually maintained its own trusts for worshipping, welfare, and educational needs, and many families had set aside some fields for these purposes.

Community organization was strong in these villages. Authority rested with an informal council of elders who met in a local temple which was used as a village office, and a headman conducted the ordinary affairs of the settlement. The corporate existence of the village as a settlement was continually emphasized, and the fortunes of its inhabitants linked together, by the daily observance of simple protective rites performed by families in turn; also by the performance of more elaborate rites at periodic intervals or at need when an unexpected event appeared to threaten the life and wellbeing of the inhabitants. The birthdays of the local temple gods were other occasions for community solidarity. In the larger villages like Shek Pik, this corporateness was augmented by the possession of property in common, generally referred to as Ah Kung, such as fields and an orchard rented out to produce an income for the village school and other community expenses. This was the general pattern, though one can invariably cite exceptions to it, such is the variety to be found in the region.

At Ngau Tau Kok and the Four Stone Hills the village organization was equally in evidence, though the settlements comprised large families rather than lineage groups. At Ngau Tau Kok there was a village school built on land set aside for the purpose, and the community held protective rites and celebrations once a year at the village shrine.

However, this was a different kind of settlement from the farming villages of Lantau. It had come together quickly due to the demand for stone, and had not taken generations and even centuries to develop. Composed of specialist artisans rather than farmers and fishermen, it was a collection of families, each of which maintained strong links with home villages in Kwangtung for the purpose of recruiting labor and wives. Ancestral halls did not exist. This gave it a different social and organizational character from the Lantau villages. The latter existed within a much more localized situation in which the villagers obtained their wives and husbands for their daughters from surrounding settlements and had largely severed links with their old homes.

In the coastal market centers the street, dialect affiliation groups, and the community were the main features of local organization. The street was a recognized unit. It was more informal at Cheung Chau than at Tai O, where the bodies known as *she* appear to have been based on substreet groupings closely linked with shrines to the gods of earth and grain. In Cheung Chau, persons from the same area or dialect group seem to have congregated in different streets, adding to their social cohesion. I have less information for the residents of the Tai O streets.

However, the dialect or fellow countrymen group was the predominent social unit for welfare purposes—broadly defined —in each of these places. Strong societies, some owning considerable property to support their activities, existed in both Cheung Chau and Tai O, and by 1899 had probably been in existence for a hundred years, perhaps longer in some cases. They were then very active in educational and charitable work on behalf of fellow countrymen, especially the old and destitute.

As in the local villages, community organization for the settlement as a whole was strong and vigorous, exercised mainly through the body known as the Kaifong. This existed in both Cheung Chau and Tai O. It was composed of the leading shopkeepers of the place, and handled a wide range of public business with the aid of receipts from property and services, and donations from wealthy residents. It handled local security measures, community projects (as opposed to schemes benefitting only that section of the population represented by the street or dialect association) and relations with the civil and military authorities. In Cheung Chau this body has always been particularly noted for its energy and capacity. There was also a Kaifong at Kowloon Street formed of the same type of person and performing similar functions.

Fragmentation was thus countered in both town and country by a sense of community. Leaders, especially in the more diversely composed coastal market centers, developed this community feeling through the wide range of interests and experience that accrued to them from the common practice of plural office holding. This sense of community was, I am sure, felt equally by the led, who saw renewed evidence of group solidarity every time there was a local festival or religious rite. It is, indeed, difficult to overstate the vital importance of the religious element for the emergence and training of leaders and the development of community solidarity in this region.

To summarize the results of this survey of diverse communities, we have here the form and, less certainly, the substance of local organization for self-direction and local management. It is difficult, of course, to be uniformly sure of the latter with the source materials at my disposal; though I consider that there is sufficient evidence for this from Cheung Chau and Pui O—besides other less concentrated instances—through the actions detailed in the record of the Tung-kuan association and the various local records made use of in the geographical chapters.

Turning away from the villages and coastal market centers to view the higher local organization of the Lantau area we immediately notice a marked difference in the local scene. The ample organizational structure noted in the individual communities is not to be found, and group activities other than for religious purposes are generally wanting.

Groups of villages existed in 1899, but their size and nature varied and their organizational mechanisms were weak or almost nonexistent. These Lantau groups ranged from genuine confederations of a sizable number of villages—Tung Chung had 17 member settlements—to clusters of no more than two or three in which the smaller ones were satellites rather than equals. There was no uniformity whatever, and some villages remained on their own, unlinked. Where the larger groupings existed, they were characterized by certain features. They possessed sets of rules (written or unwritten) governing local life and custom in matters where disputes or misunderstandings were likely; they had a common interest and financial responsibility in one or more temples; and participated in the performance and celebration of protective rites (*ta chiao*) that were held at regular intervals or when a special need arose.

Local leadership directly reflected the organizational tailing-off described above. It was strong and plentiful at lineage and village level in the countryside, and at a street, dialect association, and community level in the coastal market centers, and it was generally effective. Above the village and market, leadership was weak and, in most of the places described above, insufficient. There was no mechanism for linking one rural market center with another or for combining rural groups, either for routine purposes or for special need. The local populations and the district government had apparently considered that such arrangements were not necessary.

However, the Kowloon material shows that this situation was

not typical of the region as a whole. The discussion of the institutions serving the districts round Kowloon and its submagistracy shows that alliances between villages had been established on a wider and larger scale than on Lantau, and that there were meeting houses for communication and liaison between groups and between them and the authorities. In another part of Kowloon, the Four Stone Hills meeting house not only served as the community organization for the quarrying villages but also assisted the magistrate in the collection of revenue from stone cutting and in keeping the peace. One cannot therefore, generalize with accuracy even in a few subdistricts of a small county like Hsin-an.

Six Locations without Gentry Direction in Local Affairs

I have, thus far, regarded the six communities under study as being without resident gentry and not subject to direction by gentry, whether from inside or from outside. This decision is crucial to my thesis, which seeks to emphasize complete management of internal affairs in the villages and market towns by local persons who were either peasants or shopkeepers and merchants, albeit some of them were in possession of purchased degrees.

In arguing that my areas of study were without gentry or gentry management, I have to dispose of two groups which might otherwise compromise this proposition: first, the resident managers with degree or "honor" status who might *prima facie* appear to be gentry; second, nonresident families of undoubted gentry status who owned large areas of land in the region. In the case of the first of these groups, my defense rests on an examination of what constituted gentry and its applicability to the local scene. Neither Chang Chung-li's nor Ping-ti Ho's classifications of gentry really fit the local case. If I use Chang's rather wide definition,[1] I find that I cannot argue successfully that these areas were gentryless, since it includes degree holders by examination or purchase, with or without official position. This means that all such persons encountered in the areas of study must be defined as gentry, which, for the reasons given below, I decline to do.

If, on the other hand, I use Professor Ho's narrower classification,[2] in which he excludes the lower gentry from the group, I would be ignoring a large body of persons whose significance is far greater at the periphery than at the center. Though possessing (from the national viewpoint) petty honors, they had access to the official class at county and subcounty level, a consideration of prime importance to this study.

Philip Kuhn has noted the difficulty of applying these categorizations at the local level. In his study of militarization in nineteenth century China, he has commented, with reference to the village with effective leadership and surplus wealth, which he styles "the simplex *t'uan* or local defence association":

> Leaders on this level were often lower degree holders—*sheng-yuan* or *chien-sheng*—or those degree aspirants, the *tung-sheng*. Such leaders might also be holders of purchased brevet rank. But the leadership of simplex t'uan was by no means confined to men with formal degree status, and we can find in the record many examples of commoners who, by virtue of their wealth and community influence, were functionally indistinguishable from titled scholars in community defence.[3]

Earlier in his study he refers more specifically to the "fit" of Chang and Ho's classifications at the local level, and states:

> To my purposes neither of these views is entirely applicable: neither is quite successful in relating status to the context in which it is recognized, or power to the context in which it is wielded. I shall therefore work toward a broad functional definition of an "elite" segmented according to its power and prestige on various scales of organization.

He describes "national" and "provincial" elites, and finally the "local elite" which, he says, "lacked the social prestige and powerful connections of the former two groups but might still wield considerable power in the society of village and market town."[4]

My present study affirms the correctness of this reclassification at the local level. Indeed, since it concerns the village, the rural market, and the smallest kind of unit above the village—and within a very small geographical compass—I have encountered the problem of "fit" in a yet more acute form.

With the above in mind, it is clearly inadvisable, as well as highly artificial, to decide on the basis of Chang's definition—though it is more applicable to the local scene than Ping-ti Ho's—that there *were* "gentry" in the villages and market towns of this study. While there were persons who could be so termed, it is very misleading to classify them as such. They were individuals, not members of established gentry families. In the case of the rural elites, this is very clear from an overall scrutiny of the villages from which they came, the records of their lineage, their own houses, holdings, wives, even their graves, and from the comparisons that can be made with other local people from the land records and other genealogies. They, and others like them in the region at large, were isolated examples of men who had "got on" in a modest way. They had neither come from, nor did they hand down, a gentry status. Their background was wholly local and peasant and, along with the degreeless brothers and cousins with whom they associated in management functions, they are more accurately classified as elites. Their presence, too, was intermittent and does not justify use of the term "gentry direction" to village affairs under their management. Also, the effect of the addition of such men to the "local elites" in no way resulted in the type of (often deleterious) "gentry management" reported from other areas.[5]

I turn now to my second theme; that the presence of non-resident gentry connected with my areas of study did not *per se* provide for gentry management in local affairs. Excluding the Wong clan of Nam Tau and Cheung Chau for the present, there were two such groups in the rural areas. The Li family was the ground landlord for much of Lantau at the end of the nineteenth century, and the Tangs of Kam Tin were in the same position in Kowloon and elsewhere. Both had held landlord status in these areas from Sung times. From this it might seem that my claim that these districts were without gentry or gentry management is both unfounded and misleading.

However, this situation cannot be taken at its face value.

In the first place, these families were nonresident. Secondly, a field study shows that, by the end of the century and probably for much earlier, they did little more than collect rent. They were largely ignorant of the plot boundaries of the land they owned, and did not know the identity of their tenants, though most of the latter belonged to village clans settled in the area for many generations. This situation arose in part because the land was subject to a double ownership, whereby payment of the rent charge was all that was required of the village cultivators. The villagers dealt freely with the land, and I have already shown how, every time a plot subject to rent changed hands, the rent charge was specified as the responsibility of the "purchaser." This was at the initiative of the seller, not at the command of the true owner who probably remained ignorant of the transaction.

Thirdly, the field inquiry shows that these gentry landlords did not direct or manage village business. There is neither evidence of such action nor a local memory of it. The villagers were free to manage their own affairs, and proceeded to do so through a variety of institutions of their own devising. (I exclude from this estimate the occasional defense of rent that led gentry landlords to take cases to the magistrate, or take direct action to confiscate produce or livestock considered owing. These occurred, but cannot be considered as interference with, or direction of, local affairs.) The situation is in no way consistent with gentry management of local affairs, which must be rejected in the face of so many indications that local people directed their own communities and their interactions with others in the area.

The two coastal market centers were no more under gentry management than the farming villages. One of them, Tai O, had no resident merchants with titles in the late nineteenth century. The other, Cheung Chau, appears to have had a few, as befitted its more flourishing condition. Such persons may, again, be classified as "local elites" rather than gentry. The ground landlords in each place were undoubtedly gentry, the Li family at Tai O, and the Wongs at Cheung Chau. Some of the latter even resided there and appear to have been degree men by purchase and examination.[6] However, as in the villages, local management was not affected by this consideration. In each place the management of community affairs rested firmly with the Kaifong, the body of leading shopkeepers of the town. It is clear that the men who comprised the Kaifong operated in an independent way, using their gentry status or contacts only when required to effect a desired end.[7]

In short, local management in these towns and villages lay with local people. A very small number of these might, from time to time, have degrees by purchase, but these persons are to be regarded more as town or country elites. Their presence does not alter the essentially "gentryless" condition of these areas, and its corollary, the independent management of local affairs by elders and local elites.[8]

District Government and Local Leadership

The nature of the district government is another factor in a reappraisal of local leadership and its relation to the gentry. In my assessment of the situation in the villages and market centers studied in this book, neither the county authorities nor the scholar gentry exhibited a powerful controlling influence at the subdistrict level.[9] I find it hard, for instance, to recognize any sign there of the situation painted by Balazs:

> The bureaucracy was a hard taskmaster, and its tentacles reached everywhere. It marked every member of society and every sphere of life with its stamp. Nothing escaped it; for the least deviation from prescribed paths had to be kept in check lest it should lead to rebellion, and any dislocation, however slight, was a threat to the system as a whole...for the ordinary subject, the cardinal virtue was absolute obedience....[10]

It is true that many observers in the last century pointed, like Rutherford Alcock, to the government's practice of identifying and punishing the individual who could be detected in actions against society and the state.[11] Despite their usual apprehension of popular strength[12] and their eagerness to escape the penalties of maladministration by minimizing trouble or failing to report it,[13] the authorities believed in making drastic examples when they were in a position to do so. The occasional severity meted out to villages suspected of robbery and piracy,[14] and Viceroy Yeh's wholesale execution of actual or suspected rebels in Kwangtung in the 1850s,[15] are instances of the vengeance wreaked against the individual once he was identified by officialdom. The nature and practice of the law also support Balazs' description of "the cumbrous, gigantic machinery of government...the great steamroller,"[16] and any collection of documents can provide examples of what he styled "its many victims."[17]

There is, however, a vast difference between the grinding, inexorable nature of the statutes and administrative regulations with an occasional savage bout of repression, and the routine methods for securing local control. Drastic measures were adopted only when individuals in the society, or in Yeh's case almost the entire population, had got out of hand. In normal times, the government relied on the self-regulating society for local control;[18] and, as I have attempted to show, at the nongentry village and small town level, control was probably undertaken in many places by villagers and shopkeepers without much guidance of any kind. There appears to have been a basis of competence and common sense that kept things moving to local satisfaction, and thereby removed the necessity for either gentry or officials to get involved in the direction of village and subdistrict affairs in the normal course of events.

The availability of leadership in old China appears to have presented no problem: willing and competent personnel existed at all levels, in the educated sector of society, and outside it. Perhaps the most striking impression with which I am left from my inquiries into local village and smalltown society in the Hong Kong region has been the readiness to form and man associations of all kinds to meet a wide range of purposes.

In this context, one of Franz Schurmann's observations is of particular interest. "There is," he writes, "little in the traditional literature of China that prepares the researcher for grappling with Communist China. One can look far and wide in the traditional literature for discussions on leadership, whereas the literature of Communist China often consists of nothing else."[19] If this is so, it is paradoxical that the Communists, who have given the masses a political consciousness, should have thereby to grapple with the problems of leadership for, in my reading of the situation, the old system provided leaders in abundance.

It is, too, strangely at variance with the facts of traditional society that the mandarinate largely ignored—or perhaps took for granted—the capability of the masses for social and political leadership now recognized by the Communists. Its members spent their time writing benevolently about the people, and wrote frequently for them on morals and conduct. On their part the people, in petitioning the officials, did so in what now seems an unnecessarily self-depreciatory way, especially as, in daily life, they got on quite well with the job of organizing the regular sequence of religious and social events that, with some variation, was common to all South China communities at the time.

This capacity for association and leadership on the part of poorly educated ordinary people did not escape contemporary Western observers like Wells Williams, and it was given further expression in the emigrant communities of overseas Chinese[20] and in the community organization of Chinese newcomers in British Kowloon.[21] This was not a new flowering of the Chinese genius but, rather, a quality in all probability practiced unobstrusively, but pervasively, in all the Eighteen Provinces and wherever ordinary Chinese have found themselves.

One reason why the ability of the ordinary man in management at the basic level has been so little recognized is that he was well below the educational and operational levels of officials such as the Governor Han and his principal assistants who appear in the pages of Wade's textbook on Chinese documents quoted above. In the ordinary course of events, such men must have seen little of peasant and shopkeeper leaders and their work. Until events overwhelmed the local leaders by involving them in situations and problems beyond their experience and competence, there was little call for senior officials to have contact with them, or to cultivate an awareness of what was happening in the ordinary course of daily life in the localities. It was left to the minor military officers and noncommissioned officers—if we may style them such—who had most to do with the workings of the local communities among whom they were stationed all over each district, to express and appreciate their worth.

Unfamiliarity with peasant leadership in everyday life extends from imperial officials to most modern scholars. Even Kung-chuan Hsiao, despite his major contribution to our understanding of rural China and imperial control, is not sufficiently aware of the peasant contribution and underplays their capacity and active role in the creation and elaboration of rural society. Quotations from his major work indicate his belief in the incapacity of the people and the lack of infrastructure in nongentry Chinese society:

> Data on. . . cooperative activities are meager. The peasants probably had few such activities, and local historians were inclined to attribute little significance to them.

> Since village leadership often remained in the hands of the gentry or literati, the participation of the bulk of the villagers in community undertakings rarely went beyond the contribution of manual labour or perhaps modest sums of money. It was the gentry or scholars who usually initiated the ideas, drew up the plans, directed the enterprises, and supplied or collected the necessary funds. The peasants did not play a prominent role in any work that called for organizing ability or for personal prestige.[22]

Other instances of Hsiao's predilection in favor of the gentry contribution to the motivation and continuance of rural society include the following. When describing village activities he states that "ordinary people had no control over religious activities." This is very much at variance with my findings in the Hong Kong region. In his discussion of clan activities he writes that "the ordinary villager-clansmen, whose chief concern was to keep themselves and their immediate families alive, probably had little interest" in keeping genealogical records. This does not allow for the production of modest records—handwritten instead of printed, gentrytype ones—of the kind collected in considerable numbers recently by Baker for the British Museum. Again, there is his comment on the incorporation of commoners into the *hsiang-yüeh* system as long ago as the K'ang Hsi reign, that such men "frequently must have been of lesser calibre, whose social and moral influence on their fellow villagers or townsmen was limited or negligible."[23] In short, Hsiao paints altogether too unfavorable a picture of the capacity of villagers and townsmen than is acceptable for the Hong Kong region of Hsin-an. Wider research would establish whether this is so for other areas.

To some extent, Hsiao has, it seems to me, already refutated his own statements in what he has to say in his lengthy consideration of the *li-chia* structure.[24] There was a great need for rural leaders below the gentry there and in the *pao-chia* structure, in which the Ch'ing government sought to include the gentry but exclude them from its leadership.[25] If these systems to assist the district administration's financial and community control were to operate at all—and some obviously did for a time—where did these men come from, if not from their ordinary duties in town and village?

To conclude this study of village institutions and leadership, it will be recalled that historians have long discounted the statements made by earlier generations of Western observers and sinologists on "the village republic," of which the writings of E.T. Williams and E.T.C. Werner may serve as an example.[26] I consider it time to take seriously some of the earlier statements on local management and independence in handling local affairs that were discarded along with more untenable claims for the existence of democratic institutions and practices in the villages of late imperial China.[27] Separated from theory, the facts then recorded have a direct relevance for a revised estimate of rural organization and leadership, and of the true and complex nature of the foundations of imperial control in the nineteenth century.

Postscript

The Nature of the Political Situation in 1898, and Its Relevance for Local Leadership Patterns

By way of a postscript to this account of local institutions and leadership as they evolved in one outlying part of Hsin-an by the end of the 19th century, I would like to hazard a few guesses about the wider regional situation, including the mainland areas of the New Territories which were the home of the "Five great clans."[1] In the course of preparing the main work, I found myself agreeing, yet disagreeing, with some points made by Howard Nelson on the political system that operated in the New Territories before 1899. These may be found in his perceptive and stimulating review of Hugh Baker's book on Sheung Shui, one of the major lineage seats in the New Territories.[2] They are germane both to the background and to the continuing discussion on institutions and leadership. My comments and projections based on them take the issue beyond the scope of my geographical research; so my suggestions will remain no more than speculation until someone undertakes detailed work on the "Five great clans."

Nelson takes up Baker's emphasis of disturbances between competing lineages, and contrasts it with the "remarkably little we are told about the peaceful settlement of disputes," which he styles "an essential dimension of any political system."[3] He expresses surprise that Baker should accept "so uncritically the early British description of the orderliness of the local political scene," and that he does not bring out the paradox of disturbed times and the alleged smoothness of a working system above village level for settling disputes and facilitating dialogues with the magistrate and his assistants. He suggests that "the standard means of political expression at the local level was violence, and that this was the main reason why the British failed in their attempt to get the local leaders to act as arbitrators in the tribunals that they established by ordinance in 1899 and repealed eleven years later."[4] In his view this failure "stemmed from their near total unfamiliarity with such a role," which by implication could not have been practiced before the changeover to British rule.[5]

This is an interesting assessment of the local situation; but one that is so far removed from that described in this book that it raises the immediate question. Is it accurate, or the whole truth? Did violence rather than order characterize the prevailing political system? Did Lockhart describe the mere facade of an order that did not exist? Was this the case everywhere?

The description of the local political system given in contemporary British reports may be ascribed mainly to J.H. Stewart Lockhart. The Kuk, its village elders, and their constables, as described by him and elaborated here and there in the colonial records, were, it seems, one part of a complicated subadministrative system by which the district was in part governed by the district authorities and in part managed by its own leaders. The governmental machinery included the security and taxation systems, *pao-chia* and *li-chia*, to which Kung-chuan Hsiao has given space in his Chinawide survey.[6] The details, and even the framework, of this system are still far from clear. The matter is exceedingly complex, and, as Maurice Freedman observed in 1966 after a review of the information then available, "a great deal of research has yet to be done on local government and structure in the area."[7]

Since Freedman and Baker wrote in 1966 and 1968, John Brim of the University of Washington, Seattle, has written an as yet unpublished doctoral thesis "The Modernization of Local Systems in the New Territories of Hong Kong" (1970). This is based on 16 months' field work in the Yuen Long district of Hong Kong. In it he attempts to set out what he calls "four distinct local systems" forming the "major components of supra-village, local level social structure in the Yuen Long and nearby areas on the eve of British takeover." These he classifies as "lineage organization, the marketing system, the formal administrative system, and the non-official local government."[8] These structural components, he estimates, were for the most part interlocking and mutually reinforcing; and he noted that only the formal government structure appears to have been relatively independent of the other three "natural" systems.

Brim continues, in his summary,

> This lack of correspondence between the territorial units of the formal administrative apparatus and those of the other systems was no doubt made possible by the fact that the formal Government's sub-*hsien* agencies were to a great extent "legal fictions." That is to say, they had a formal existence but were of little consequence for local affairs which generally were left to the disposition of the non-official local government.[9]

He provides an interesting layout in support of his four categories; but though it may fit the Yuen Long situation it is too orderly for other parts of the New Territories, particularly the coastal regions and the outlying islands.

The inability to be more definite about the administrative and fiscal mechanism represented by the *li-chia* and *pao-chia* systems for the area,[10] and its quasi-governmental institutions such as the *tung*, the *lo* and their *chü*, besides the local systems of *yueh* alliances, is of prime importance. Until they can be elucidated we shall not possess a full appreciation of the realities of local systems in Hsin-an.

There is therefore insufficient evidence, as yet, to support Nelson's criticism that Dr. Baker accepts too readily British descriptions of the machinery for settling rural affairs. As for Mr. Nelson's thesis that violence was the only means of political expression that counted for anything in local society, this is presumably based on the interlineage situation among the "Five great clans" and does not take in the rest of the New Territories' villages, about which little has been written to match the work done on the major lineages. I would challenge this interpretation of the total local situation on the basis of the details provided in the six geographical chapters of this book.

To my mind, the background to leadership is as important as the precise number and nature of the local institutions and systems. I suggest that there were two political systems in operation, and that in the second of them, in which the peasantry and shopkeepers acted on their own initiative, the nature of the local land tenure system and the resultant pattern of landlord (tax lord) behavior were crucial to a proper understanding of the situation.

The first of these systems comprised a number of similar sized, more or less equally balanced lineages, each of which had to maintain a wide-awake posture against its fellows. The other was composed of a congeries of smaller settlements in a less critical situation. There is a world of difference between, say, the Liao lineage of Sheung Shui and the Lantau villages of Shek Pik, Lo Wai, and Tong Fuk. The one had long been locked in an interlineage struggle situation and the others were individual settlements pursuing a seemingly uncomplicated life, free from intense feuds and dreading disease, the supernatural, and robbery from outside more than trouble with adjoining settlements.

The interlineage "struggle situation" of the first of these systems is very well described by Baker in his chapter on the lineage and its external relationships as applied to the Liaos of Sheung Shui.[11] The outlook and policies of the lineages of the "Five great clans," it appears, were determined by the situation in which they found themselves and led to their becoming differentiated from lesser single and multilineage settlements in having more distinct economic and political aims. These were reflected in an organizational structure in which lineage wealth could be centralized and channeled to achieve corporate ends.

The difference between the villages of the two systems becomes most pointed in the respective amounts and proportions of trust or clan land. Baker reported that in 1966 the Liaos owned some 4,144 lots of agricultural land (of varying size and quality) totalling 973.33 acres and 726 house lots.[12] Of these, 1,943 land lots (47% of total) and 50 house lots (7 per cent of total) were communally owned, that is, were owned by trusts of one kind or another."[13] In the Yuen Long district, Brim's sample of land ownership for one-third of the local villages showed that 44% of their land was lineage owned at this time.[14] In comparison, Brim's small multilineage village with its 136 persons in 1911 had 2.51 acres of trust land, less than 6% of the village families' total holdings.[15] At Shek Pik and Pui O these figures were 2.69 acres (4.1%) and 18.39 (10.8%) respectively.

The gap between the two types of settlement was further

widened, since to this numerical difference in holdings in genuine ownership (i.e., as accepted by the British at the New Territories land settlement) must be added the large areas over which the major lineages collected charges.[16] Though its extent has still not been adequately charted, being completely obscured by the land ownership situation recorded in the 1904 settlement, sufficient evidence remains to show its importance to them, and that they still recall this abbreviation of their authority and income with bitterness.[17]

Another difference between the two political systems was the need for the lineage villages to produce gentry. The ability of gentry members to effect an "interest" with the authorities often proved its worth during lawsuits and other troubles, and was one of the keys to continued existence and successful struggle against other lineages and combinations.[18] It appears that gentry production was almost entirely a prerogative of the large lineages. Brim points out that the recorded scholars of the Yuen Long area all came from four lineages representing less than half the population, and that one of them, the Tang lineage, accounted for no less than 64% of the total ever recorded for the area.[19]

This does not mean that other lineages and other areas never secured examination successes, but when they occurred they were the result of individual brilliance, against heavy odds.[20] They were even heavier than they appeared because, as Freedman stresses, the major lineages could, if they wished, concentrate their wealth to secure continued successes and the maintenance of their supremacy rather than spread opportunities amongst their poorer kinsmen.[21] The poorer Hakka lineages were additionally handicapped, since even by the 1850s, when they were already resident in considerable numbers, the *hsien* examination quotas for the first degree were 8 for Puntis and only 2 for Hakkas.[22]

The age of the major lineages of the area in 1899 was yet another major difference between them and lineages in poorer areas. The "Five great clans" had long been great, and had been settled since Sung and Yuan times.[23] The Tangs had produced scholar-officials from the start, and the others had intermittent successes that underlined their higher status and economic strength vis-à-vis neighbors and newcomers. Baker describes the progress of one of their number, the Liaos, in the three centuries between the return from the Evacuation of the Coast in 1669 and the British takeover of the New Territories:

> Change was apparently in degree rather than in kind—that is to say, the lineage may have seen changes in its internal balance, as wealth and fertility saw fit to confer their favours, and its position of power in relation to the outside world may have fluctuated from time to time, but in large it still retained the same attributes of internal organisation *and it still pursued the same policies of aggrandisement which were determined by its standing as a single lineage settlement in a wider society which continued to be composed primarily of other similar settlements.*[24]

The underlining is mine. It brings out the fact that the major lineages were implicated in a continuous power struggle. As Baker points out, there was a constant search for more land and larger spheres of influence. The political power reflected in land holdings and the amounts of rent charges levied over client villages in wider areas made for a struggle situation, and guaranteed its continuance. Lineages could not afford to have their holdings or their overlordship eroded.[25] Cessation of effort on their part was paid for by decline and even extinction. Expansion could, of course, be pursued by peaceful as well as by warlike means. The accretion of holdings and client settlements by purchase and negotiation was less spectacular than obtaining them by fighting,[26] but steady attention to this point was more rewarding in the long run.

Herein, as I have said, lies the difference between the major clans and the smaller single or multilineage settlements. I suggest that this amalgam of systems—here necessarily contrasted in black and white—the one locked in long-term struggle and the other free to go its own way in peace or war makes up the true political condition of the region before 1899.[27]

With regard to the villages of the second of these political systems, I have suggested elsewhere that the development of the local land system, with its perpetual lease and its twofold division of the soil, enabled peasants to become virtual proprietors, increased peasant independence and fostered belligerence. I have also indicated that with weakened landlord authority over land, there was an associated noninterference in village management. Combined, these two elements in the local situation made for a rugged independence that enabled the two systems to operate side by side without the one swallowing up the other. The occasional exercise of "force majeure," and the bullying of minor by major clans so quickly picked up by the incoming British[28] should not obscure the workable contradiction that was the reality of the local situation.

The taxlord activities of the major lineages are now almost too well known. It has been too readily assumed that their control over land had led to interference and bullying. My reading of the local situation is that it was more complex than has hitherto been imagined and is not subject to such easy generalization. Moreover, the local peasantry have always been a tough and difficult lot.[29] The evidence for peasant independence, noninterference by gentry (and other) landlords in local management, and the virility of local organization is so strong that I question whether by the late nineteenth century the rent charge *was* the start of an unjustified excursion into the control of family and village affairs by personnel of major lineages or their lackeys. On the evidence before me, I believe that there was an incongruity in full scale operation in the region. It existed not only between the active and passive systems, but within the active system, whereby the major lineages practiced their known and documented exactions on client villages in the form of rent charges but otherwise interfered little with local management and daily routine.

Without such an explanation, it is difficult to explain how such a flourishing, self-regulating community life could exist in the areas studied. Bullied and depressed communities would not have had the spirit, much less the opportunity, to manage their own affairs.

This contradiction may help to explain why the *tung* and *lo* systems of local government-gentry-local elite consultation and peaceful settlement of outstanding matters could exist in the *luan* situation created by the infighting between lineages, the major lineages' collection of rent charges, the confused land registration system, peasant independence under the Fukien system of tenure, and the limited authority of the district administration.

Somewhere in this confusion there was order; and I believe that there was a good deal more than meets the eye. I have certainly been assured by old men that there was, and I have been told on so many occasions in many small and mediumsized villages that the elders were the seat of authority, that they settled all disputes, that some among them had area prestige, that there was no interference with village and local affairs by either the gentry or the magistrate, that it is difficult for me to think otherwise.

Reliance on oral evidence raises the doubts cast by Nelson that such statements incorporate elderly persons' unconscious "ideal statements" about their own society.[30] Therefore their statements must—when we get more evidence—be checked against records of actual behavior. Yet it is most encouraging that Freedman has also sensed this basic order in the midst of apparent chaos. He wrote, in 1966, of "that very complexity of social ties which made it possible for some sort of order to be maintained in a part of China that one might have superficially supposed was well on the road to anarchy."[31]

Appendix

Note on Weights and Measures

(with particular reference to Land Tenure)

> Owners or occupiers report their land in *maus* or Chinese acres, but as it has not been the general custom in the districts to calculate the area of land by *maus*, but rather by the amount of grain required to sow a field, they also report the area of their land in this manner.[1]

Throughout this book, the unit of land measurement used in the tables is the English acre, because this was adopted by the Hong Kong authorities in their land survey and settlement of titles to land in the New Territories after 1899 and is used in the Block Crown Leases and all later official papers and documents. However, the units of land measurement used in the New Territories and the Hong Kong Region under Chinese rule were the *tou chung*, and its superior decimal unit the *tan chung*, and these appear in all local deeds of sale and mortgage.[2]

The *tou* itself is a wooden container which varies in size, but normally holds some ten catties of rice seed, (about 13.333 lbs). The *tou chung* is the area of land required to grow one *tou* of rice seed. This area varies: firstly because the *tou* is not uniform, there being "tall" and "low" *tou* of 12 and 10 *shing* respectively; secondly because, dependent upon the quality of the field (1st, 2nd, or 3rd, according to Chinese and English grading, largely determined by irrigation)[3] the clumps of padi seedlings will be more, or less, concentrated so that 1 *tou* of seed on first class land will take up less space than if planted on second class land.[4]

These measures were uniformly used in determining and agreeing tenant rentals, and payment was taken in the requisite number of *tou* of unhusked rice.[4] Here again variation occurred as the rent could be fixed in "heaped" or "level" *tou.*[5]

However, as indicated in the opening quotation, a different system was in use for official purposes, based on a measurement called a *mou* which determined measured areas and fixed the land tax, although the "fiscal *mou*," as it was called, was an elastic measure whose relationship to the linear *mou* was varied by official decision.[6]

The subject becomes more complicated locally as more evidence comes to light, such as may be found in Chinese title deeds, property and rent books, disputes over tax or rent whose settlement was recorded on commemorative tablets in prominent places with official consent, and the like, dating from the 18th and 19th centuries, and in discussion with elders. This brief notice serves to advertize the fact, not to explore it.

For weights as well as measures see sections 3–4 of S. Wells Williams' *Chinese Commercial Guide*, 1863, pp. 278–88. For a more detailed study, see Wu Ch'eng-lo, *Chung-kuo tu-liang-heng shih*, Vol. VII of *Chung-kuo wen-hua shih ts'ung shu* Wang Yün-wu and Fu Wei-p'ing, editors, Shanghai Commercial Press, 1937; and on the multifarious systems prevailing in the different provinces, Liu Keung-cheng and Ch'en Chieh, *Chung-kuo tu-liang-heng*, Shanghai Commercial Press, 1934.

Notes

Notes to Introduction

1. Fairbank 1948: 105. The words *lead and* are added in the 1958 and 1971 (p. 103) editions.

2. This passage is worded identically in the 1958 and 1971 editions of Professor Fairbank's book. Its wording in the 1948 edition is different after the first sentence, but the sense is not altered, and for convenience I have used the most recent edition (p. 29) being that readily available to readers.

3. Hsiao: 316–17, 321. I have been selective, but not to distort the sense or content of Professor Hsiao's argument.

4. Balazs: 153–56.

5. Cited in Schurmann and Schell: 26.

6. Wells Williams 1883: II, 87–88.

7. Fitzgerald: 109.

8. Some of these points are well known and covered in the existing literature; others are discussed at various points in this book. See, in general, Krone 1859; Eitel 1895; Balfour 1941; Barnett 1957; Endacott 1958; Peter Y.L. Ng 1961; and Lo 1963. My account of the Chinese historiography of the Hong Kong region and the principal events since the establishment of Hsin-an in 1573 appeared in JHKBRAS 14, 1974. For the Evacuation of the Coast, an enforced, seven year removal and a major watershed in the district's later history, see Hsieh's article; also Lo 1963: 89–105, Sung 1939, and Mai's article in Chinese. For a description of the geography and climate of the present British crown colony, generally applicable to the region, see CR 1975: 168–70, and for a more detailed account Tregear 5–24.

9. HNHC: 1/1b, 3a and KTKKTY: 1/1b. Also New Atlas: 52.

10. PSN 2 (1): 3–4. See also Powell in PSN 1 (3): 94–99. It should be noted that in their social and cultural aspects, the coastal market centers were only once removed from peasant society, in that many of their shopkeepers were former members of the peasantry of Kwangtung who had made good in their new homes and occupations. See Selby: 46 for a general statement on the shopkeepers of Canton and Foshan in the 1870s.

11. Freedman 1963: par. 6.

12. Even so, the introduction to Jarvie and Agassi 1969 devotes a section to the lack of sociological studies of Hong Kong.

13. Endacott 1958: 1.

14. The works mentioned in this and following paragraphs will be found in the bibliography. A useful detailed survey of recent studies appears in Topley "Published and Unpublished Materials on Hong Kong by Overseas Affiliated Scholars," 1970.

15. I have, in this largely historical study, used "lineage" as defined by Freedman, *Chinese Lineage and Society*, 1966, chapter 1.

16. 602 are listed for the northern district alone at the 1911 colony census, SP 1911: 103 (27–36). Another 71 villages are given for the southern, from which many are, however, omitted, SP 1911: 103 (37–38).

17. These are indicated in detail in the bibliography.

18. Compare Hayes in Topley (ed.) 1967: 96–98 with HNHC 7/12b–18b. This partial listing in gazetteers is apparently common, e.g. Graham: 203–204 found the same thing in west China.

19. Skinner 1964: 5.

20. Commemorative tablets are usually included in gazetteers. HNHC has some in chüan 23 *chi hsü* but is typically weak in this sector. Their intrinsic usefulness, whether obtained from gazetteers or fieldwork, has been recognized: e.g. Yang 1967: 22 and David Buck's article in CSWT 1974. They have been collected for Singapore and Malaysia by Chen and Tan, *A Collection of Chinese Inscriptions in Singapore*, in Chinese (Hong Kong: The Chinese University of Hong Kong, 1970.)

21. Myers 1972: 413.

22. For a recent appraisal see Vansina.

23. The recollected youth of my informants covered the thirty years 1885–1915, so that some of these statements refer to the early period of British rule in the New Territories. However, the colonial authorities did not intend to change or interfere with the existing system of internal control. (See Blake's Chinese proclamation on taking over the New Territory in Extension: 21 and his farewell address to the Legislative Council of Hong Kong in Hansard 1903: 52). In those aspects of local society in which I am interested, the situation at village level continued much the same as under Chinese rule. Freedman [article] 1966: 8, took the same view.

24. The relations between land and boat people are placed on a more practical and commonplace basis by interviews with each side than by the literature. The Shek Pik people could not see the point of my questions about the extent of intermarriage with the local Tanka and when pressed said "How could we take their women for wives when they don't know the first thing about farming": given added point at Shek Pik where this was left largely to women.

25. I could only have discovered from interviews that the vague knowledge of landlords reported by the New Territories Land Court was real. My Lantau informants all said that the rent collectors came "from Sha Wan" but most did not know the landowner's family name and none of

them knew the name of its estate management organisation, the Li Kau Yuen Tong. Again, on local participation in piracy, a local elder (born 1883) said, with a broad smile, that he had been "in all lines of business."

Notes to Chapter 1

1. K.M.A. Barnett's various articles come nearest to providing this: see bibliography.
2. Detailed reports of finds and excavations can be found in Finn (1933–36) Schofield (1940) and Davis and Tregear (1959). The Journal of the Hong Kong Archaeological Society from 1969 on contains accounts of recent work.
3. Barnett 1957: 261.
4. For a general description of Hakka and Punti see Barnett 1957. There is no modern work on the Cantonese, but see Forrest in Purcell, Appendix 1. For the Hakkas, Lo 1971 is the principal Chinese work. See also Cohen 1968, and the illustrated article by Edge in *Echo*, October 1973. Among older works see Lechler, Piton, and Vaillant.
5. Barnett 1957: 261. Also McCoy, JHKBRAS 5 (1965): 46–64.
6. See JHKBRAS 10 (1970): 197–202. Also Sewell: 75 for Canton.
7. Orange: 184, 312, and 377.
8. Eitel 1895: 132.
9. James Johnston: 263–64; Orme: par. 53.
10. E.g. folders of Rev. Roberts and Rev. Dean for the early 1840s and ABMM vols. 23 and 24 for the same period (from Carl T. Smith).
11. Orme: par. 53. See also ARDONT 1919: J13, and CR 1947: 10.
12. A local petition of 1318 mentions two tribes named Yao and Shanlao: see Barnett 1958: 2. Wiens: 272 states that the Chuang and the Yao are the principal tribal peoples of Ling-nan. The tribes of Kwangtung are described in YTPC chüan 7 and Imperial Encyclopaedia, 1389–94.
13. Wiens: 269–76. See also Eberhard 1962: 198–201, and Drake (editor): 101–109, 115–19.
14. Barnett 1958: 2; Yang: 1959 12; Schofield mss quoting "Selections from Toi Shan History," *Chinese Nationalist Daily* (New York) 16 January 1943.
15. Barnett 1964: 59.
16. Wiens: 168–84, and for Lingnan in particular 180–84.
17. HKGG 8 April 1899 (hereafter styled Lockhart): 542–43 and SP 1912 (hereafter styled Orme) after par. 6 (the numbering in my copy is defective). See also Lo: 104–105 and 143.
18. Orme: par. 6.
19. CR 1957: 38.

20. Barnett 1967: part 3, "The Riddle of the Hakka."

21. I have recorded the first type of conversion from Pa Mei, (now called Shan Ha), Ma Wan Chung and Tung Chung Hang (all three located in the Tung Chung Valley), Tai and Siu A Chau, and Luk Tei Tong at Mui Wo. See Gazetteer: 76–77, 79, 82 for these places. Instances of the latter type came from Lo Wai at Pui O on Lantau; Pak Lap on High Island in the Sai Kung subdistrict; Tai Nam Wu in Ho Chung; and Sheung Sz Wan in Clear Water Bay. Gazetteer: 80, 132, 139, 109. These all relate to small lineages, but conversion is not lacking among the major lineages of the region. The Liao of Sheung Shui were originally Hakka (Baker 1968: 28 and 41) and Michael Palmer tells me that the Hau of Ho Sheung Heung, Kam Tsin, Yin Kong, and other places were also Hakka though now classified as Punti (Gazetteer: 205–206). See also, generally, Eberhard 1962: 114–15.

And yet the separate identity of Hakkas, and even of their individual villages, was generally marked and maintained through generations by the finely decorated woven colored bands known as *fa tai* made and worn by Hakka girls and women. Both unmarried and married appear generally to keep to the colors and patterns of their native village. Dr Betsy Johnson's unique study of these fascinating items of Hong Kong ethnography will appear in JHKBRAS 16 (1976).

22. Informants in Chuk Yuen village, Kowloon, who are *wai tau wa* speakers, tell me that the reference in AR 1947: 10 to such mixed villages as "pun kong cham," the half-filled pitcher, refers to this speech, which is also known by at least one uncomplimentary term, being apparently not highly regarded among Hakkas or Cantonese. The subject is worthy of detailed specialist examination before it is too late. Mongrel speech is not unusual in Kwangtung with its mixed population: see Eitel's Dictionary: v, viii. For mixed population, see Eitel in *China Review* 20 (1892–93): 264 which lists 6 districts of the Canton Delta area with mixed Hakka, Hoklo, and Punti settlements including Hsin-an. Another instance is given by Johnston, 272, who mentions a mixed Hakka-Hoklo area in northeast Kwangtung.

23. Lockhart: 543. For conflict see, *inter alia*, Wells Williams 1883: 2: 590–91 and Dyer Ball 1903: 326. And more recently Kuhn: 421–23, 431.

24. Balfour: 139.

25. Hsiao: 421.

26. Orme, par. 6.

27. Barnett 1957: 263.

28. The main Punti villages of Sai Kung in the eastern New Territories all received regular visits from Tang collectors.

29. Potter 1968: 19–21. See also Baker 1968: 154–61 for minor families at Sheung Shui, although he does not say whether they were Hakka or Punti. Serfdom, in one form or another, appears to have lingered long in China: see Elvin: 235–50, particularly 247, for adjacent parts of Kwangtung.

30. Freedman reached the same conclusion. See Freedman 1963: par. 93.

31. Orme, par. 53.

32. SP 1911: 103 (22); by addition.

33. CR 1957: 39.

34. See, *inter alia*, CO 129/12, no. 53; Orme, par. 53; HNTES 1908 Report.

35. Hoklo boat people at Peng Chau, Lantau (1885, 1888; 1971).

36. CR 1938: 50. See also Lin 1939: 6–8 and Burkhardt 1957: 271.

37. Summarized in Ward 1965: 287–89. Also Kani 1967: chapter 1 and notes.

38. John Davis: 195. See also T'ung-chu Ch'ü 1961: 128–35.

39. See chapter three, p. 00 for the long continuing cooperation between land and boat people at Tai O in the repair of local temples 1802–1930: also Hayes 1964: 84–86 and notes 39–45; and Hayes 1969.

40. *Eastern No. 88* (hereafter styled Nathan).

41. Encl. B to Nathan. As the major farming product, rice was well developed. The HNHC 3/1a–b states that the county is good for paddy which has many names and varieties, and it lists 26 types. Nearly a hundred years later, SP 1907: 223 gives 19 varieties. See also the details for some yields given in *Report of the Agricultural Department*, Hong Kong government, 1948–49: 4–7.

42. Governor Blake's report for 1901 in SP 1902: 348a. For earlier see CO 129/12, no. 53 (3 May 1845) par. 12.

43. Lockhart: 543. Hong Kong Island's thriving western district was built on this foundation in the 19th century.

44. Arlington: 158.

45. Lockhart: 543.

46. See HKGG, GN no. 557 of 1901; also CSO 1901 Ext, vol. 2/1240, minute of 30 July 1902, and CSO 1904 Ext/6929, minute of 29 August 1904.

47. Lockhart: 544; and Enclosure C to Nathan. See also SP 1903: 209.

48. SP 1901: no. 28, p. 6. I have found abandoned stone mills in villages in the Clear Water Bay and Sai Kung subdistricts and on Lantau. See also Baker 1968: 15; and Blackie: 78. A description of sugar cane and of sugar production in northeast Kwangtung is given in Campbell Gibson: 127–28. It is not known whether the cooperative methods of producing sugar in that region as described in Kulp: 88–89, 203–206 were practiced here.

49. Enclosure B to Nathan.

50. These entries and much other information on local salt-making will be found in JHKBRAS 7, 1967: 138–51.

51. Annex on Native Trade to Governor of Hong Kong's Despatch no. 38 to Gladstone, Secretary of State for the Colonies, 11 April 1846.

52. Orme, par. 79.

53. See Orme, par. 76, and Blue Book 1906: U 2.

54. Lockhart: 544; and Hayes 1968 and 1971 for notes on weaving and calendering.

55. SP 1907: 221; and Blackie: 118. It is difficult to give a date for the tea plantations, but the 1688 edition of the Hsin-an gazetteer states that Tai Mo Shan, the highest mountain in the present New Territories, was famous for its tea, HNHC 1688, chüan 3.

56. Enclosure B to Nathan.

57. Orme: par. 80. See also CSO 1904 Ext/6929, minute of 29 August 1904.

58. Lockhart: 544; Orme: par. 83; Enclosure B to Nathan; and CSO 1904 Ext/6929, as above. Also JHKBRAS 15: 290–1.

59. Lockhart: 544; Enclosure B to Nathan.

60. Orme: par. 84.

61. Lockhart: 544; Enclosure D to Nathan; and CSO 1901 Ext/151, minute of 5 July 1901, CSO 1903 Ext/1474. Water wheels also worked the clay crushing mills at the Wun Yiu potteries, CSO 1904 Ext/6929.

62. Orme: par. 85.

63. ARDONT, I17. See also Welsby: 3–7, 21–23, 29–30 and 47.

64. Krone: 122; also Orme: paras 58–60; CSO 1905 Ext/17, minutes of 6 April and 5 May 1905, and Fortune: 9–11.

65. Krone: 108; Enclosures C and D to Nathan; and Orme, app. F.

66. Krone: 105 and 124.

67. One case is recorded at length in CSO 1903 Ext/586, Pang Wai-leung's petition of 16 Jan. 1903.

68. E.g. Ross in ARDONT 1909, 1910, 1916.

69. Lockhart: 552.

70. Hon Gershom Stewart, HAN 1910: 113.

71. Lo 1963: 80–88.

72. TCITCCY 41/1a.

73. Krone: 124. Some time later, traveling in the Hakka country near Hong Kong in 1884, Rev. Frank Damon wrote "Truly this is a land of 'burden bearers.' Men and women and children passed us in a continuous stream bearing great baskets and bales and parcels of every description." Char 1975: 25. See also the figures in "Traffic on the Principal Roads of the New Territory," Enclosure E to Nathan.

74. The markets of Hsin-an are shown in the 1688 and 1819 editions of the district gazetteer at chüan 3 and 2 respectively. No market schedules are given. The 1880 edition of the prefectural gazetteer KCFC lists the markets of Hsin-an in chüan 69 but does not give this information either. The products of Hsin-an are listed in HNHC 1819: 3.

75. Tablet dated Tao Kuang 17th year, 11th month, lucky day. See HNHC 1688: 3 and HNHC 1819: 2/12.

76. Tablet dated Kuang Hsü 18th year, 5th month, 14th day, now lost. See HNHC 1688: 3 under Tai Po Tau, and HNHC 1819: 2/13a under Tai Po.

77. HNHC 1819: 2/13b.

78. Enclosure C to Nathan.

79. Skinner 1964: 5–10. See also Baker 1968: 6.

80. Sung 1934: 94. Cheung Chau and Tai O had no proper market

places before the British administration designated them in 1914 and 1918 respectively, and applied rules to them. See HKGG, 10 July 1914 and 30 August 1918. Local people explained that marketing had been done in certain streets.

81. Some of these were very large concerns. See Hayes 1964 for an account of the San Tai Li shop on Peng Chau. There were similar large, multifarious businesses in Sai Kung and Cheung Chau.

82. Skinner 1964: 20–21.

83. Nacken in JHKBRAS 8 (1968): 130; and Bowring in JHKBRAS 5 (1965): 34.

84. I would expect to find it all along the China coast, wherever small communities are settled in places where a sheltered anchorage provides a convenient refuge for a floating population and there is room for boat building, running repairs to craft and fishing equipment, and a supply of water.

85. Waley 1958: 101.

86. Hayes 1964: 77–78.

87. The Tangs of Kam Tin let out nine sites on Tsing Yi at $6 per annum each, (see CSO 1903 Ext/8551) and the Wongs of Nam Tau and Cheung Chau let out thirteen fishing stations on the southern part of Hong Kong Island as shown on a map in their printed genealogy (Huang-shih Tsu-p'u, *t'u hsing* section).

88. Alice Memorial Hospital, Hong Kong, annual reports for 1904 and 1905. This practice was prohibited by law: see Alabaster, 1: 1074.

89. Hayes 1964: 76–77, 81.

90. SP 1903: 348a. It is a pity that, in his otherwise exhaustive and valuable work on the fisheries of Hong Kong, S.Y. Lin scarcely touched on the village fishing, perhaps because by the late 1930s it had already declined greatly in importance and numbers.

91. China, IMC; 111 Misc. Series, no. 11: 5–10.

92. Wells Williams 1856: 306.

93. E.g. Wong Chuk Shan and Pak Kong Au in Sai Kung subdistrict. Aijmar 1967: 50–51 mentions that the Hakkas of Grass Field Village (Mau Ping), Sha Tin, were also long engaged in this trade. (Woodside: 31 writes of itinerant families of Vietnamese carpenters and bricklayers in 19th century Vietnam).

94. Lechler in *Chinese Recorder* September–October, 1878: 359. See also my note in JHKBRAS 8 (1968): 162–65.

95. See e.g. Dyer Ball 1903: 325.

96. Boxer: 232 n. 1 reminds us that geomancers had specialized functions and were not one-line experts. Li Shu-fan: 9 states that they were often physiognomists as well. By way of comparison, Fairbank, Banno and Yamamoto, 8.2.13 p. 238, lists an article by Naoe Hiroji (1947) which lists geomancers and itinerants in North China villages and ascribes to them the additional function of transmitters of folk tales and legends.

97. Among them two persons from the Cheung lineage of Pui O's home district of Kim Hau, Fukien, which it had left nearly three centuries before. See also HKNTES, 1911 report.

98. I have given a few examples in Hayes 1962: n. 55.

99. It is also necessary to take into account the favorable bias of the work load associated with rice farming in a predominently rural society. D.Y. Lin has calculated that to work an average-size farm of 12.5 tou (his figure), 100 days of animal labor and 225 days of human labor would be required, and that if no catch crop is grown during the winter months there will be an idle period of 140 days or more than one-third of a year (Tregear: 64–65). Bear in mind, too, that in this region, as elsewhere in the southeast the women often did much of the field work (Campbell Gibson: 136). I propose to develop, elsewhere, this interesting question of time available for community work at various levels, and the priorities awarded to it in local society. A full examination of time available in a life style bounded largely by natural daylight and reduced by reliance on traditional means of production, preparation and manufacture, would e.g. take into account the division of work between men and women, and the time needed to travel on foot to market, usually with loads and reportedly more often by men than women, and to perform the self-sufficient parts of household economy like unhusking rice by traditional means.

100. Field Officer: 75.

101. Lockhart: 542. E.R. Hallifax, then serving in the New Territory gives further information in a memorandum dated 30 June 1903 in CSO 1903 Ext/3690.

102. J. L. Buck 1937: 443.

103. See John Davis: 163 and Ryckmans: 6.

104. See Wu: 23, 25, and 45.

105. One seldom encounters the history of ordinary dwellings. An interesting brief record of one such house is contained in a manuscript genealogy of the Pang family of Shek Pui Ling, Pang Tong, Tung-kuan district, Kwangtung. This records a *mao wu* or thatched house descending from an unknown time to a 11th generation ancestor (1728–1803), through the next (1762–1830); rebuilt as a tiled house measuring 17 *hang* across by the 13th generation (1814–93); affected by the collapse of a neighboring earthwalled house after rain in 1899; compensated with seven silver dollars and rebuilt five months later. It was sold in 1904 to a mother and son of the same lineage and finally, in 1912, was rebuilt to provide three connecting houses.

106. E.g. Wells Williams 1883: 1: 40; Gutzlaff: 141 and Simpson: 4.

107. Goodwin: 109, 123.

108. See e.g. its report for 1936.

109. SP 1898: 235.

110. The minutes of HKNTES for 5 November 1917 mention that the mistress of their school on Cheung Chau had given notice because she was "suffering from boils and eruptions due to the state of the drinking water in the place." Also ADR, DCNT 1955–6: par. 24.

111. There is a useful summary of communicable diseases and of factors facilitating the spread of disease in Lamson 1935: 274–88. See also Kulp on health in Phenix Village, northeast Kwangtung: 54–61. Li Shu-fan has also remarked of his home village in Toi Shan, Kwangtung that the

heat of the tropical sun on tender skins "often caused boils that left ugly scars," whilst "the merest cut often resulted in suppuration." And about 1905 he recalls treating 70 cases of dysentery in his maternal grandmother's nearby village while on vacation from the Hong Kong College of Medicine (Li: 11, 13, 27). However, village practices were sometimes beneficial. The use of traditional methods of processing rice "in a stone basin with a wooden hammer contrivance worked by foot" retained the nutritious pericarp and safeguarded the village population from beriberi, the disease resulting from a deficiency of vitamin B. This covering was usually removed in the imported machine-polished rice of Southeast Asia. (Li: 162.)

112. Yang (1967: 14) reported that 80% of the worshippers in the temple at Nanching, Kwangtung, prayed for the return of health.

This spiritual protection was also sought for animals. Ng reports that a cure for cattle diseases and infections was 'the hanging of a piece of red paper folded in the shape of a triangle, blessed at the village temple [and hung] around the neck of the affected animal': Ng in Jarvie and Agassi: 62. Protection was further extended for both men and animals by placing lucky papers on agricultural tools at the Lunar New Year, a practice still to be seen in local villages.

113. Hong Kong Meteorological Records (R.O.T.M. 5): 1.

114. The damage done in the New Territories by the 1937 typhoon, one of the worst in the colony's history, is described in ARDONT 1937: J7.

115. Hayes 1964: 75–76, 91–92. See Gray II: 286 for descriptions of losses to the boat populations of Macao and Canton in 1857 and 1862 respectively.

116. HNHC 1819: 13/1b–6b. The droughts of the two preceding years are noted on a tablet in the Tao lineage ancestral hall of Ping Shan, Yuen Long, dated the 52nd year of Ch'ien Lung (1787–88).

117. ARDONT 1917, 1918, and 1928.

118. They were a regular part of farming life in the Far East. Thomas C. Smith reports of 17th–19th century Japan "Some records kept by peasants, recording little else than the size of the harvest each year, read like chronicles of disaster: 'poor harvest,' 'crop failure,' 'harvest reduced by one-half,' and so on appear every few years." Smith: 159c.

119. See e.g. Hume: 47, 214, and chapter 25; Moody: 102–103, 107; and Li: 21. For some associated ideas see Topley in *Man*, 1970.

Tree spirits were also pressed into protective service by villagers, and may still be seen in present day Hong Kong. Trees are pasted with lucky papers announcing that such and such a child is their *kai tsai* (seen in Sheung Kwai Chung and Tung Chung, Lantau).

120. See Moody: 110. For the background to Chinese geomancy see March.

121. See Foster: 87. This was applied less to outbuildings, which, in the Hong Kong region, tended to be sited haphazardly and at need.

122. Some were given in a short lived Chinese periodical, *Hsin-chieh chou-pao* in 1962–63. Many others are to be found in Sung Hok-pang's articles on the Tangs in *The Hong Kong Naturalist*, 1935–38.

123. See the case in CSO 1904 Ext/6269, minute of 17 January 1908.

124. Gazetteer: 214.

125. I have described some of these cases in JHKBRAS 3 (1963) and 9 (1969).

126. This disease was called *chü mo ping* by the villagers, and appears in Eitel 1910: 619 as follows, "a common disease in South China. It begins with high fever and after vigorously rubbing the chest, bristles an inch long appear through the skin, after their removal the fever goes down".

The problem of depopulation early intruded itself into my village studies. It came first to my attention through the preoccupation with *feng-shui* noted in the text, so much of it linked to a reported decline in local populations. Besides the statements of old persons in the villages and the few documentary indications on the subject, there is other evidence to support a large population in, say, midcentury. First, close acquaintance with the hills and valleys of the southern district of the New Territories suggests that practically every piece of land, high or low, that could be planted with rice had been opened for that purpose at one time or another. This presumes a large and settled population, since the opening of paddy fields and their irrigation dams and channels involves considerable labor, and once rice is cultivated there is continuous farming unless the number of cultivators available in a family or village drops to the point where fields go out of use. There was dry and shifting cultivation in addition, for ancillary crops such as peanuts and sweet potatoes that, old villagers say, were more extensively cultivated in the past. Writing in 1958, Tregear: 42–44 states "There is a surprising amount of land, formerly under cultivation, which has been abandoned. In all it amounts to some 3,000 acres. The map. . . shows this to be fairly generally distributed but with a rather greater concentration in districts to the north and east." Poor water supply, lack of communications, poor farming, pests and epidemics, and other more recent factors are attributed by the author; but in my view the extent of depopulation and the reasons for it have not yet been realized or understood. A second factor that points to a larger population is the widespread and intense fishing of local waters that was such a marked feature of village life seventy and more years ago, as revealed by my inquiries all over the New Territories. Local affirmation is reinforced by the many fishing stations that can be discerned at places all along the coastline of the mainland and islands. If fishing at its most intensive coincided with farming at its most widespread, one may conclude that, subsidiary reasons and incentive factors apart, all this activity was required to provide for the existence of a large population in the villages.

Thus village tradition and the evidence of the countryside and coastline combine to support my belief that depopulation was an event in the later history of the Hong Kong region. Though it is tempting, and speculative, to suggest that emigration and the establishment and rise of Hong Kong had something to do with attracting men away from the villages and helping to reduce the birthrate,—but on these points see Li Shu-fan: 4, 121—I believe that more vital and serious reasons exist to explain what amounted to a major disaster in rural life. In the light of my surmises it is interesting to find that Perkins notes a sharp reduction in the population figures for Kwangtung between 1851 and 1873, not fully recovered by 1893. This would, of course, take in the ravages of the Tai Ping time and the Hakka-Punti wars; but there is more to it. Using available demographic and economic materials, much work can yet be done to show that Professor Ping-ti Ho's postulate of a "declining rate of growth" in the population of Kwangtung, 1850–1953, covers reductions as well as increases at the local level. See Ho 1959: 270, 277–78.

127. Da Silva 1972: 62–64.

128. Wells Williams 1883: II: 246.

129. See CSO 1904 Ext/4893. I have elaborated on some of the inadequacies of the Block Crown Leases in a forthcoming article "Rural Society and Economy in Late Ch'ing: A Case Study of the New Territories of Hong Kong (Kwangtung)" to appear in CSWT 3, No. 5 (1976).

130. KTKKCY 6/4a.

131. Illegally, according to the Lis. See CSO 1899 no. 8, Confid. 153, and CSO 1903 Ext/7466.

132. I do not know how to account for this situation, nor when it began. The earliest date for a deed not concerned with Li land is Ch'ien Lung 37 (1772–73).

133. KTTC 270. Also Lo 1956: 217, n. 29.

134. See Hsieh. Also Lo 1963: 89–105.

135. Legal suits could pile up. It is said that in the 1820s a newly appointed provincial judge of Kiangsi cleared up, within four months, some four thousand accumulated cases. Hummel: 702.

136. Fei: 189 found that old people in Kaihsienkung in the Yangtse valley regarded similar rent payment as a "moral duty."

137. First Year, Appendix 8, par. 12. This situation occasioned the taxlord controversy which caused the British much concern and major clans like the Lis and Tangs much heartburning, impoverishment, and loss of prestige. They and other owners of land given out on perpetual lease were the "rent charge owners or taxlords" referred to by the president of the New Territories Land Court in SP 1902: 557–64, par. 14, but elsewhere referred to as "tax-collecting families," (SP 1906: 143–52, par. 82). The former is the correct description, in my view. Some taxlords were compensated by the Hong Kong government—see Orme: par. 21 (1) and Clementi's minute of 28 August 1906 in CSO 1904 Ext/6269. Others, including the Li family of Lantau, the Chans who owned much of Peng Chau (see Hayes 1964: n. 27–28 and CSO 1903 Ext/7466) and some smaller "taxlords" were not (see CSO 1904 Ext/1625, minute of 29 February 1904). See also Potter 1968: 23 and 100.

138. Rawski 1972: 19–24. Elvin: 245 suggests that its origin there may be traced to a 15th century rebellion.

139. from First Year: Appendix 3.

140. CSO 1904 Ext/1560, minute of 5 August 1904.

141. CSO Ext/1823, minute of 9 April 1904. A similar two-fold division of the soil was to be found in Fukien, Kiangsu and Kiangsi: reference

7.6.8. in Fairbank, Banno and Yamamoto: 191. See also Fei on Kaihsienkung, 188–89.

142. First Year: 4. Rawski (1975: 71) reports a like situation in the settlement of the Han River Highlands on the borders of Szechuan, Hopei, and Shensi, citing an early 19th century report.

143. CSO 1903 Ext/8551, minute of 6 July 1904.

144. CSO 1904 Ext/436, minute of 27 March 1904.

145. CSO 1904 Ext/1625, minute of 29 February 1904.

146. See, *inter alia*, the translated letter from the provincial treasurer of Kwangtung to Sir John Davis attached to no. 76 in CO 129/7; the *Friend of China* 24 July 1858 for the translation of a Chinese notice on this subject; Lobscheid 1858: 36; Report of the Anglo-Chinese Land Commission in CO 129/85, no. 82 of 30 April 1862; and CSO 1898 no. 2982. However, by the 1860s the position was obscure and chaotic, leading to the doubts expressed—wrongly I believe—by the surveyor-general of Hong Kong in par. 6 of no. 19 in CO 129/98.

147. See e.g. CSO 1904 Ext/1625 and 3420, minutes of 29 February and 26 April 1904.

148. Alabaster: 1897.

149. Rawski 1972: 19, citing Niida Noboru.

150. It continued well into the British period. A district officer wrote in 1922, "Although the waste land round villages are now technically the property of the Crown the villagers continue to regard them as theirs, and resent encroachments by individuals accordingly." (ARDONT 1922, under D.O. North.)

151. Yasaburo Takekoshi: 121.

152. See par. 6–10 of his no. 82 in CO 129/85. See also the surveyor general's resumé in CO 129/98.

153. Elvin: 250–60.

154. There is no trace here, so far, in the areas studied, of the "powerful domination" which landlords and bursaries were able to exert over their land and tenants in late Ch'ing and early Republican Kiangnan. Muramatsu: 595–99.

155. Rostow: 105.

156. Ho 1962: 86–91 has an important section on the permeation of society by Confucian ideology. Chiang Monlin's autobiography tells the same story: "These moral precepts came from the Confucian classics. Moral ideas were driven into the people by every possible means–temples, theatres, houses, toys, proverbs, schools, history and stories–until they became habits in daily life." (Chiang: 9.) For state action see Hisayuki Miyakawa, especially 43–46, on the Ch'ing confucianization of Formosa, and also on that subject Colquhoun and Lockhart: 184–190, 204. See also Fairbank, Banno and Yamamoto, 8.8.1, p. 255, which lists an article by Tsukishima Kenzo (1951) which stresses the permeation of the so-called Confucian morality into the lower social strata of China and the persistant influence of the traditional morality even in persons seemingly rather detached from the old social order.

157. See the library list of holdings in the Fung Ping-shan Library, University of Hong Kong in Lo 1971: 211–40, to which additions are being steadily made.

158. Kept in the Department of Oriental Printed Books and Mss. My own fieldwork in the Tsuen Wan subdistrict of the New Territories is producing additional family records, both printed and manuscript, and my forthcoming article in CSWT 3, No. 5 (1976) will have more to say on the Confucianization of the small lineage.

159. Chung: 26–27. See also for Nanching, Kwangtung, in the 1940s Yang 1959: 182.

160. These pursuits are listed in YTPC 1/1a. Some of the folktales and legends were collected in the 1920s by the National Sun Yat-sen University at Canton. See Eberhard 1973: x–xi and Schneider 137–38, 142–43 for Ku Chieh-kang's and Chung Ching-wen's work there, and part 2 of this interesting book for the folklore movement and popular culture. The class of female entertainers in towns and cities was another repository of old stories; Sewell: 126. Also Peplow: 52 on riddles. A rare translation of some New Year riddles appears at pp. 66–69 of L.G. Hopkins' *The Guide to Kuan Hua* (Shanghai, Kelly and Walsh, Fifth edition, 1921).

161. Cantonese, Hoklo and Chiu-chou opera troupes perform in present-day Hong Kong, along with Cantonese, Chiu-chou and Fukienese puppet troupes.

162. See Werle in JHKBRAS 13 (1973).

163. Fitzgerald: 140. See also Chiang: 19, Sewell: 91 and Llewellyn: 101–102. Gamble 1954: 329–97 gives many useful comparative details of *yang ke* plays, other recreation, festivals, and customs for Ting Hsien, including texts. Many more texts are given in Gamble 1971.

164. See Kulp: 268–70. In Hong Kong the verses are usually taken from Tang poetry. See also Paul Ng: 82, 87–98.

165. Kulp: 276 makes this point. His whole chapter 9, 261–83, on art and recreation is a valuable and seldom-found account of these influences at village level, as observed over fifty years ago. See also Yang 1959: 96, and, especially, Ho 1962: 91.

Notes to Chapter 2

1. Introduction to an inscription dated 1870 (T'ung Chih, 9th year, 3rd moon, lucky date) recording the repair of the Chen-an She of the present Pao-an District Association.

2. Gazetteer: 88; about 592 acres.

3. SP 1911: 103 (26) and 103 (38). The figure for the floating population may be the figure for the census district as at 103 (38).

4. HKNTES: 1916 report.
5. Arlington: 159. He was in charge of the Imperial Maritime Customs station on Cheung Chau, 1893–99.
6. CSP: 443.
7. Arlington: 158.
8. BB 1906: V2–11.
9. It is not possible to give an exact figure for the late 19th century but the number probably exceeded one hundred. Businesses were often stable and long lasting, as befitted a prosperous place. A survey made in 1962 gave 26 shops founded before 1918. Ten of these had been established in the 19th century, the five earliest in 1833, 1843, 1853, 1854, and 1860.
10. SP 1911: 103 (38).
11. SP 1911: 103 (22).
12. Tablet of 1866–67 (T'ung Chih, 5th year, winter).
13. Cheung Chau is shown on a plan entitled "Chang-chou Yü-t'u" in the *t'u hsing* section of the *Huang-shih tsu-p'u.* The land officer in Hong Kong reported in 1903, "I find there, all the houses are held under one landlord, the tenants holding varying leases from one year to perpetuity.' (CSO 1903 Ext/3690: minute of 18 August.) See also ARDONT 1909: H5.
14. *Huang-shih tsu-p'u.* The Cheung Chau members of the family say they have been twenty-seven adult generations at Nam Tau.
15. Comparison of entries in the *ch'ang-yeh* section in chüan 7, *Huang-shih tsu-p'u* and the preamble to a surviving woodblock-printed lease of land dated January 1904.
16. 91.07 acres of agricultural land were surveyed and registered by the New Territories Survey and Land Court: see BCL for Cheung Chau.
17. The Tong was still collecting rent from sand beaches in 1958: see the printed statement of account, "Huang Wei Tse T'ang Cheng Hsin Lu," for 1958.
18. CSO 1905 Ext/5914, petition dated 31st July 1905. It refers to houses and shops, but also involved agricultural lots.
19. The last appears to confirm the position reported by my older informants, that the Tong did not lead or direct the management of local affairs.
20. CSO 1905 Ext/5914.
21. ARDONT 1909, H 5. Not only was the decision unusual; it also appears that the land work was badly done. See Orme: par. 19.
22. Skinner 1958 calls such bodies "speech group organizations." Their formation was usual in the Hong Kong region, where numbers permitted. For instance, the associations of Hsin-an and Tung-kuan men at Tai O are described in chapter 3; and on Ap Lei Chau, off Hong Kong Island (population 1,437 at the 1911 census) there were two similar associations for Hsin-an and Tung-kuan people and a third for residents of other places. See Hayes in JHKBRAS, 7 (1967): 166–68; also Osgood 1975: 2: 487–88, 491–93.
23. A recent review of their overseas aspects is given by Aline K. Wong in JHKBRAS 11 (1971): 62–73.
24. The Wai Chiu Club also provided a school before and after 1899.

One of my informants attended it in 1885–86: see Hayes 1963: 97 and 105, n. 28.

25. In all this work there is an interesting parallel with the Tung Kwun Tung Yee Tong of Hong Kong (*Chu-chiang Tung-kuan Tung-i-t'ang*) established in Kuang Hsü 19th year (1893–94). Its record, published in 1931, describes its main objects as to establish a charitable grave, carry out the customary worship and sacrifices to feed hungry souls and transport them in spirit to their native place, and to found a charitable school for poor children of the district. (*Chu-chiang Tang-kuan Tung-i-t'ang shih-lu*: 4).

26. Hayes 1963: 97.

27. ADR by the social welfare officer for the period 1948–54, par. 72. I have here altered the capitals to match the differentiation adopted above. I have found a reference to the Kaifong of a section of Canton City in Clementi: 100. He quotes from a letter by Harry Parkes dated 12 November 1859 in which the latter had got some gentry and a deputy magistrate "to call in the Kai-fong, or principal men of the neighbourhood—men who have a voice in the municipal arrangements of that quarter—" to listen to an explanation of the workings and objects of an emigration depot established in the area. For later Kaifong in Hong Kong see Wong 1973.

28. It is still standing. The lintel is inscribed "Kung-so" and is dated Tung Chih, 1st year, mid month of summer. There had been earlier developments before the Kung-so was established, indicating that the early Chinese community of Hong Kong was taking steps to organize itself as a group and in the several districts of the new town. See Carl Smith 1971: 76 (7), 81; Lethbridge 1971: 117–18; and Topley and Hayes 1967: 139–41.

29. Hayes 1966: 129–30.

30. The community of Hung Hom, a large village beside the Hong Kong and Whampoa Dock Company's yards at Kowloon, erected two temples, a meeting hall, and a clinic between the 1870s and 1910. See the note in JHKBRAS 15 (1975): 318–24.

31. Tablet dated T'ung Chih 12th year, autumn, lucky day.

32. See M. Hugo-Brunt's article on this church in JOS 1, no. 2: 327–44.

33. Kuang Hsü 22nd year, 6th month, 17th day.

34. Head tablet inscribed T'ung Chih 12th year, 6th month. Giles 1912: 363, describes *i-chung* as "a public cemetery—for the temporary accommodation of the bodies of strangers." This grave is stated conclusively by all elders to be the Kaifong's scheme.

35. See the petition to this end from leading Kaifongs in CSO 1901 Ext/44.

36. Hayes 1963: 98 and 106, n. 31.

37. BCL, Lot 340 where it is styled *chai lau so* or "asylum."

38. One is reminded, probably unjustly in this case, of the satirical "eight thoughts of a Chinese official" current just before the Revolution of 1911. "When he meets a Chinese merchant from Singapore, Java, San Francisco etc. he thinks of charitable endowments i.e. of the opportunities of squeezing such presents for good causes." (Tyau: 111.)

39. For more details see Hayes 1963: 92, 94–95 and n. 18 and 22. The tablet listed 21 persons with rank or title of whom sixteen were Wongs and probably members of the Tong, from the main as well as the Cheung Chau branches. However, I believe that this was outside "interest" exerted in an emergency rather than a sign of Wong direction of local affairs. Since 1963 I have also discovered that several Cheung Chau shopkeepers had purchased degrees.

40. Personal communication, 1962.

41. This importance is reflected by the local honors paid to committeemen of this type. Stevens: 16 includes among his "Cantonese Apothegms" the phrase *Tsip sung chik sz* (*Chieh-sung chih-shih*) and comments "The ceremonies of welcoming a new and escorting home an old, street councillor are carried out with a fanfare of trumpets, beating of gongs and firing of crackers."

42. See DAR, DCNT for 1954–55, par. 48, and for 1960–61, pars. 121 and 126.

43. E.g. the "Sun Hing Street Luen Yee Wui" registered on 8 October 1949 by the registrar of societies; and the unregistered Pak She Street Kung Sor formed in 1955 but originating in a prewar youth group for lion dancing and music training.

44. On the 18th of the first month at Pak She; and on the Earth God's festival on the 2nd day of the second month at Tai San and San Hing Streets.

45. See the note in JHKBRAS 15 (1975): 311–18.

46. Giles 1912: 161, calls it "the festival of All-Souls." There is a good description of different types of *chiao*, as practiced in present day Taiwan, in *Echo*, January 1974: 28–44. Of these, the *ping-an chiao* is closest to the Cheung Chau rite.

47. There is here a striking similarity to the proceedings in late 19th century Formosa described by Rev. G.L. Mackay who calls the bun towers "cones." (Mackay: 129–31.) See also *Echo* 6, No. 2: 13–18, 60.

48. See Topley 1967: 108–109; Werner: 196–97; and Wells Williams 1856: 308 and 531.

49. The modern practice is not new, however. Adele Fielde reported it from Swatow in the 1870s (Fielde: 68–71) and J.A. Turner gives details of such a procession at Fatshan in the 1880s "in which several hundreds of boys, girls, and men take part" (Turner: 140). See also Lobscheid 1883–84: 403.

50. Dated Kuang Hsü 15th year, third winter month.

51. Tin Hau dated Hsüan Tung 1st year, and Pak Tai Kuang Hsü 29th year.

52. The Tin Hau (Pak She) has a bell dated Ch'ien Lung 32 (1767–68) and an incense burner dated Ch'ien Lung 50 (1785–86). The Tin Hau (Chung Hing Street) bell is dated Ch'ien Lung 37 (1772–73). The Pak Tai's bell is dated Ch'ien Lung 49 (1784–85) and the Hung Shing temple's bell is dated Chia Ch'ing 18 (1813–14).

53. From Mr. Lo Tin-yan of the Tung Yu shrimp sauce business established in 1843.

54. This was not the first time that Kuang-chou natives had presented items to the temple; a pair of imposing granite lion-dogs standing outside it were donated in 1861. Individuals had probably also contributed amounts in the past. But 1904 was the first time an approach was made to Kuang-chou groups to associate them in the management.

55. Bell dated Ch'ien Lung 39th year (1774–75).

56. A nearby tablet commemorating the construction of the road to this temple gives Tao Kuang 20th year (1840–41) for the date of the work.

57. I have here regarded the temples as institutions and vehicles for leadership, especially in the activities at the time of their gods' birthdays. I have not studied their year-round social and ritual activities or the persons connected with them. Some information on what was likely to take place in them, as in other temples of their kind and other religious institutions, is provided by Topley 1967 on Chinese occasional rites in Hong Kong, and Topley and Hayes, included in the same RAS Symposium brochure under her editorship. Topley's two articles on Chinese Religion in Singapore (1956 and 1961, see bibliography) are also of assistance in this specialized field. See, too, Graham: 195–214.

58. The fare provided for these events did not always meet with satisfaction from members. An elder recalled that on one occasion there were twenty-eight tables with over 220 people. He named the caterer and the cost, and added, "The food was no good, and those present were dissatisfied and there was a lot of grumbling."

59. The Hoklo and Cantonese elements on the island were particularly antagonistic to each other: see HKNTES 1908. There is much evidence for these animosities which, as might have been expected, also came to the fore on emigrant ships. In 1859 Rev. Lobscheid advised an agent that "some care should be taken to separate the clans, for example Hak-ka from Pun-ti, so as to prevent quarrels in the ship." Three years later trouble on two ships was attributed to taking on a mixed complement of Chinese from Hong Kong, Canton, Amoy, and Swatow, and the surgeon-superintendent of the ship *Persia* gave a graphic description of the troubles that ensued, "They spoke different dialects, could not understand and cordially hated each other . . . came on board fighting and during the ten days the ship lay at Hong Kong these faction fights were of almost daily occurrence." (Clementi: 79, 130–33.)

60. In the course of a long life, many of them have not found it necessary to take much interest in anything else. One old man, born in 1885 and usually a mine of information, was unable to tell me anything about an institution in the next street, though it was located only a few hundred yards from the house in which he had lived all his life. He explained his ignorance by saying that he lived in Pak She Street "whereas over there is San Hing Street."

61. HKGG, 15 July 1899: 1,117. Sir Henry Blake, governor of Hong Kong at this time, explained the background to, and intentions of, this legislation in his farewell address to the Legislative Council. Hansard, 1903: 52.

62. See CSO 1901 Ext/44 and CSO 1905 Ext/5914, petitions dated 5 March 1901 and 31 July 1905 respectively.

63. HKGG, 15 July 1899: 1,117.

64. Ts'o Tsing's name appears as one of the managers for the property on lots 421, 482, 502, and 599 belonging to the Tung Kwun association. Descendants of some of the others are registered as managers of the Hoklo community's Chiu Chau and Wai Chau Club property on lots 229 and 379.

65. I have not yet been able to establish, in an outline study, whether this was a temporary absence from local leadership or whether the Tong's leaders were not normally included in Kaifong direction in the 19th century.

66. This emphasis on the human element in the management of local affairs, at the expense of rigid demarcation of personnel, duties, and finance, is another manifestation of what D.E. Willmott: 144, writing in 1960 of the Chinese of Semarang, styles the "continuing preference for face-to-face trust relations rather than contractual relations."

67. I have no information on what happened in a crisis requiring measures to placate the gods: as in the case of plague related by Peplow: 223–26, said to have occurred about 1910.

68. Eitel 1910: 345, 780: not in Giles.

69. As happened in 1946: see Paul K.C. Tsui's minute in file 11/631/45 on the Pak Tai Temple, Cheung Chau (kept in the Directorate of Home Affairs, Hong Kong).

70. Skinner 1958: 5, 11–12.

71. See ARDONT 1910: I 11–12; 1911: I 15; 1912: I 13; and 1914: I 9.

72. ARDONT 1919, 1920, 1921: J 12, J 12, and J 13 respectively.

Notes to Chapter 3

1. By comparison with Cheung Chau, present day Tai O appears to have fewer old families with members prominent in its 19th century management, most likely due to the economic stagnation that kept the population fluid and sent many enterprising people elsewhere. Partly because of this, I have not attempted to deal with the economic relationship between land and boat people—despite its obvious bearing on the community aspects of their interaction—because there is insufficient 19th century material and a lack of suitable informants.

2. ARDONT 1915: J 9.

3. SP 1911: 103 (38) and (26).

4. SP 1911: 103 (38).

5. CSO 1904 Ext/3165, minute of 21 April 1904.

6. Also seen in old shops on Ap Lei Chau, Hong Kong island.

7. Memorial 28000 in the Hong Kong Land Registry, dated 6 July 1900, concerns the sale of a shop at Tai O in Kuang Hsü 23rd year, on which there was a yearly ground rent of 2 mace payable to the Li family.

8. ARDONT 1911 and 1916: I 14 and J 12.

9. See JHKBRAS 10 (1970): 197–202 for an account, written in 1937, of the dwellings of Tai O boat people.

10. ARDONT 1916, 1926, 1927: J 12, J 13, and J 11.

11. Orme, par. 70. HNHC mentions them (3/13b) 'caught in the sea near Tai O. From the ninth to eleventh moons fishermen hear their croak at night and catch them with nets, encircling them. The tactic is 'beat the yellow croaker'.

12. ARDONT 1911: I 15; 1915: J 9; and 1926 and 1927: J 13 and J 11.

13. ARDONT 1918: J 11; 1920: J 12; 1921: J 12; 1922: J 11.

14. BB 1906: J 2–11.

15. Colonial Reports—Annual, no. 314, Hong Kong, 1899: 14.

16. Orme: par. 65.

17. J.F. Davis: 343.

18. The salt production for these years, taken from ARDONT, is summarized in JHKBRAS 7 (1967): 145–49.

19. Lo 1959: 212 and 216 (n. 28).

20. See also Cheng Kam-man's complaints about junks bringing salt to Tai O for sale and his workmen selling salt in the night in CSO 1903 Ext/4904 minute of 22 June 1903.

21. This man's name (Cheng Kam-man) appears in the BCL for Tai O and the CSO papers (1903 Ext/4904 and 1904 Ext/2140). Some of his own and his father's purchases of land in the Hong Kong region, mainly of fishing stations and an abandoned salt pan, are shown in deeds recorded in the Hong Kong Land Registry (memorials 26918, 27998–28000).

22. Local information, and CSO 1904 Ext/3420, minute of 26 April 1904.

23. CSO 1904 Ext/7304, petition of 17 July 1906.

24. JHKBRAS 7 (1967): 139.

25. See JHKBRAS 7 (1967): 149.

26. NTLC 1900–1905 in SP 1906: 150.

27. Schofield, personal communication; also Lo 1963: 172.

28. For accounts of these places see JHKBRAS 3 (1963): 144–45; 4 (1964): 146–52; 8 (1968): 82–95 and 165–67.

29. The troops came from the Tai Pang battalion and were under the overall command of the Kowloon garrison commander.

30. HNHC 2/19a onwards.

31. Tablet dated in the winter months of Tao Kuang 18th year.

32. See chapter one, also Hayes 1964: n. 40.

33. HKNTES 1910.

34. HKNTES 1915.

35. HKNTES 1917. See Anderson 1972: 21–32 for useful background.
36. Lot 152 in DD 313.
37. Lot 258 in DD 313.
38. No transactions have been listed for either the Hip Wo She Hok or the Po On Study since the initial registration of 1905. Consequently no leads for further inquiry were available.
39. In every case these premises were regarded as public property at the land settlement, and were registered in the block crown lease for Tai O in the name of the registrar general.
40. According to the district land registers, lot 133 was sold in 1922, and lots 134–35 the following year. Lot 263 was vested in a private person in 1910, and lot 275 has remained in the name of the registrar general, now the director of home affairs.
41. Yang 1967: 96–99.
42. Brim (1970: chapter 2) reports it from Sun Fung Wai near Castle Peak (Gazetteer: 162), and I have recorded it from Shek Pik and Tong Fuk on Lantau Island.
43. Personal communication, 1962.
44. Nevius: 219 reports it from Ningpo, and Clark: 133 from Chefoo.
45. Personal communication, 1962. Prewar (and postwar) the Kaifong also operated a *fong pin so*, similar in type and purpose to the Cheung Chau Fong Pin hospital but much smaller. It was repaired by them in 1934 but was originally provided as a charitable work with subscriptions collected mainly from Hong Kong by the Kuan Yin temple at Keung Shan nearby. The Kaifong appointed a keeper for this 'dying house' to look after the indigent sick near to death, and it provided coffins at need.
46. ARDONT 1926: J 13. Unfortunately GN 394, HKGG, 15 July 1899, does not list the committeemen (i.e. Kaifong) for Tai O market, as it does for Cheung Chau. The names shown there are only those for the surrounding villages.
47. This *Tei Po* is probably the same functionary as the *Yeuk-po* (*Yüeh-pao*) Cheng Lam-sau who was writer and middleman for the sale of an old house at Tai O in T'ung Chih 5 (copy of deed in my possession).
48. There was, for instance, a *tei po* (tepo) at Kowloon Street before 1899: he reported a stabbing to the assistant magistrate of Kowloon, as mentioned in a Chinese deed of Kuang Hsü 25th year (Memorial 28037 in the Hong Kong Land Registry).
49. This temple has three main sections within the one structure: the temple to Kwan Tai after whom it takes its name; a side temple to Tin Hau with its own commemorative tablet of 1835; and the guest hall-community office.

Tai O has a fifth temple, a small building in Wang Hang village on the edge of the salt fields styled the Chung Sheng temple (lots 58–59 in DD 313). It seems to be a village temple erected and maintained by the residents of this small multi-lineage place, and had been built or reconstructed in the 1890s.
50. However, the Yeung Hau Wong temple directors at its major

repairs of 1877—the only one for which a commemorative tablet exists—were not only from the boat population. The tablet was erected by *ho-ao chih-li*.

51. The bells are dated as follows: Kwan Tai-Tin Hau, Ch'ien Lung 6 (1741–42) and Ch'ien Lung 37 (1772–73); Hung Shing, Ch'ien Lung 11 (1746–47); Yeung Hau Wong, K'ang Hsi 38 (1699–1700) and Tin Hau, K'ang Hsi 52 (1713–14).

52. See chapter one, also Hayes 1964: n. 39–45, and Hayes 1969: 41–43.

53. The *ssu-hsiang* were the Tai O villages of Wang Hang, San Tsuen, Leung Uk and Nam Chung. (SP 1911: 103 (38).)

54. These included reaching mutual agreement on the auspicious times at which each of the major events in the rebuilding projects were to be undertaken. For example, a Sai Kung temple tablet (1916) lists eleven stages, from the erection of the scaffolding to the fixing of doors and the installation of the several gods. (Hayes 1967: 89 and n. 14.)

Notes to Chapter 4

1. See Schofield 1940.

2. Hayes and Watt 1970. It is considered by some scholars that the name of the smaller of the Shek Pik villages, Fan Pui ("the back of the tomb"), may denote the existence of a royal burial, one of the last two boy emperors of Sung. The events of this sad time have lived long in local history. Dr. Li Shu-fan's home village of Heung Tau Fan ("Sandalwood-Head Tomb") in Toi Shan district has similar connections. The name commemorates the fate of a loyal minister of the Sung Dynasty "who was finally caught and decapitated on the same hill where his remains now lie in a tomb, with a head carved from sandalwood in place where his natural head should be." (Li: 4.)

3. Lin T'ien-wei 1964. Two rocks with carved geometric patterns probably date from this time. See S.G. Davis 1963: 19–21.

4. 4,142 separate lots were registered in the demarcation district sheets nos. 312, 315, 318, 319, 321, and 323. See BCL.

5. E.W. Hamilton, private communication, 1960. Also ARDONT 1922: J 12.

6. SP 1911: 103 (38).

7. The closeness of these two lineages is noted by Giles 1912: 573: "Certain families (e.g. the 徐 and the 余) will not intermarry because their surnames, now different, were once the same."

8. Krone noted this tendency elsewhere in the Hsin-an district in the 1850s through for different reasons, Krone: 124. This phenomenon is apparently not confined to peasants. I have a Chia Ch'ing edition of a book of collected moral instructions first published in the 7th year of Ch'ien Lung (1742–43) which advises gentry not to be ashamed of their own family and seek to enter more important ones (implying those of other *hsing*). (Ch'en Hung-mou: 4/53.)

9. Most of these fields lay round and above Shek Pik Wai in DD 312.

10. These figures tie in roughly with an irrigation engineer's survey of 1952. He estimated 136 acres in cultivation, and 40 abandoned acres in the upper village. (File IO 115/52 of DCNT's office.)

11. The plight of a landless rural laborer in a late 19th century "small crowded village, a few miles from Hong Kong" subsisting with his wife and two children on "six baskets of rice which were paid, twice a year for my father's duty as a night watchman" and the proceeds of odd jobs, is described in Char: 247–49.

12. I have since come to believe that the BCL registers are not a reliable guide to the lineage and other institutions to be found in Shek Pik and many other smaller villages of the region. In this particular case the Chan and Tsui lineages recall their ancestral halls, and the Chi lineage hall is mentioned in a deed of partition of 1789. See Hayes 1976: 46–47, 63.

13. Said to be common in the Tai Po district of the New Territories. Morrison: 98, describes *cheng ch'ang* as sacrifices in winter and autumn.

14. The Yeung Hau Wong temple owned 0.06 building and 1.67 acres agricultural at the land settlement, and the Hung Shing temple 0.04 building and 0.10 agricultural. The school was registered in the first temple's name (lot 566 in DD 312). Max Weber: 91–93 has seized upon the administrative position of the temple in Chinese villages of this sort, and states that its "significance . . . lay in its secular, social and legal practices." He continues, "the village legally and actually was capable of acting as a corporate body through the temple." In Shek Pik and other local cases, the temple lay at the center of corporate life, while the concept of "Ah Kung" was its outer manifestation.

15. The customary religious activities at Shek Pik and adjoining villages appear more numerous and regular than those mentioned by Yang 1967, chapter 4; and more specifically, for Nanching, in Yang 1959: 191–96.

16. Stevens: 100 and Jenyns: 169.

17. See Kulp: 209–10.

18. In the Hong Kong region, dancing lions (*wu shih*) are generally associated with Cantonese villages and unicorns (*ch'i lin*) with Hakka settlements. There is, I am told, considerable variation in the style, shape, and design of these very old art forms.

19. For an account of the organization and functions of the lineage (clan) in Nanching, see Yang 1959: 92–99. See also Baker 1968: chapters 1–5 and the lineage passages in Potter 1968.

20. An engrossing account of such accountability is given in Selby:

63–68 for a village in north Kwangtung apparently in the 1870s. See also a case from early British Hong Kong concerning a clan in Hsiang-shan district in CO 129/23 no. 19 of 4 March 1848.

21. SP 1921: 161–62, mentions "the common practice of purchasing a small girl ('*sanpotsai*') as prospective bride to be brought up in the family of the future husband . . . very prevalent in San On, especially among Hakkas." I recorded earlier cases at Shek Pik, and also those in which engagements had been made before puberty but without the daughter being reared in the boy's family.

22. It is explained, I think, by their highly personal nature which discourages their production for study purposes.

23. Yang 1959: 11, and Hayes 1970: 165. A 19th century deed of sale for a village house illustrates this clearly for Shek Pik, "The house in question is situated in Shek Pik village, facing south, with Cheung Yung-tai's house on the left, Kung Kwai-fat's house on the right, Chan Wang-ho's house in front, and Tsui Lung-choi's house at the back."

24. See FO 233, vol. 136, e.g. 1845, nos. 20, 30, and 24, and 1848 nos. 5 and 7. Where literati or other elites were involved this is usually indicated by the use of degree titles or other terms indicative of special status, but these are seldom encountered in the old Southern District.

25. Yang 1959: 99. Baker 1968: 52, could not find evidence of one at Sheung Shui, but then this was a single, not a multilineage village.

26. Myers 1970: 259 also reports village councils "of half a dozen or more peasants, who selected a headman and his assistant from among their number" in his recent study of four villages in Shantung and Hopei, 1890–1949. For a village council in Yunnan see Osgood 1963: 117–8.

27. Lockhart: 546. He was here describing its jurisdiction rather than its executive functions.

28. Yang 1959: 99.

29. Seventy years after the event it is impossible to trace the local power groups and the informal political order at Shek Pik in the way reported by Yang for Nanching, 1959: 109–18. However, one person was clearly of importance in late 19th century Shek Pik. This was the schoolmaster Kung from a local village who built up an estate there by purchase and mortgage, and maintained an influence, through his holdings and his superior education.

30. He was styled "village representative" in the post 1945 period: see ARDONT 1947–48: 2–3.

31. Similar statements about the post of headman, and how it was manned, were made to me in many of the multilineage settlements of Lantau.

32. Berkowitz and Poon: 17–18.

33. As the manager of the branch of the powerful Tang lineage claiming possession of Tsing Yi told Cecil Clementi: "I have been manager for two years, I remain manager so long as I give satisfaction." (CSO 1903 Ext/8551, minute of 16 June 1904.)

34. See Ordinance No. 13 of 1844, Ordinance No. 3 of 1853 and Colonial

Estimates 1854–61. These appointments were discontinued in 1861. See Endacott 1964: 37–38.

35. The CO 129 and FO 233 series show that they were extensively used by the authorities. See e.g. CO 129/10, no. 45; CO 129/16, no. 47; CO 129/19, no. 11; CO 129/47, no. 89; CO 129/80, no. 2. Also FO 233, vol. 186, nos. 20, 30 of 1845; nos. 5 and 7 of 1848: and no. 22 of 1847 in vol. 187. After 1861, though not paid, headmen were still recognized and sometimes styled Tepos. See *Authorities* and also Eitel 1895: 166.

36. This much is certain, though the nature of their duties is not always clear and the literature is sometimes confused. See Hsiao: 64–66, 267; Chü: 3–4, 203–204; Watt: 190.

37. Werner: 161–62.

38. Baker 1968: 133–34.

39. Yang 1959: 103. This transition is shown clearly by Myers 1970: 97–98 for a village in Li-ch'eng County, Shantung.

40. Kulp: 110–17.

41. They were apparently needed. Peplow: 154–155 explains the less welcome aspects of village festivals which attracted many persons to the site besides relatives and friends.

42. Collectively, these represent the "non-economic, communal religious observances" described by Yang 1967: 86–96. Yang does not mention the *Ta chiao* ceremonies by name, and it may be that they had lapsed at Nanching by the 1940s, as they had in many places, including the Hong Kong region. (See Yang 1959: 194, and Potter 1968: 171.) Yang 1967, chapter 13, and Fei 1939: 130–31, note the discontinuation of old ceremonies. The latter relates the "deterioration of social life" that this represented in the minds of ordinary people.

43. Such lands had apparently been under lease from the Chinese government; see SP 1901: 307.

44. Fortune: 9–11 mentions the "very fair orchards containing the Mango, Leechee, Longan, Wangpee, Orange, Citrons and Pomelows" of the Hong Kong region. It was customary in local villages for the produce to be auctioned well before each crop and the proceeds credited to village funds, as at Shek Pik itself. Consequently it was forbidden to pick fruit in common ownership.

45. No doubt following local custom, British forestry licenses included graves within forest lots, but forbade desecration and stipulated a clear space of grass one *chang* in width (10 Chinese feet) to be left round them (Forestry Licence No. 95 of D.O. South for 1925–26).

46. These are mentioned in a lease of fields for 15 years, drawn up at Shek Pik in 1954. Scattered evidence is given in surviving deeds of mortgage and in an old property book listing rents and cultivators in the late 19th century and after.

47. For comparison, Baker's lineage village "possessed only the most sketchy of village rules" (Baker 1968: 134). Kulp's Phenix Village had no written rules, but he gives an account of offenses and punishments (Kulp: 129 et seq., 320–321). For a written local example from Tung

Chung on north Lantau, revised once after being drawn up in 1894, see Hayes 1962: 84. These particular rules were not comprehensive. They covered theft from crops and plantations and trespass by cattle. Other matters had apparently to be covered by the elders' collective memory of past precedents: see Ng in Jarvie and Agassi: 59.

48. As reported from Tung Chung in connection with its rules. They were described as *ch'un t'ing*.

49. Until the early 1950s, it was usual to summon Shek Pik and Lo Wai (Pui O) villagers by gong for this duty. The determinant of involvement was the dam; there were four in the Shek Pik valley and three at Pui O. Disputes regarding water supply from communally constructed irrigation works were apparently solved by the memory of what had been done before on a similar occasion: as reported for Tung Chung by Ng in Jarvie and Agassi: 59.

When the new Civil and Criminal Codes were being elaborated by the Kuomint'ang Government, the place of local custom in the matter of irrigation and other rights was much in its mind. The Introduction to the Civil Code states (p. xvi): "It was the wish of the Commission that many traditional agricultural customs, which had grown out of the geographical or economic conditions of particular districts, should be preserved so long as they were not contrary to public order or good morals". It is noteworthy that the articles of the Civil Code in this and related matters (for water rights see Articles 775–785) provide that local custom shall have precedence over the Code if there be a difference in provision. See the English translations of *The Civil Code of the Republic of China* and *The Criminal Code of the Republic of China*, Shanghai, Kelly and Walsh, 1931 and 1936 respectively. Article 252 of the Criminal Code makes the impairment of farm irrigation an offence punishable by imprisonment, detention or fine.

50. These are sometimes recorded by memorial tablets, and can be glimpsed in the prewar administrative reports of the DONT, e.g. for Shek Pik in ARDONT 1922.

51. The involvement of village elders with teachers is shown in AR 1913: N16–17.

52. Neumann: 97–125 and Montalto de Jesus: 231–48. Pirate fleets from a later time are described in *Illustrated London News* for 28 March 1857: 283. See also Fox and Dalrymple Hay.

53. Some strong-minded, capable headman or elder in the smaller villages might take everything on himself, despite the heavy burden. This happened at Tong Fuk fifty or sixty years ago when, the elders recall, one such person determined all public business.

54. This happened in the lineage as in the village: see also Yang 1959: 95.

55. In theory, the district land records should provide a record of the successive managers of landed trusts, since registration of managers was required by the New Territories Ordinance, Cap 97; but in the pre-1941 period villages often did not register changes, even on the death of a manager. This tendency in other registrations was early remarked by the British district administration; ARDONT 1912: I 11.

56. For a similar process in appointing clan managers see Yang 1959: 94. For village office holders in Yunnan see Osgood 1963: 118–9.

57. Eberhard 1962: 212 mentions such *p'ao* in South China and Taiwan as "typical attempts towards self-defense of colonial settlements."

58. *Chang-shi Tzu-p'u.*

59. *Illustrated London News*, 9 and 16 May 1857: 463, 473–74, and Szczesniak: 262–66.

60. CO 129/99, no. 115; 37–45.

61. Ramon Myers has described the existence of a specialist (*t'o ku*) skilled in handling property divisions in Taiwan rural families and other matters requiring mediation, and went on to observe "The role of such special individuals has scarcely been touched upon by students of traditional Chinese society" (Myers 1972: 3: 422). I agree with him, though my information shows that villagers in this region may have done some of this work themselves. Myers 1970: 94–95 gives the only detailed account I have seen of steps in sale negotiations.

62. Examples of local deeds can be found in Appendix 3 to *First Year*, in SP 1900: 266–77. See also Meadows 1859.

63. Smith: 156.

64. Money loan associations in the Hong Kong region are described at Appendix E to Orme, and by Dyer Ball: 632–45. See also L.S. Yang: 75–78. They are now generally described in the literature as "rotating credit associations." See Ardener in bibliography.

65. Proof that money loan associations were in operation twenty years before is given in another of the Shek Pik land papers, a mortgage deed of 1858, in which failure to repay 18 taels of silver "being a share in a money loan association" led to the mortgage.

66. The operation of money loan associations was further complicated by weather and its effect on crops, and hence on ability to pay debts. See ARDONT 1916: J 4; 1929: J 2.

67. Kulp: 134.

68. The extent of village organization in the Hong Kong region in the late 19th century appears, on a superficial comparison, to be considerably greater than that reported by Myers for sixteen North China villages from information provided by Gamble and Japanese researchers (Myers 1970: 262). The weight of evidence for the importance of folk and village religion in providing for the functions and exercise of local leadership in the Hong Kong region is particularly striking, and the apparent lack of this element in leadership in the areas of Hopei and Shantung reported on by Myers is puzzling to me (Myers 1970: 40–122). His statements that "the household must be considered the basic economic and social unit" (p. 126) in these villages, and that their peasants "lacked a strong sense of village identity" (p. 125 and also p. 80) are based on solid Japanese research. Nonetheless, while variety is encountered everywhere, I am inclined to suggest that a closer study of village religion in these areas might have modified opinions reached from inquiries with an economic and institutional emphasis.

Notes to Chapter 5

1. In the 19th century. Two others, Cheung Sha Lan in the Shap Long peninsula, and Lower Cheung Sha have been added since 1899; see Gazetteer: 80–81 (which is not accurate for Pui O itself).

2. SP 1911: 103 (37).

3. Gazetteer gives 11.90 square miles for an area that includes Silver Mine Bay (Mui Wo) which is another separate group.

4. For aspects of Chinese family organization see Chapter 3 of Cohen 1976. With regard to the registrations contained in the Block Crown Leases for Pui O and elsewhere in the New Territories, I think we should beware of taking registration of ownership within lineages at its face value until we know more about the pre-1899 arrangements in any one location from other sources such as land deeds, rent books, account books, and the like.

5. See the sizes of lineages given in Freedman 1958: 5–6 and Freedman 1966: 4n. 16, and 19.

6. All told, these holdings amounted to 11.73 acres of agricultural land and 0.21 acres of building land in 1904; out of a total clan holding of 93.30 acres and 2.33 acres respectively.

7. This deed, registered with the Hsin-an magistrate, is dated Ch'ien Lung 37th year.

8. This clan's demography gives point to the great increases shown in the early Ch'ing census records: see Perkins: 206–208 and 212–14.

9. *Kuo-hsueh-sheng* and *chün-kung*. It would be both interesting and useful to compare such men with e.g. the many *kuo-hsüeh-sheng* and holders of similar lesser titles listed in the Lo genealogy of Chiu-lin subdistrict of Hsin-hui, Kwangtung (chüan 22/27a–32a for *Kuo-hsüeh-sheng*) to ascertain whether their property, income, life-style and background were similar or not. An easier comparison, aided by field investigation, could be done with, say, the minor degree holders of the Tang lineage of Kam Tin, New Territories. I suspect that great variation could be shown.

10. Cheung Kwong-chuen is said to have owned ten houses and fifty to sixty *tou chung* of fields, His wife was a Ho from San Tsuen, and he seems to have had a concubine from the local boat population. He would be a good subject for investigation of the degree of exploitation practised by 'small landlords' and 'rich peasants' of the Hong Kong region. Elvin: 259–60 cites a Communist document that alleges that such persons exploited more ruthlessly than large landlords. It seems unlikely from my inquiries that the Li Kau Yuen Tong, the subsoil owner, was much of an exploiter—at least in the 19th century—so that such exploitation as there was was likely to come from persons like Kwong-chuen. Regrettably the materials are not fully available to determine the issue; but it was undoubtedly in the detailed nitty-gritty of daily economic life, in the matter of interest on loans of all kinds and in small dealings in farm produce and running small stores, listed in the paper cited by Elvin, that the greatest impact of the 'rich peasant' like him could lie.

11. Similar organizations are shown in the Block Crown Leases for

Sheung Ling Pei and Tung Hing villages at Tung Chung, Luk Tei Tong at Mui Wo, and Tong Fuk east of Pui O.

12. Other trusts in the registers are specifically stated to be *tu t'i hui*, e.g. for the Lantau villages of Pak Ngan Heung at Mui Wo and Shek Mun Kap at Tung Chung. A *ta wang hui* is listed for Tai Tei Tong, another of the Mui Wo villages. These three are all multilineage settlements, so that the trusts are shared. Yet such is the diversity of the local scene that we can find, at Lo Wai village, Pui O, *each* of the three clans with its own earth shrine.

13. ARDONT 1947–48, section on "Rural Organisation."

14. They were big enough for self-defense and to have their own organization for religious rites, and most possessed their own local temple. However some of the villages within linkages also had their own temples.

15. Freedman 1963: pars. 17–28 discusses these and other *yüeh* complexes in the New Territories.

16. These groupings can be found in Gazetteer: 170–72, 166–68 and 182–83 respectively, but in the case of the first two the number of the villages in the group is now much greater than their names suggest. This use of *hsiang* places it (and these settlements) within the definition given in Hsiao: 11–12, "a unit of intervillage cooperation or organization: it had semiofficial recognition and occupied a definite place in the pattern of rural life." See also Hsiao: 559–60 n. 12. Under the Kuomintang the *hsiang* became a legally established unit of self-government: see Linebarger: 107, 324, 389–91 with chart.

17. See Freedman 1963: pars. 8–22.

18. HNHC 1688: chüan 3, and HNHC 1819: 2/13b et seq.

19. Tong Fuk *Hsiang* ("Tong Fuk village") appears on a bell of 1802 in the Hung Shing temple at Tong Fuk. At Tung Chung the rule board of 1894 described the subdistrict as Tung Chung *ho-hsiang* ("the united villages of Tung Chung"). At Tai O a tablet listing contributions to a temple repair of 1877 is worded *ko-hsiang* ("each of the villages").

20. A tablet of 1883 in a Taoist religious hall in the hills above Tai O calls the area Luk Wu Tung, but this is surely in its descriptive usage, as there were only a few settlements in the surrounding area.

21. Dated July 1899 and now in the PRO, Hong Kong. For Ordinance No. 11 of 1899 see HKGG 18 April 1899.

22. GN 394 in HKGG 15 July 1899.

23. Only the Tai O, Mui Wo, and Tung Chung villages are listed. All the South Lantau villages and many outlying ones are omitted.

24. According to Freedman 1966: 8, they were in some cases the latter; but I am not yet sure of this.

25. HNHC 1819 2/19a et seq.

26. Tax receipts from Pui O and Shek Pik, dated in the Hsien Feng and Kuang Hsü periods respectively, list the payers as residing in the Mut *chia*, Yau *tu* of 3rd *t'u*. Registration of a sale of fields at Shui Hau, dated early 1895, also lists the parties to the transaction as belonging to these tax divisions. However, the same divisions are used for land in Kowloon

Tong, Kowloon (Hong Kong Memorials 28116, 28120, and 28145 registering deeds dated 1876, 1897, 1897 respectively). The tax divisions are confusing, as seen in local deeds, and their operation is clearly a complex matter requiring investigation.

27. In this respect the existence of unlinked settlements is a good indication of the comparative unimportance of the group on the local scene, since it must be supposed that they could do without whatever advantages it was presumed to have.

28. The Wan lineage of Pui O, settled there for two hundred years, stems from a family whose senior branch has long been in the adjoining Mui Wo group. The Tsui lineage of Shek Pik have a branch that went generations ago to Mui Wo and continues there today.

29. Sitings often led to quarrels at the outset or periodically thereafter. These are also recorded. A grave would not normally stay long in a place without the prior consent of the local elders or a later adjustment.

30. Old villagers stress the element of cooperation and mutual aid in the group system. Asked to illustrate how it operated in Pui O, one old man (b. 1886) said "If Cheung Sha people asked for help in trouble, they would get it. If Tong Fuk asked, they would not."

31. Old people have even told me that the gods, not men, were intended to benefit in the expectation that their help would be forthcoming when required.

32. They would not otherwise have been described as *Ta-ao ko-hsiang*.

33. The Tung Chung villages used the Hau Wong temple as their meeting place, and the rules of the group were displayed on a board that hung on one of its side rooms.

34. The 1899 map referred to above is accurate only in its representation of the Tung Chung area.

35. There were six schools at Tai O in 1912; see Orme: Appendix G.

36. See Hayes 1967: 97–100.

37. The Kwan Tai temple at Tai O has an inscription commemorating a repair of 1852 to which the Li Kau Yuen Tong contributed 10 taels (maximum donation 33.5) and the 1852 tablet at the Hung Shing temple at Sha Lo Wan lists it as giving 3.6 taels (maximum donation 11.8 taels).

38. These ceremonies appear similar to the *chau shen fu chiao* (thanking the gods in advance) and *yuan min fu chiao* (thanking the gods for favors granted) rites in present-day Taiwan. See *Echo*, January 1974: 28–44.

39. There was no formal organization for this twice-yearly ceremony despite its importance to the continued well-being of the Pui O villages. However, the management duties followed the pattern mentioned above. The organizers at the 12th month rituals in the lunar year 1972–73 were a Cheung, a Ho, and a Law. At the 2nd month ceremony in 1973–74, they were two Cheungs and a Ho.

40. Dated Chinese Republic, 3rd year, lucky day in the third winter month. It has now disappeared at a recent rebuilding.

41. Dated Tao Kuang 19th year, lucky day in the 3rd spring month.

The Cheung names lead all the others on the two memorial boards, as befitted their leading position in the locality.

42. Dated Chia Ch'ing, 4th year, lucky day in the 1st summer month.

43. Curiously enough, the solidarity of the Pui O villages was not reinforced by the periodic "Ta Chiu" reported from many other places on Lantau. The oldest men said to me on many occasions, "We Hakka do not *ta chiao*." However, this did not prevent villagers from adjoining settlements from taking the portable images of the gods in the Pui O temples to their Ta Chiu, as allowed by local custom.

Notes to Chapter 6

1. The old village was cleared for redevelopment in May, 1966.

2. Ngau Tau Kok, Lei Yue Mun, Cha Kwo Ling, and Sai Cho Wan: see Gazetteer: 126–27. The population of these four villages at the 1911 colony census was 440, 255, 211, and 58 respectively. Of these 314, 142, 134, and 35 were males: SP 1911: 103 (39).

3. Orme: par. 79.

4. HKN: 8: 109–10.

5. Obtained from them by inquiries made since 1966.

6. Smith: 74–75.

7. Colonial secretary to British consul-general, Canton, 21 February 1901 in CSO 1903 Ext/6550 (originally no. 384 in 1902 Ext/32). This man is the Ho Lap Pun referred to by Gompertz in a querulous memorandum to the colonial secretary, dated 16 August 1901, in CSO Ext 1901/201.

8. Included in the viceroy's reply dated 28 June 1901 in CSO 1903 Ext/6550.

9. Gazetteer: 128.

10. Memorials 27231, 27371 and 26891 in HKLR.

11. Memorials 28549, 28550 and 28551 in HKLR.

12. CO 129/92, no. 121 of 24 April 1863.

13. Lockhart: Appendix 6.

14. A proclamation by another acting magistrate of Hsin-an set out rules for the management of the stone quarries, and shows the troublesome nature of the place, requiring regulation by a permanent control mechanism.

15. Quoted in Endacott 1964: 96–97.

16. See BCL, SD No. 3, Lots 926–1029.

17. A deed of perpetual lease to the first Liu to settle in Ngau Tau Kok, to cultivate land and occupy four houses already built thereon, dated 18

April 1877, is translated in Memorial 26891 in HKLR.

18. Aijmer, *Interim Report* 3: 23–28.

19. Lockhart: 543.

20. Orme: par. 79. Kweishin was a district in the Hui-chou prefecture, not far from Hsin-an. In fact, it is the former name for the present Wai Yeung (Hui-yang) which received this name at the beginning of the Chinese Republic (*New Atlas*: 33).

21. E.g. Dyer Ball 1896: ix.

22. The Hong Kong Blue Books list the current wages in various employments, year by year, and stonecutters figure among the higher paid Chinese trades.

23. Report NTLC up to 31 December 1901, par. 10, in SP 1902: 559–60.

24. See Hayes 1970: 164.

25. Some information is given in CSO 1901 Ext/292.

26. It is dated Kuang Hsü 19 year, 3rd moon, 13th day and is included in CSO 1903 Ext/6550.

27. HKGG 24 June 1904.

28. This information is taken from one of a printed series of reports on Hong Kong labor and commercial guilds prepared by Cecil Clementi in the early 1900s and kept (1965) among his papers at Holmer Court, Bucks. This one is headed "Masons."

29. For an explanation of *Tung* and *Hsi* in connection with masters and men, see Wade and Hillier: 2: 143.

30. The temple was removed to another location about 1950 to make way for an oil storage depot.

Notes to Chapter 7

1. For descriptions of typical areas see Parliamentary Papers, China, 1861–66: 16, and dispatch no. 73 of 14 February 1863 in CO 129/91.

2. "List of Villages of New Kowloon in the Southern District" printed in Victoria Gaol, Hong Kong. It came from Walter Schofield who had added five more in Ms.

3. Report of the Anglo-Chinese Land Commission of 1862, annexed to dispatch no. 82 of 30 April 1862 in CO 129/85. The later settlements of Old Kowloon are listed in table 13 of the 1901 census return included in SP 1902.

4. The five Cheung Sha Wan villages in west Kowloon had recorded populations of 157, 151, 68, 55, and 61 at the 1911 census (Hayes 1970:

157). Ma Tau Wai and Ma Tau Chung, near Kowloon City, had 318 and 243 persons at the same census (SP 1911: 103 [24]). The largest and oldest settlements of the area, Nga Tsin Wai, Chuk Yuen, and Po Kong, are unfortunately not included in any census record, though the number of houses in each is given in the Block Crown Lease for Kowloon SD no. 1.

5. See Hayes 1970: 161–62.

6. SP 1911: 103 (22).

7. It is shown on the map of Tung-kuan *hsien* at Chüan 11905 of the early 15th century Yung Lo Encyclopedia.

8. Lockhart: 552. For earlier mentions see Krone, and Wade in HKGG, 25 April 1857, GN no. 62.

9. Although it is not listed as a market in HNHC 1819: 2.

10. One visitor from Hong Kong described the suburbs in the 1840s. See Sirr: 60–61, 66. For descriptions before and after the British takeover in 1899 see Wesley-Smith 1973 and 1975.

11. See CSO 1904 Ext/6564, Wood's report on survey district no. 1 dated 17 August 1904. Only the superstructure on two lots in the city was allowed to private individuals, in consequence of a mortgage.

12. As in the land settlement of Old British Kowloon in 1862. See CO 129/85 no. 82 par. 8 which gives a very clear statement of this point.

13. Entries numbered HKLR 28126, 27228, 27386, 27381, 27382, 26816, 26611, and 28124. I am indebted to Carl T. Smith for copies of these papers. They are in English translation only, the Chinese originals not being retained in the registry.

14. In two cases, deeds of the 16th and 20th years of the Ch'ien Lung reign are cited.

15. See, e.g., the wording in memorial 27585 registered 4 May 1900 in the Hong Kong Land Registry. "As Ip family (purchaser) have no household name in the Sun On Magistracy he is unable to register it in his name, therefore he shall have to pay tax to the vendor forever (who is responsible for the Tax)." See also par. 9 of "Some Notes on Land Tenure" in HKGG 17 August 1901; and Weber: 273–74, quoting Bumbaillif's article on Land Tenure in China.

16. See, e.g., CSO 1904 Ext/430, 1560, 1625, 5956, and 6564.

17. See Anglo-Chinese Land Commission's Report 1862, and CSO 1898, no. 2982, minute of 12 December 1898; also memorials 28118 and 28117 in HKLR.

18. The remarks columns of the Block Crown Lease for Kowloon SD1 give occasional indications of the former situation. For the Ngs see against lot nos. 5309, 5312–14, 5341–43, 5900. For others see, e.g., 1313–14 connected with lots on pp. 43–46 of the register; also 1406–07, 1413, 1472, 1690.

19. I attribute these late developments to the increased importance of the Kowloon post following the cession of Hong Kong to Britain. Krone mentions that the Tai Pang colonel was transferred permanently to Kowloon thereafter. Also to the need for a closer liaison with and over-

sight of the local civil population.

20. The memorial tablet has disappeared since the 1941–45 war, but its text has been preserved. For Wang see KCFC: 27/11b.

21. It is likely that it was used for consultations between civil and military officials and local leaders from Kowloon and the surrounding districts during the hostilities of 1857. See Wade in HKGG 1857: GN no. 62.

22. HKGG 1901: GN no. 274.

23. Lot 6625.

24. This was wholly in keeping with Chinese practice: see Yang, 1967: 335–36.

25. It was removed for redevelopment of the area in 1963.

26. Memorial 28037 in HKLR.

27. JHKBRAS 7 (1967): 158–60.

28. This man's name also appears on the list of directors responsible for the repair of the Hau Wong Temple at Kowloon city in 1879. Both men were *Kuo-hsüeh-sheng*.

29. See dispatches no. 61 of 21 August 1854 and no. 67 of 9 September 1854 from acting governor Caine to Sir George Grey in CO 129/47 on the rebels' capture and withdrawal from Kowloon City.

30. Tablet dated Tao-kuang 1st year at the Hau Wong temple.

31. Schofield papers and contents of Hau Wong and Tin Hau temples, Kowloon City.

32. Schofield papers.

33. According to old residents, part of the Tong's income came from the one cent fee paid to enter the Kowloon City vegetable market, and another one cent charge levied at the open space where grass and firewood were weighed on public scales. This was the kind of revenue that would normally belong to a Kaifong, and must have been passed to, or instituted for the Tong where it was established in 1880, to help finance its activities.

34. Krone: 116, and HNHC 1819: 2/19a et seq.

35. E.g. Chang 1955: 51–70; Ch'ü 1962: 180–85; Watts: 14.

36. Hirth: 2: 211–22. Lobscheid refers to the "understrappers" in government offices (Dictionary: 3).

37. See the chapter on mandarin offices in Medhurst: 76–83. Ralph: 31, 129–30 describes the dignity of official traveling on the waterways of Kiangsu and Chekiang. Des Voeux: 2: 237 noted the roughness of mandarins' attendants in Shanghai.

38. Ch'ü 1962: 21–22; Watts: 20–22; Woodside: 83–84.

39. As given in Appendix 2 to Chang 1962: "a consistently high proportion of gentry members were engaged in public works and relief organisations in all areas" (p. 215). See also Appendix to Ho 1962, and the biographies in Chow.

40. Lockhart: 546. This "Tung Lo" is clearly not to be confused with the east, west, and central *lo* of Kwangtung itself which were connected with organization for coastal defense, and took in much larger areas than one part of a *hsien*. See KTKKCY: 30/4a, 8a, and 9b; and the late Ming

work *Wu-pei chih*: chüan 215.

41. Lockhart: 546. *Kuk* is the Cantonese for *chü*.

42. Referred to in Groves: 52–55.

43. See CSO 1902 Ext/202 for the Kuk's undated petition, the Special Summons (translation only) of the Hsin-an magistrate of 3 October 1904, and C. McI. M.'s minute of 27 December 1904.

44. CO 129/184, no. 242.

45. It is very likely that old members of the leading families of the Northern District might have known about the Tung Ping Kuk, but I missed the opportunity to question them on the subject.

46. CSWT, issue 1, no. 1.

47. Especially when a little over one hundred taels could purchase a title. See Ho 1959: 60–65 and Ho 1962: 33–38.

48. See da Silva 1968.

49. A full list of these and other local garrison places in the T'ung Chih reign, with the numbers of men supposed to be at each of them is given in KTTS 13/14–20. At that time the Cheung Chau post (*hsün*) had 45 men, the posts at Tai O and Tung Chung 30 each, with smaller numbers in other places down to the 5 each at the other Lantau *hsün* of Mui Wo, Tai Ho, and Sha Lo Wan.

50. Harry Lamley (personal communication, 1974) has told me that similar evidence can be found in Taiwan and the Pescadores.

51. HNHC: chüan 6 lists (up to 1819) names and often origins. KCFC, chüan 30–31, gives more information up to a later time.

52. CSO 1899/9, Confidential 190.

53. Hui-chou Bulletin: 109, and JHKBRAS 15 (1975): 311–318.

54. The *Ch'ou Hai T'u Pien* (1802 ed.): 3 gives similar details, as does Ku Yen-wu's *T'ien-hsia chun-kuo li-ping shu*: 97–104 and the *Wu-pei chih*: 215; all for the late Ming period.

55. Parker: 260–61.

56. The provincial authorities issued prohibitions in the Ch'ia Ching and Tao Kuang periods against military, naval, and customs personnel harrassing fishing craft in the delta. There are inscribed stone tablets to this effect at the Hsin Miao at Macao dated in the 11th month of the 6th year of Tao Kuang (1826) which refers to a similar tablet dated in early Ch'ia Ching; and another outside the Tin Hau temple at Peng Chau, Lantau, dated in the 15th year of Tao Kuang (1835–36).

57. Sayer: 33.

58. First tablet referred to in n. 56 above.

59. Krone: 118. Perhaps because pay was often in arrears?

60. Krone: 114, 119.

61. Hsiao—he sees their duty as that of defense, e.g. p. 66.

62. Waung: 11 states "Military officers with their detachments . . . were also stationed in the provinces, but they played little or no part in local administration."

63. Myers 1971: 503.

Notes to Chapter 8

1. Chang 1955: 3–6.
2. Ho 1962: 38–41.
3. Kuhn: 67. He adds that considerations of this sort lead one to doubt the utility of an overly formal definition of elite status in rural China.
4. Kuhn: 4. See also Schoppa's article on Szechuan elites, CSWT 1973.
5. Where gentry leaders harassed the countryside and even the magistrate at will: see, e.g., Hsiao: 317–20 (various examples from Kwangtung) and Campbell Gibson: 299–309 (from Pu-ning, Kwangtung).
6. Hayes 1963: n. 16, 22 on pp. 102–104.
7. Hayes 1964: 92.
8. It is interesting that, in his study of Hopei and Shantung villages, Ramon Myers (1970: 258) comments "from the surveys of Sidney Gamble and the Mentetsu researchers, there is no evidence that the gentry resided in villages or played any role in village affairs." He implies that this was the situation from 1890 on, though he is not certain whether this was so in the early Ch'ing.
9. See Skinner 1971: 2. The "peasant platform" apart, it may be the case that we have, indeed, greatly overstated the role of the degree-holding gentry in some areas. Keith Schoppa has recently given another pointer in this direction. In his investigation of the composition and functions of local elites in Szechuan 1851–74, as recovered from biographical material in gazetteers, he has shown that in such fields as *t'uan* leadership, the provision of military forces, public works, charity, and in the mediation of disputes the majority of persons engaging in these activities were nondegree-holders. Even in the exception, education, 41% of those listed were nondegree-holders. On this basis, he suggests that claims that degree-holding gentry "dominated the social and economic life of Chinese communities" (as stated by Franz Michael at p. xiii of his introduction to Chang's *The Chinese Gentry*) obscures the richness and complexity of the forces at work in society (Schoppa, CSWT 2 (no. 10, November 1973): 7–23).
10. Balazs: 155.
11. See MacNair: 216.
12. See MacNair: 216, 223, 259, 330.
13. Cooke: 436 quoting Tseng Wang-yen, later viceroy of Szechuan.
14. See, e.g., the *Hong Kong Daily Telegraph*, 13 March 1879 quoting from the *Catholic Register*; and Forbes: 232–34.
15. Wakeman: 149–50 on the "purge" of 1855.
16. Balazs: 149.
17. See, e.g., Governor Han Wen-chi's memorials in Wade 1867, especially no. 74 which gives his recommendations for the punishment of certain rebels, members of an affiliated society.
18. Myers 1971: 503.
19. Schurmann: lii. Besides providing leadership at the local level,

traditional China may also have prepared the way for the modern apparatus of social control and direction through its proliferation of associations and organizations in the villages. In the course of reading Pi-chao Chen's review of Martin K. Whyte's 1974 study, *Small Groups and Political Rituals in China* (*China Quarterly* 63 (September 1975): 543–45) it seemed to me that these primary devices (sic) for effecting change in mainland China since 1949 may build heavily on pre-liberation organization and practise. The contents of my present study imply that the peasant was accustomed to operate small groups of various kinds, whilst rural life involved him in rituals of many different sorts, not always understood!

20. J.M. Gullick, a former member of the Malayan Civil Service, writing in 1963 of the Chinese in Malaya notes their "remarkable facility for organizing themselves into societies and associations for welfare and the prosecution of common interests" (Gullick: 20). Earlier this genius expressed itself in the formation of secret societies to which, the protector of Chinese in the straits settlements estimated in 1876, sixty percent of the Chinese population belonged (Jackson: 51).

21. Hayes 1966: 128–31.

22. Hsiao: 313, 275. This does not square with Ramon Myers' recent study of the traditional economy of Ch'ing Taiwan in which he had occasion to note the common people's "ingenuity and skill to create organizations and share scarce resources among themselves." (Myers 1972: 2: 408).

23. Hsiao: 281, 333–34, 198.

24. Hsiao: 521–48.

25. Hsiao: 68–69.

26. Werner: 161–65; Williams: 118–36, and as assessed by Max Weber: 88–95 who wrote of "the organized self-government of the (Chinese) village". Also G. Jamieson, *Chinese Family and Commercial Law*, Shanghai, Kelly and Walsh 1921, p. 74 with his description "a pure democracy": his Chapter IV pp 56–75 is entitled "Village Organization".

27. Especially as they are supported by Chinese accounts; see, e.g., Chiang Monlin: 12–13 on the "self government" of his sixty-household, three-hundred-persons, five-century-old settlement in Yu-yao district, Hang Chou Bay, Chekiang. Freedman wrote of "the high degree of local autonomy" in Liang Chi-chiao's ancestral region in another part of coastal Kwangtung (Freedman 1966: 88n.) as described by Liang.

Notes to Postscript

1. See Baker 1966.
2. Nelson 1971: 101–104.

3. Nelson 1971: 103.
4. HKGG 1910: 593 and Hansard 1910: 113, 115.
5. The Hong Kong authorities gave other reasons, principally the easy access to "the stronger authority of the [British] magistrates" (Orme: par. 15).
6. Hsiao: chapters 3–4 and Appendix 1.
7. Freedman 1966: 81n.
8. Brim: chapter 1, 26. For Yuen Long see Gazetteer: 166–69.
9. Brim: chapter 1, 26.
10. About which little or nothing is known, though I have in my possession a copy of a woodblock *pao-chia* form dated in the 2nd month of the 32nd year of Ch'ien Lung completed for a family living in Chai Wan, Hong Kong Island. *Li-chia* nomenclature is used on some local land deeds, but many more are required to construct the divisions and their meaning.
11. Baker 1968: 164–203.
12. Baker 1968: 92. Shek Pik had about the same number of agricultural lots. The difference in acreage between the two places, 973 at Sheung Shui to 177 at Shek Pik, underlines the difference in terrain and the much greater agricultural wealth of the former.
13. Baker 1968: 92.
14. Brim: chapter 1, 24.
15. Brim: chapter 2, 2.
16. See Hayes 1970: 170–73.
17. Potter 1968: 100. I have come to believe that there was somewhere a legitimate basis to this ownership or overlordship (whichever it was), and think Nelson's statement of the major clans' "totally spurious claims" is inadequate: but more research is required.
18. E.g. Campbell Gibson: 299–309.
19. Brim: chapter 1, 25.
20. After much inquiry, I have discovered only one *hsiu-ts'ai* by examination and only several failed ones for Southern District villages in the late 19th century.
21. Freedman 1966: 74–75.
22. Krone: 95, and the useful note in Freedman 1966: 71n.
23. Baker 1966: 26–27.
24. Baker 1968: 204.
25. The virtual independence of their tenants mattered little so long as they paid their rent charges, which seems to have been always or mostly the case.
26. For an example of land by conquest see Shepherd, par. 11 in SP 1900: 278.
27. In fairness to Mr. Nelson, there was a deal of violence about: see Lamley's assemblage of information on the subject of *hsieh-ton*, especially on the southeastern provinces of China. However, the latter's evidence, if tested against local information, may relate mainly to *lineage* struggle.
28. Extension: 47 and 57. Also Orme: par. 6.

29. Yang 1959: 115 says of a village leader of Nanching "His piercing eyes revealed a fierceness characteristic of many of the natives of this province." I concur.

30. Nelson 1971: 102, and Murphey 1970: 27–30.

31. Freedman 1966: 64. See also Schurmann: 229–31 on "the extraordinary capacity" of Chinese society "to link human groups by intermediary devices." To conclude, a good example of some unexpected ties at work is provided by two presentation boards in the Tung-kuan Chamber of Commerce in Hong Kong, one dated 1911–12 and the other undated but a little later. They had been given in appreciation of the chamber's successful mediation in intervillage conflicts in Tung-kuan *hsien*.

Notes to A Note on Weights and Measures

1. *First Year:* 3.

2. As in the many examples of "white" or unregistered deeds that have come to my notice. However, the examples of land documents "A" or "B" in *First Year:* 21–24 use *mou* measurements, being concerned with tax registers and payment of the land tax.

3. *First Year:* 15.

4. See Taylor in JHKBRAS 6 (1966).

5. Information from Pui O, Lantau.

6. Ho 1959: 104–23.

GLOSSARY

Glossary of Chinese names and terms (in Cantonese or Mandarin romanization, or both, as appropriate to their use in the text). Local place names are excluded from this list, since they may be found, in a form of Cantonese romanization, in the *Gazetteer*.

Ah Kung 亞公
Chan clan 陳族
chai lau so 栖流社
Chan On She 鎮安社
Chan Tak-hang 陳德亨
chang 丈
chang-chien-jen 掌建人
Chang-shi ts'u-p'u 張氏族譜
chang-ye 嘗業
Ch'ao-chou 潮州
chau-shen fu chiao 酬神福醮
Chen An She 鎮安社
cheng-ch'ang-tien 烝嘗田
Cheng Kam-man 鄭鑑文
Cheng Lam-sau 鄭林壽
Cheung-chou Yu-t'u 長洲輿圖
Cheung clan 張族
Cheung Kwang-chuen 張廣全
Cheung Lam-to 張麟吐
cheung p'ai 長批
Chi clan 池族
chi-lao 耆老
chi-min 耆民
Chi Wing Shing Tong 池永勝堂
Ch'i Yüeh 七約
chia 家
chia p'u 家譜
Chieh-fang 街坊
Chieh-fang ssu-hsiang ko-fou 街坊四鄉各埠
Chieh-shang wang-ch'uan ko-hsiang ko-fou 街商網船各鄉各埠
chieh-shih 街市
chin-shih 進士
ch'ing-chuan shih chiao 清磚石脚
Ching Ming Chung Yeung 清明重陽
Chiu Chau 潮州
chiu long yap she 招郎入舍
chou 州
chü (kuk) 局
Chu-chiang Tung-kuan Tung-i-t'ang 駐港東莞東義堂
Chu-chiang Tung-kuan Tung-i-t'ang shih-lu 駐港東莞東義堂事略
chü mo ping 猪毛病

chuk po 族譜
chün-kung 軍公
ch'un-t'ing 巡丁
Chung clan 鍾族
Chung Hing Street 中興街
chung-jen 中人
Chung-shan 中山
Chung Sheng 衆聖
En-ping 恩平
fa tai 花帶
fang-chang 方長
Feast of Lanterns (teng chieh) 燈節
Feng-hsiang-shen 奉香神
feng-shui 風水
Fo-shan 佛山
Fong Pin Hospital 方便醫院
Fong Yi Hop (shop) 方義合(號)
fu 符
fu-lao 父老
Fuk Luk She 福祿社
Fuk Tak Chi (Fu-te Ts'u) 福德祠
Fung clan 馮族
Ha Wan 下灣
Ha-ao keng-chi wang-lai
kuan-yuan shang-ku shui-lu
shi-shue yue-chiao jen tang
闔澳衿耆往來官員商賈水陸
士庶漁樵人等
Hai-lu-feng 海陸豐
Hai-ping 開平
Hakka 客家
hang 桁
Hao-shan 鶴山
Hap Hing Tong 合興堂
Hing Lung Street 興隆街
Hip Wo She Hok 協和社學
ho-ao chih-li 合澳值理
ho-hsiang 合鄉
Hoklo 學(福)佬
Hsi Chia Hsing 西家行
hsiang 鄉
hsiang-chang 鄉長
hsiang-chin 鄉津
hsiang-lao 鄉老
Hsiang-shan 香山
hsiang-shih 鄉仕
hsiang-yu-tien 香油田
hsiang-yüeh 鄉約
hsien 縣
Hsin-an 新安
hsin-chien 信監
Hsin-hui 新會
hsin pao tzu 新抱仔
hsing 姓
hsü 墟
hsün 汎
huan-shen 還神
Huang-shih tsu-p'u 黃氏族譜
Hui-chou 惠州
Hung clan 洪族
hung k'ai 紅契
hung-meng-teng 孔明燈
Hung Shing 洪聖
i-chung 義塚
Kam Chan-lun 金湛霖
kai tsai (nui) 契仔(女)
kang tsai 耕仔
kau-pui 珓杯
kei-lun 麒麟
Kim Hau 鉗口
ko-hsiang 各鄉
Kong clan 江族
ku-ch'uan 罟船
Kuang-chou fu 廣州府
Kung-so 公所
kuo-hsüeh-sheng 國學生
Kwan Tai 關帝
Kwei-shin 歸善
Kwong On She 廣安社
Kwun Yam (Kuan-yin) 觀音
Lady Kam Fa 金花夫人
Lai Chun-pin 賴鎮邊
Lai Hing 黎興
Lam Lai 林禮

Lam Yuk-mo 林玉戊
Li Chung-kan 李忠簡
Li Kau Yuen Tong 李久遠堂
Li Mau-ying 李昴英
Li Ping-ngam 李炳顏 (?)
Li-chia 里甲
Ling-nan 嶺南
Liu Shing 廖盛
lo 路(?)
Lo Tang Pang 老燈棚
Lo Tin-yan 羅天恩
Lo Wu Village 羅湖
Lok Shin Tong 樂善堂
luan 亂
Lui family 呂家
Luk Yeuk Tsuen, Sai Heung, (Hsin-an) 新安,西鄉,六約村
Lung Chun Yee Hok 龍津義學
Man Mo Temple 文武廟
Mau clan 繆族
mau wu 茅屋
Mo sz k'u yik 舞獅驅疫
mo-shih 舞獅
mou 畝
mut/yau 末/又
nam mo lo* 喃嘸佬
Nam Tau 南頭
Nam Tong, Shum Chun (Hsin-an) 新安,深圳,南塘
Ng clan 吳族
Ng Shue-fan 吳樹藩
Ng Shue-tong 吳樹堂
Ng Wah 五華
ni-shui-lao 泥水佬
pai-kung 伯公
pak k'ai 白契
Pak Kap (Hui-chou) 惠州,八甲
Pak Mong Fa (Hui-chou) 惠州,白望花
Pak She 北社
Pak Tai Temple 北帝廟
pao 堡
Pao-an 寶安
pao-chang 保長
pao-chia 保甲
Pau Kung Temple 包公廟
pau shan 包山
p'au tai 砲臺
Pen-ao ch'uan 本澳船
Peng Wo Tong 平和堂
pin-hsing-kuan 賓興館
ping-an chiao 平安醮
Po Cheung Kung (pao-chang-kung) 保長公
Po Mei Heung 布尾鄉
Po On Shue Shat 寶安書室
Po On Wui Sho 寶安會所
p'o t'ou 坡頭
Punti 本地
Sam Pa Mun 三把門
samshu, 三燒 Eitel 1911: 875
san-hang 三行
San Hing Street 新興街
san po tsai 新抱仔
Sei Yap 四邑
Sha Tseng (Hsin-an) 新安,沙井
Sha Wan 沙灣
Sha Wan (Chia-Ying-Chou) 嘉應州沙灣
she 社
she-t'an kung 社壇公
shen 神
Shen-chin ch'i-lao shang hsi-shih ch'uan-chih hu-hsiang cho-ting k'ai-pu 紳衿耆老商善士船隻互相酌定開簿
shen-chu-p'ai 神主牌
shen-shih 紳士

*Itinerant lay Taoist priests, normally engaged to perform protective rituals of many kinds. See Davis 1865: 154–55 and Topley 1967: 104, 136.

shen-t'ai 神枱
shih 石**
Shin Yik She 信益社
shing (sheng) 勝
shu-shih 書室
Shui Shang Tong 遂生堂
(Sui Sheng T'ang)
shui tsun 水圳
Shum Chun 深圳
Shun-te 順德
shun(hsün)-t'i-kuan 汎地官
Sik Tsz She 惜字社
sok-kwu (so-ku) 索罟
Ssu-i 四邑
Sun Hing Street Luen Yee Wu
新興街聯誼會
Swabue 汕尾
tan chung 担種
t-o ku 託孤
Ta Chiu (ta chiao) 打醮
Ta-ao ko-hsiang 大澳各鄉
ta-wang-hui 大王會
Tai Pang 大鵬
Tai Ping Street 太平街
Tai Ping Shan Street 太平山街
Tai San Street 大新街
T'ai-shan 台山
Tai Wong 大王
Tam Ah-che 譚阿車
Tam-shui 淡水
tam-shui 擔水
t'ang 堂
Tanka 蛋家
Tepo (ti-pao) 地保
Teng 鄧
ti kwat 地骨
ti min 地面
ti-p'i 地皮
ti tai 地底
tiao-t'ing 釣艇
Tin Hau 天后
t'o-ch'uan 拖船
Toi-shan 台山
Tong Chu Wan 劏豬灣
tou chung 斗種
Tsip sung chik sz (chieh-sung
chih-shih) 接送値事
tso (tz'u) 祖
tso-shen 作神
tsu-chang 族長
Tsui clan 徐族
ts'un 村
Tsung, e.g., Pui O Tsung 衆
t'u 圖
t'u-hsing 圖形
tu 都
tu kung 督工
t'u-ti-hui 土地會
t'u-ti-kung 土地公
Tun Shin shrine 敦善社
tung 洞
Tung Chia Hsing 東家行
t'ung-hsiang-hui 同鄉會
Tung-kuan 東莞
Tung Kwun Wui Sho 東莞會所
Tung Lo (C) 東路(?)
Tung Ping Kuk (C) 東平局
Tung Wah Hospital 東華醫院
Tung Yu 同裕
tzu 族
Wai-chiu 惠潮
Wai Chiu Club 惠潮會所
wai tau wa 圍頭話
Wai Yeung 惠陽
wang-t'ing 網艇
Weng Shing Tong 永勝堂
Wing Fuk She 榮福社
Wing On Street 永安街
Wong clan 黃族
Wong clan, now Wong 汪族現黃族

**A local measure used for calculating yields and rents in grain. See Wells Williams 1856: 441.

wong fa 黄花
Wong Wai Tsak Tong 黃維則堂
Wu-i 五邑
yang ke 秧歌
Yao 猺
Yao-chi shui-lu chung-hsin sui-miao kung-i
邀集水陸衆信聚廟公議
Yee Chi (i-ts'u) 義祠
Yeuk Po (Yueh-pao) 約保
Yeung Hau Wong 楊后王
(otherwise in its shorter form 后王)
Yik Shin Tong 益善堂
Yim Tin, Nam Tau (Hsin-an)
新安,南頭,鹽田
yuan min fu chiao 圓滿福醮
Yue clan 余族
yüeh 約
yung-chun tuan-lien 勇壯團練
Yung Sheng T'ang 永勝堂

Bibliography

In English

Aijmer, Göran. "Expansion and Extension in Hakka Society." *JHKBRAS* 7 (1967): 42–79.

———. *Sha Tin Project, Interim Reports*, No. 6, "Being Next of Kin"; No. 7, "Marketing"; No. 8, "The Neighbourliness of a Neighbourhood." (Mimeographed). Also No. 3.

Alabaster, Chaloner Grenville. *The Laws of Hong Kong*. 3 vols. Hong Kong: Noronha and Co., Government Printers, 1913.

Anderson, Eugene N. *Essays on South China's Boat People*. Taipei: The Orient Cultural Service, 1972.

Anderson, Eugene N. and Anderson, Marja L. *Mountains and Waters: Essays on the Cultural Ecology of South Coastal China*. Taipei: The Orient Cultural Service, 1973.

Ardener, Shirley. "The Comparative Study of Rotating Credit Associations." *Journal of the Royal Anthropological Institute of Great Britain and Ireland*. 94, parts 1 & 2 (Jan–Dec. 1964).

Arlington, L.C. *Through the Dragon's Eyes: Fifty Years' Experiences of a Foreigner in the Chinese Government Service*. London: Constable, 1931.

Baker, H.D.R. "The Five Great Clans of the New Territories." *JHKBRAS* 6 (1966): 25–47.

———. *A Chinese Lineage Village: Sheung Shui*. London: Frank Cass, 1968.

Balazs, Etienne. *Chinese Civilization and Bureaucracy Variations on a Theme*. Translated by H.M. Wright. New Haven: Yale University Press, 1964.

Balfour, S.F. "Hong Kong before the British; being a local history . . . before the British occupation." *T'ien Hsia Monthly* 11–12 (1940–41): 330–52, 440–64. Reprinted in *JHKBRAS* 7 (1967).

Ball, J. Dyer. *Hakka Made Easy*, Hong Kong: Kelly and Walsh, 1896.

———. *Things Chinese or Notes Connected with China*. 4th ed. Hong Kong: Kelly and Walsh, 1903.

Barnett, K.M.A. "The Peoples of the New Territories." In *Hong Kong Business Symposium*, compiled by J.M. Braga. Hong Kong: South China Morning Post, Ltd., 1957, pp. 261–65.

———. "Introduction on Hong Kong Place Names." In *Hong Kong Gazetteer to the Land Utilisation Map of Hong Kong and the New Territories*, by Thomas R. Tregear. Hong Kong: Hong Kong University Press, 1958, pp. 1–13. Reprinted with additions in *JHKBRAS* 14 (1974): 136–159.

———. "Hong Kong before the Chinese: the Frame, the Puzzle and the Missing Pieces." *JHKBRAS* 4 (1964): 42–67.

———. "Hong Kong before the Chinese." "Technological Revolution in 900 A.D.," "The Riddle of the Hakka." Hong Kong: *South China Morning Post*, 24–26 April 1967.

Berkowitz, Morris I., and Poon, Eddie K. "Political Disintegration of Hakka Villages: a Study of Drastic Social Change in the New Territories of Hong Kong." *Chung Chi Journal* 8, no. 2 (May 1969): 16–31.

Berkowitz, Morris I., Brandauer, Frederick P., and Reed, John H. *Folk Religion in an Urban Setting, a Study of Hakka Villagers in Transition*. Hong Kong: Christian Study Centre on Chinese Religion and Culture, 1969.

Blackie, W.J. *The Kadoorie Agricultural Aid Association*. Hong Kong: K.A.A.A., 1972.

Bodde, Derk, and Morris, Clarence. *Law in Imperial China, Exemplified by 190 Ch'ing Dynasty Cases (translated from the Hsing-an hui-lan) With Historical, Social and Juridical Commentaries*. Philadelphia: University of Pennsylvania Press, 1967.

Boxer, Baruch. "Space Change and *Feng-Shui* in Tsuen Wan's

Urbanization." *Journal of Asian and African Studies* 3, nos. 3–4 (July and October 1968): 226–40.

Bowring, Sir John. "The Population of China, A Letter on the Population of China Addressed to the Registrar General London." *C.B.R.A.S. Transactions* 5 (1855): 1–16, reprinted in *JHKBRAS* 5 (1965): 27–45.

Brim, John A. *The Modernisation of Local Systems in the New Territories of Hong Kong.* Ph.D. dissertation, University of Washington, Seattle, 1970.

Brown, C. Campbell. *China in Legend and Story.* Edinburgh: Oliphant, Anderson and Ferrier, 1907.

Brunt, M. Hugo. "An Architectural Survey of the Jesuit Seminary Church of St. Paul's, Macao." *Journal of Oriental Studies* 1, no. 2 (July, 1954): 327–44.

Buck, David D. "Public Monuments as a Guide to Political Leadership." *Ch'ing-shih wen-t'i* 3, no. 1 (November 1974): 62–70.

Buck, J.L. *Land Utilization in China.* Shanghai: The Commercial Press, 1937.

Burkhardt, V.R. *Chinese Creeds and Customs.* Hong Kong: South China Morning Post 1 (1953), 2 (1955), 3, 1958.

———. "The Water Folk." In *Hong Kong Business Symposium,* compiled by J.M. Braga. Hong Kong: South China Morning Post, 1957, pp. 271–75.

Chang, Chung-li. *The Chinese Gentry: Studies on Their Role in Nineteenth Century Chinese Society.* Seattle: University of Washington Press, 1955.

———. *The Income of the Chinese Gentry.* Seattle: University of Washington Press, 1962.

Char, Tin-yuke, compiler and editor. *The Sandalwood Mountains: Readings and Stories of the Early Chinese in Hawaii.* Honolulu: University Press of Hawaii, 1975.

Char, Tin-yuke and Kwok, C.H. *The Hakka Chinese—Their Origin and Folk Songs.* San Francisco: Jade Mountain Press, 1969. Originally published in *The Chinese Social and Political Science Review,* April 1929.

Chiang, Monlin. *Tides from the West.* Reprint of Yale University Press, edition of 1947. Taiwan: China Cultural Publishing Foundation, 1957.

Ch'ing-shih wen-t'i: a Bulletin Issued Irregularly by the Society for Ch'ing Studies. New Haven and St. Louis, 1965 to date.

Chow, Yung-teh. *Social Mobility in China: Status Careers among the Gentry in a Chinese Community.* New York: Atherton, 1966.

Chü, T'ung-chu, *Law and Society in Traditional China*, Paris and The Hague; Mouton & Co., 1961.

Ch'ü, T'ung-tsu. *Local Government in China under the Ch'ing.* Cambridge, Mass.: Harvard University Press, 1962.

Chung, Kun-ai. *My Seventy Nine Years in Hawaii (1879–1958).* Hong Kong: Cosmorama Pictorial Publisher, 1960.

Clark, Charles Allen. *Religions of Old Korea.* Reprint of the first edition of 1930. Seoul: The Christian Literature Society of Korea, 1961.

Clementi, Cecil. *The Chinese in British Guiana.* Georgetown: The Argosy Company Ltd., 1915.

Coates, Austin. *A Summary Memorandum on the Southern District of the New Territories, Spring, 1955.* Hong Kong. Headquarters of the New Territories Administration, Hong Kong government. Mr. Coates was District Officer, South, 1953–55.

Cohen, Myron L. "The Hakka or 'Guest People': Dialect as a Sociocultural Variable in Southeastern China." *Ethnohistory* 15, no. 3 (1968): 237–92.

———. *House United, House Divided: The Chinese Family in Taiwan.* New York: Columbia University Press, 1976.

Colquhoun, A.R., and Stewart-Lockhart, J.H. "A Sketch of Formosa." *China Review* 13 (1884–85): 161–207.

Cooke, G. Wingrove. *China: Being "The Times" Special Correspondence from China in the Years 1857–58.* London: G. Routledge & Co., 1858.

Davis, J.F. *The Chinese: A General Description of China and Its Inhabitants.* Rev. ed. London: Charles Knight & Co., 1840.

Davis, Sir John Francis. *Chinese Miscellanies: A Collection of Essays and Notes.* London: John Murray, 1865.

Davis, S.G., and Tregear, Mary. "Man Kok Tsui Archaeological Site 30, Lantau Island, Hong Kong." *Asian Perspectives*

4, nos. 1–2 (Summer-Winter 1960): 183–212.

Davis, S.G. "Regional Reports 4, Hong Kong." *Asian Perspectives* 7, nos. 1–2 (Summer-Winter 1963): 19–21.

Des Voeux, Sir G. William. *My Colonial Service in British Guiana, St. Lucia, Trinidad, Fiji, Australia, Newfoundland and Hong Kong*. 2 vols. London: John Murray, 1903.

Drake, F.S., general editor. *Symposium on Historical, Archaeological and Linguistic Studies on Southern China, South-east Asia and the Hong Kong Region.* Papers presented at meetings held in September 1961 as part of the Golden Jubilee Congress of the University of Hong Kong, Hong Kong. Hong Kong University Press, 1967.

Eberhard, Wolfram. *Social Mobility in Traditional China.* Leiden: E.J. Brill, 1962.

———. *Folktales of China*. New York: Washington Square Press, 1973. University of Chicago edition, 1965.

———. *The Local Cultures of South and East China.* Leiden: E.J. Brill, 1968.

Echo of Things Chinese. Taipei: Echo Magazine Company, monthly, early 1971 on.

Edge, John. "The Hakkas: A People Apart." *Echo of Things Chinese*, October 1973: 20–27, 50–51.

Eitel, E.J. *Europe in China. The History of Hong Kong from the Beginning to the Year 1882*. Hong Kong: Kelly and Walsh, 1895.

———. "Ethnographical Sketches of the Hakka Chinese." *Notes and Queries on China and Japan* 1 (1867): 49, 65–67, 81–83, 97–99, 113–14, 128–30, 145–46, 161–63; 2 (1868): 145–47, 167–69, and 3 (1869): 1–3. See also in *China Review* 20, no. 4 (1891–92): 263–67.

———. *A Dictionary of the Chinese Language*. 2 vols. Revised and enlarged by Immanuel Gottlieb Genähr. Hong Kong: Kelly and Walsh, 1910–11.

Elvin, Mark. *The Pattern of the Chinese Past*. London: Eyre Methuen, 1973.

Endacott, G.B. *A History of Hong Kong*. London: Oxford University Press, 1958.

———. *Government and People in Hong Kong*. Hong Kong: Hong Kong University Press, 1964.

Fairbank, John King. *The United States and China.* Cambridge, Mass: Harvard University Press, 1949; new edition, completely revised and enlarged 1958; and third edition, completely revised and enlarged, 1971.

Fairbank, John King, Banno Masataka and Yamamoto Sumiko. *Japanese Studies of Modern China: A Bibliographical Guide to Historical and Social Science Research on the 19th and 20th Centries.* Harvard-Yenching Institute Studies 26. Cambridge, Mass: Harvard University Press, 1971.

Fei, Hsiao-tung. *Peasant Life in China, A Field Study of Country Life in the Yangtse Valley.* London: Kegan Paul, Trench, Trübner, 1939.

Field Officer. *The Last Year in China to the Peace of Nanking as Sketched in Letters to his Friends by a Field Officer Actively Employed in That Country.* 2d ed. rev. London: Longman, Brown, Green and Longman, 1843.

Fielde, Adele M. *Pagoda Shadows: Studies from Life in China.* London: T. Ogilvie Smith, 1887.

Finn, Daniel J. *Archaeological Finds on Lamma Island* (舶遼州) *near Hong Kong.* Edited by T.F. Ryan. Hong Kong: Ricci Hall, University of Hong Kong, 1958.

Fitzgerald, C.P. *Flood Tide in China.* London: The Cresset Press, 1958.

Forbes, Lieut. F.E. *Five Years in China from 1842 to 1847 with an Account of the Occupation of the Islands of Labuan and Borneo by H.M.'s Forces.* London: R. Bentley, 1848.

Forrest, R.A.D. "The Southern Dialects of Chinese." Appendix 1 of *The Chinese in Southeast Asia*, by Victor Purcell. 2d ed. London: Oxford University Press, 1965.

Fortune, Robert. *Three Years' Wandering in the Northern Provinces of China, including a Visit to the Tea, Cotton, and Silk Countries.* 2d ed. London: John Murray, 1847.

Foster, Arnold. *Christian Progress in China, Gleanings from the Writings and Speeches of Many Workers.* London: The Religious Tract Society, 1889.

Fox, Grace. *British Admirals and Chinese Pirates 1832–1869.* London: Kegan Paul, Trench, Trübner and Co., 1940.

Freedman, Maurice. *Lineage Organization in Southeastern China.* London: University of London the Athlone Press, 1958.

———. *A Report on Social Research in the New Territories, May–July, 1963*. Mimeographed. Will be included in *JHKBRAS* 16 (1976).

———. *Chinese Lineage and Society: Fukien and Kwangtung*. London: University of London the Athlone Press, 1966.

———. "Shifts of Power in the Hong Kong New Territories." *Journal of Asian and African Studies* 1, no. 1, Leiden, 1966.

———. "Geomancy." Presidential Address 1968 from *Proceedings of the Royal Anthropological Institute of Great Britain and Ireland*, 1968.

———, ed. *Family and Kinship in Chinese Society*. Stanford, California: Stanford University Press, 1970.

Fu, Lo-shu, compiler. *A Documentary Chronicle of Sino-Western Relations (1644–1820)*. 2 vols. Tucson: University of Arizona Press, 1966.

Gallin, Bernard. *Hsin Hsing, Taiwan: A Chinese Village in Change*. Berkeley and Los Angeles: University of California Press, 1966.

Gamble, Sidney D. *Ting Hsien, a North China Rural Community*. New York: Institute of Pacific Relations, 1954.

———. *Chinese Village Plays from the Ting Hsien Region (Yang Ke Hsuan)*. Amsterdam: Philo Press, 1970.

Gibson, J. Campbell. *Mission Problems and Mission Methods in South China, Lectures on Evangelical Theology*. Edinburgh and London: Oliphant, Anderson and Ferrier, 1902.

Giles, H.A. *A Short History of Chinese Civilisation*. London: Home University Library, 1911.

———. *A Chinese English Dictionary*. 2d ed., rev. Shanghai: Kelly and Walsh, 1912.

Goodwin, R.B. *Hong Kong Escape*. London: Arthur Barker, 1953.

Graham, David Crockett. *Folk Religion in Southwest China*. Smithsonian Miscellaneous Collections, vol. 142, no. 2. Washington D.C.: Smithsonian Press, 1961.

Gray, John Henry. *China. A History of the Laws, Manners and Customs of the People*. Edited by William Gow Gregor. 2 vols. London: Macmillan, 1878.

Groves, R.G. "Militia, Market and Lineage: Chinese Resistance to the Occupation of Hong Kong's New Territories in 1899." *JHKBRAS* 9 (1969): 31–64.

Gullick, J.M. *Malaya.* London: Ernest Benn, Ltd., 1963.

Gutzlaff, Charles. *Journal of Three Voyages along the Coast of China in 1831, 1832 and 1833.* 2d ed. London: Thomas Ward & Co., n.d.

Hardy, E.J. *John Chinaman at Home.* London: T. Fisher Unwin, 1905.

Hay, Sir John C. Dalrymple. *The Suppression of Piracy in the China Sea, 1849.* London: Edward Stanford, 1889.

Hayes, J.W. "The Pattern of Life in the New Territories in 1898." *JHKBRAS* 2 (1962): 75–102.

———. "Cheung Chau 1850–1898: Information from Commemorative Tablets." *JHKBRAS* 3 (1963): 88–99.

———. "Movement of Villages on Lantau Island for Fung Shui 風水 Reasons." *JHKBRAS* 3 (1963): 143–44.

———. "Peng Chau between 1798 and 1899." *JHKBRAS* 4 (1964): 71–96.

———. "Village Credit at Shek Pik, 1879–1895." *JHKBRAS* 5 (1965): 119–22.

———. "The Settlement and Development of a Multiple-clan Village." In *Aspects of Social Organization in the New Territories*, edited by Marjorie Topley. Hong Kong Branch of the Royal Asiatic Society, 1965, pp. 10–15.

———. "A Mixed Community of Hakka and Cantonese on Lantau Island." In *Aspects of Social Organization in the New Territories*, edited by Marjorie Topley. Hong Kong Branch of the Royal Asiatic Society, 1965, pp. 21–26.

———. "Old British Kowloon." *JHKBRAS* 6 (1966): 120–37.

———. "Land and Leadership in the Hong Kong Region of Kwangtung." *JHKBRAS* 7 (1967): 91–103.

———. "Geomancy and the Village." In *Some Traditional Chinese Ideas and Conceptions in Hong Kong Social Life Today*, edited by Marjorie Topley. Hong Kong Branch of the Royal Asiatic Society, 1967, pp. 22–30.

———. "Chinese Temples in the Local Setting." In *Some Traditional Chinese Ideas and Conceptions in Hong Kong Social Life Today*, edited by Marjorie Topley. Hong Kong Branch of the Royal Asiatic Society, 1967, pp. 86–95.

———. "A List of Temples in the Southern District of the New Territories and New Kowloon, 1899–1967." In *Some*

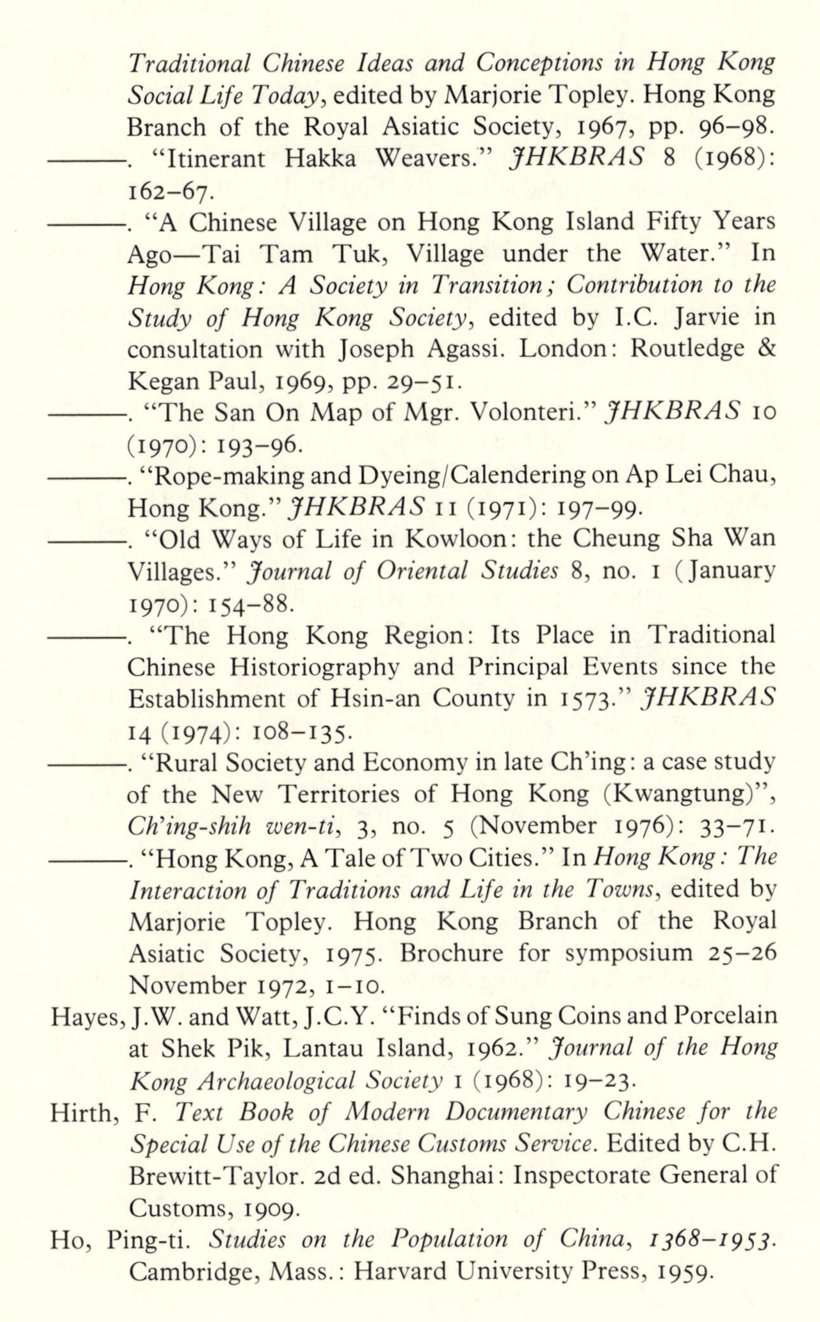

Traditional Chinese Ideas and Conceptions in Hong Kong Social Life Today, edited by Marjorie Topley. Hong Kong Branch of the Royal Asiatic Society, 1967, pp. 96–98.

———. "Itinerant Hakka Weavers." *JHKBRAS* 8 (1968): 162–67.

———. "A Chinese Village on Hong Kong Island Fifty Years Ago—Tai Tam Tuk, Village under the Water." In *Hong Kong: A Society in Transition; Contribution to the Study of Hong Kong Society*, edited by I.C. Jarvie in consultation with Joseph Agassi. London: Routledge & Kegan Paul, 1969, pp. 29–51.

———. "The San On Map of Mgr. Volonteri." *JHKBRAS* 10 (1970): 193–96.

———. "Rope-making and Dyeing/Calendering on Ap Lei Chau, Hong Kong." *JHKBRAS* 11 (1971): 197–99.

———. "Old Ways of Life in Kowloon: the Cheung Sha Wan Villages." *Journal of Oriental Studies* 8, no. 1 (January 1970): 154–88.

———. "The Hong Kong Region: Its Place in Traditional Chinese Historiography and Principal Events since the Establishment of Hsin-an County in 1573." *JHKBRAS* 14 (1974): 108–135.

———. "Rural Society and Economy in late Ch'ing: a case study of the New Territories of Hong Kong (Kwangtung)", *Ch'ing-shih wen-ti*, 3, no. 5 (November 1976): 33–71.

———. "Hong Kong, A Tale of Two Cities." In *Hong Kong: The Interaction of Traditions and Life in the Towns*, edited by Marjorie Topley. Hong Kong Branch of the Royal Asiatic Society, 1975. Brochure for symposium 25–26 November 1972, 1–10.

Hayes, J.W. and Watt, J.C.Y. "Finds of Sung Coins and Porcelain at Shek Pik, Lantau Island, 1962." *Journal of the Hong Kong Archaeological Society* 1 (1968): 19–23.

Hirth, F. *Text Book of Modern Documentary Chinese for the Special Use of the Chinese Customs Service*. Edited by C.H. Brewitt-Taylor. 2d ed. Shanghai: Inspectorate General of Customs, 1909.

Ho, Ping-ti. *Studies on the Population of China, 1368–1953*. Cambridge, Mass.: Harvard University Press, 1959.

———. *The Ladder of Success in Imperial China: Aspects of Social Mobility 1368–1911*. New York: Columbia University Press, 1962.

———. "Salient Aspects of China's Heritage." In *China in Crisis*, vol. 1, edited by Ping-ti Ho and Tang Tsou. *China's Heritage and the Communist Political System, Book One*. Chicago: University of Chicago Press, 1967, pp. 1–37, 78–92.

Hsiao, Kung-chuan. *Rural China, Imperial Control in the Nineteenth Century*. Seattle: University of Washington Press, 1960.

Hsieh, Kuo Ching. "Removal of Coastal Population in Early Tsing Period." *The Chinese Social and Political Science Review* 13 (1929): 559–96.

Hucker, Charles O. *The Traditional Chinese State in Ming Times (1368–1644)*. Tucson, Arizona: University of Arizona Press, 1961.

———. "China." In *Asia in the Modern World*, edited by Helen G. Matthew. New York: New American Library, Mentor Books, 1963, pp. 67–112.

Hume, Edward H. *Doctors East, Doctors West. An American Physician's Life in China*. London: George Allen and Unwin, 1949.

Hummel, Arthur, W., *Eminent Chinese of the Ch'ing Period (1644–1912)*. Reprint of the first edition, Washington: United States Government Printing Office, 2 vols., 1943. Taipei: Ch'eng Wen Publishing Company, 1967.

Jackson, R.N. *Pickering, Protector of Chinese*. Kuala Lumpur: Oxford University Press, 1965.

Jen, Yu-wen. *The Taiping Revolutionary Movement*. New Haven: Yale University Press, 1973.

Jenyns, Soame. *A Background to Chinese Painting*. New York: Schocken Books, 1966. (First edition, London: Sidgwick and Jackson, 1935.)

Johnston, A.R. "Note on the Island of Hong Kong." London: *Geographical Journal* 14. Also in the *Hong Kong Almanack and Directory for 1846*.

Johnston, Rev. James. *China and Formosa, the Story of the Mission of the Presbyterian Church of England*. London:

Hazel, Watson and Viney, 1897.

Kani, Hiroaki. *A General Survey of the Boat People in Hong Kong*. The Chinese University of Hong Kong, Monograph Series no. 5. Hong Kong: New Asia Research Institute, 1967.

Krone, Rev. Mr. "A Notice of the Sanon District." *C.B.R.A.S.* Transactions 6 (1859): 71–105. Reprinted in *JHKBRAS* 7 (1967): 104–37.

Kuhn, Philip A. *Rebellion and Its Enemies in Late Imperial China. Militarization and Social Structure 1796–1864*. Cambridge, Mass.: Harvard University Press, 1970.

Kulp, Daniel Harrison II. *Country Life in South China: The Sociology of Familism. Volume I, Phenix Village, Kwantung, China*. New York: Teachers College, Columbia University, 1925.

Lamley, Harry J. "*Hsieh-tou*, the Pathology of Violence in South-east China" forthcoming in *Ch'ing-shih wen-ti* 1977.

Lamson, Herbert Day. *Social Pathology in China, A Source Book for the Study of Problems of Livelihood, Health and the Family*. Shanghai: The Commercial Press, 1935.

Lechler, Rudolph. "The Hakka Chinese." *Chinese Recorder*, September-October, 1878.

Lethbridge, H.J. "The District Watch Committee: 'The Chinese Executive Council of Hong Kong.'" *JHKBRAS* 11 (1971): 116–41.

Lethbridge, H.J. "A Chinese Association in Hong Kong: The Tung Wah." *Contributions to Asian Studies* 2, no. 1 (1972): 144–58.

Li, Shu-fan. *Hong Kong Surgeon*. London: Victor Gollanz, 1964.

Lin, S.Y. *Reports on the Fisheries Industries of Hong Kong*. An apparently unpublished report dating to just before the Pacific War 1941–45. Hong Kong. University of Hong Kong Library.

———. "The Fishing Industries of Hong Kong, Parts I–IX." *Journal of the Hong Kong Fisheries Research Station* 1, nos. 1–2 (February and September, 1940): 5–101, 107–60.

Linebarger, Paul M.A. *The China of Chiang K'ai-shek: a Political Study*. Boston: World Peace Foundation, 1941.

Liu, Wu-chi. *An Introduction to Chinese Literature*. Bloomington: Indiana University Press, 1966.

Llewellyn, Bernard. *I Left My Roots in China*. London: George Allen and Unwin, 1953.

Lo, Hsiang-lin. "The Sung Wang T'ai and the Location of the Travelling Courts by the Sea-shore in the Last Days of the Sung." *Journal of Oriental Studies* 3, no. 2 (July 1956).

———, and others. *Hong Kong and Its External Communications before 1842*. Hong Kong: Institute of Chinese Culture, 1963. An English version, abbreviated, of the Chinese edition of 1959.

———. *Hong Kong and Western Cultures*. Honolulu: East West Center Press, 1963.

Lobscheid, Rev. W. *A Few Notices on the Extent of Chinese Education and the Government Schools of Hong Kong*. Hong Kong: China Mail Office, 1859.

———. *An English and Chinese Dictionary*. Revised and enlarged by Tetsuyira Inouye, Bungakushi. Tokyo: J. Fujimoto, 16th year of Meiji, 1883–84.

Mackay, Rev. G.L. *From Far Formosa: The Island, Its People and Missions*. Edinburgh: Oliphant, Anderson and Ferrier, 1896.

MacNair, Harley Farnsworth. *Modern Chinese History, Selected Readings*. 2d ed. Shanghai: Commercial Press, 1927.

March, Andrew L. "An Appreciation of Chinese Geomancy." *Journal of Asian Studies* 27, no. 2 (February 1968): 253–67.

Meadows, Thomas Taylor. *The Chinese and Their Rebellions, viewed in connection with their Natural Philosophy, Ethics, Legislation and Administration*. London: Smith, Elder and Co., 1856.

———. "Land Tenure in China. Remarks on the Acquisition, Common-tenure, and Alienation of Real Property in China, accompanied by a Facsimile and Translation of a Deed of Sale." Hong Kong: *Transactions of the China Branch of the Royal Asiatic Society*, 1859 pp. 1–16.

Medhurst, W.H. *A Foreigner in Far Cathay*. London: Edward Stanford, 1872.

Miyakawa, Hisayuki. "The Confucianization of South China."

In *The Confucian Persuasion*, edited by Arthur F. Wright. Stanford, California: Stanford University Press, 1960, pp. 21–46.

Montalto de Jesus, C.A. *Historic Macao, International Traits in China Old and New.* 2 ed., rev. Macau: 1926.

Moody, Campbell N. *The Heathen Heart, an Account of the Reception of the Gospel among the Chinese of Formosa.* Edinburgh and London: Oliphant, Anderson and Ferrier, 1908.

Morrison, R. *A Dictionary of the Chinese Language*, vol. 2, reprinted separately by the London Mission Press, Shanghai, and Trübner and Co., London, 1865.

Muramatsu, Yuji. "A Documentary Study of Chinese Landlordism in the Late Ch'ing and the Early Republican Kiangnan." *Bulletin of the School of Oriental and African Studies* 29, no. 3 (1966): 566–99.

Murphey, Rhoads. *The Treaty Ports and China's Modernization: What Went Wrong?* Michigan Papers in Chinese Studies, no. 7. Ann Arbor, Michigan: 1970.

Myers, Ramon H. "Taiwan under Ch'ing Imperial Rule, 1684–1895: The Traditional Order"; "Taiwan under Ch'ing Imperial Rule, 1684–1895: The Traditional Economy"; "Taiwan under Ch'ing Imperial Rule, 1684–1895: The Traditional Society." *Journal of the Institute of Chinese Studies of the Chinese University of Hong Kong*, 4, no. 2 (1971), and 5, no. 2 (1972): 373–411 and 413–53.

———. *The Chinese Peasant Economy, Agricultural Development in Hopei and Shantung, 1890–1949.* Cambridge, Mass.: Harvard University Press, 1970.

Nacken, J. "Chinese Street-cries in Hong Kong." *China Review*, 2 (1873): 51–55. Reprinted in *JHKBRAS* 8 (1968): 128–34.

Nelson, H.G.H. "British Land Administration in the New Territories of Hong Kong and Its Effects on Chinese Social Organisation." Paper for the London-Cornell Project for East and Southeast Asian Studies Conference, Adèle en Haut, 24–30 August 1969.

———. "Review of H.D.R. Baker: 'Sheung Shui, a Chinese Lineage Village.'" *JHKBRAS* 11 (1971): 101–104.

Neumann, C.F. *Translations from the Chinese and Armenian with Notes: I History of the Pirates who infested the China Sea from 1807 to 1810*. London: John Murray, 1831.

Nevius, Rev. John L. *China and the Chinese: A General Description of the Country and Its Inhabitants*...Rev. ed. Philadelphia: Presbyterian Board of Publication, 1882.

Ng, Shui-wai, Paul. *Decorations and Ornamentations in Chinese Architecture (in Hong Kong)*. Macau: 1971.

Ng, Peter, Y.L. *The 1819 Edition of the Hsin-an Hsien-chih, A Critical Examination with Translation and Notes. Hong Kong, Kowloon and the New Territories (1644–1842)*. M.A. thesis, University of Hong Kong, 1961.

Ng, Ronald, C.Y. "The San On Map of Mgr. Volonteri. On the Centenary of the Copy in the R.G.S. Collection." London: *Geographical Journal* 135, part 2 (June, 1969): 231–35. Reprinted in *JHKBRAS* 9 (1969): 141–48.

———. "Culture and Society of a Hakka Community on Lantau Island, Hong Kong" at pp. 53–63 of I.C. Jarvie in consultation with Joseph Agassi, *Hong Kong: A Society in Transition, Contributions to the Study of Hong Kong Society*. London, Routledge and Kegan Paul 1969.

Orange, James. *The Chater Collection. Pictures relating to China, Hong Kong and Macao 1655–1860. With Historical and Descriptive Letter-press by James Orange*. London: Thornton Butterworth, Ltd., 1924.

Orme, G.N. *Report on the New Territories for the Years 1899 to 1912*. In SP 1912, no. 11.

Osgood, Cornelius. *The Koreans and Their Culture*. Tokyo: Charles E. Tuttle Co., 1954.

———. *Village Life in Old China*. New York: The Ronald Co., 1963.

———. *The Chinese, A Study of a Hong Kong Community*. Vols. 1–3. Tucson, Arizona: University of Arizona Press, 1975.

Parker, E.H. *China, Her History, Diplomacy and Commerce from the Earliest Times to the Present Day*. London: John Murray, 1901.

Peacock, J.E., *Hong Kong Meteorological Records and Climatological Notes, 60 Years 1884–1939, 1947–1950, R.O.T.M. 5*. Hong Kong: Government Printer, 1952.

———, ed. *Supplement to R.O.T.M. 5, Hong Kong Meteorological Records for the 72 Years 1884–1939, 1947–1962. Hong Kong: Government Press*, 1963.

Peasant Studies Newsletter: History, Politics and Economy of Traditional Societies. University of Pittsburgh, vol. 1, no. 1 (January 1972) to date. (Quarterly).

Peplow, S.H. *Hong Kong About and Around.* Hong Kong: The Commercial Press, 1930.

Perkins, Dwight H. *Agricultural Development in China 1368–1968.* Chicago: Aldine Publishing Company, 1969.

Piton, Rev. Charles. "On the Origin and History of the Hakkas." *China Review* 2 (1873–74): 222–26.

Potter, Jack M. *Capitalism and the Chinese Peasant, Social and Economic Change in a Hong Kong Village.* Berkeley and Los Angeles: University of California Press, 1968.

———. "The Structure of Rural Chinese Society in New Territories." In *Hong Kong; A Society in Transition, Contributions to the Study of Hong Kong Society*, edited by I.C. Jarvie in consultation with Joseph Agassi. London: Routledge and Kegan Paul, 1969, pp. 3–28.

Powell, John Duncan. "On Defining Peasants and Peasant Society." *Peasant Studies Newsletter* 1, no. 3 (July 1972): 94–99.

Purcell, Victor. *The Chinese in Southeast Asia.* 2d ed. London: Oxford University Press, 1965.

Ralph, Julian. *Alone in China and Other Stories.* London: Osgood, McIlvaine and Co., 1897.

Rawski, Evelyn Sakakida. *Agricultural Change and the Peasant Economy of South China.* Cambridge, Mass.: Harvard University Press, 1972.

———. "Agricultural Development in the Han River Uplands." *Ch'ing-Shih wen-t'i* 3, no. 4 (December 1975): 63–81.

Rostow, W.W., in collaboration. *The Prospects for Communist China.* Cambridge, Mass.: M.I.T. and New York: John Wiley, 1954.

Ryan, Thomas F. *The Story of a Hundred Years, The Pontefical Institute of Foreign Missions (P.I.M.E.) in Hong Kong, 1858–1958.* Hong Kong: Catholic Truth Society, 1959.

Ryckmans, Pierre. *The Life and Work of Su Renshan, Rebel,*

Painter and Madman. Paris, Hong Kong: Centre de Publication de L'U E.R. Extrême-Orient–Asie du Sud-Est, 1970.

Sayer, G.R. *Hong Kong: Birth, Adolescence and Coming of Age*. London: Oxford University Press, 1937.

Schneider, Laurence A. *Ku Chieh-kang and China's New History: Nationalism and the Quest for Alternative Traditions*. Berkeley and Los Angeles: University of California Press, 1971.

Schofield, Walter. "The Proto-Historic Site of the Hong Kong Culture at Shek Pik, Lantau, Hong Kong." In *Proceedings of The Third Congress of Pre-historians of the Far East*. Singapore: Government Printing House, 1940.

Schoppa, R. Keith. "The Composition and Functions of the Local Elite in Szechuan, 1851–1874." *Ch'ing-shih wen-t'i* 2, no. 10 (November 1973): 7–23.

Schurmann, Franz, and Schell, Orville. *China Readings, I, Imperial China, The Eighteenth and Nineteenth Centuries*. London: Penguin Books, 1967.

Schurmann, Franz. *Ideology and Organization in Communist China*. 2d ed. enlarged. Berkeley and Los Angeles: University of California Press, 1968.

Selby, Thomas G. *Chinamen at Home*. London: Hodder and Stoughton, 1900.

Sewell, William G. *The Land and Life of China*. London: Edinburgh House Press, 1933.

Shanin, Teodor. "Peasantry: Delineation of a Sociological Concept and a Field of Study." *Peasant Studies Newsletter* 2, no. 1 (January 1973): 1–8.

Silva, A.M. da. "Fan Lau and Its Fort: An Historical Perspective." *JHKBRAS* 8 (1968): 82–95.

———. "Some Notes on Ethnobotany in the New Territories of Hong Kong." *JHKBRAS* 9 (1969): 124–30.

———. *Tai Yu Shan, Traditional Ecological Adaptation on a South Chinese Island*. Asian Folklore and Social Life Monographs, vol. 32. Taipei: Orient Cultural Service, 1972.

Simpson, Dr. W.J. "Report on the Causes and Continuance of Plague in Hongkong, and Suggestions as to Remedial

Measures." London: Waterlow and Sons, 1903.
Sirr, H.C. *China and the Chinese. Their Religion, Character and Manufactures, etc.* 2 vols. London: William S. Orr and Co., 1849.
Skinner, George William. *Chinese Society in Thailand: An Analytical History.* Ithaca, N.Y.: Cornell University Press, 1957.
———. "Marketing and Social Structure in Rural China." *The Journal of Asian Studies* 24, no. 1 (November, 1964): 3–43. 24, no. 2 (February, 1965): 195–228. 24, no. 3 (May, 1965): 363–99.
———. *Leadership and Power in the Chinese Community of Thailand.* Ithaca, N.Y.: Cornell University Press, 1958.
———. *Some programmatics on the local-systems approach to the study of regions.* Mimeographed paper prepared for distribution at the Canton Delta Conference, University of Washington, Seattle, 13–15 June, 1971.
Smedley, Agnes. *The Great Road: The Life and Times of Chu Te.* New York: Monthly Review Press, 1956.
Smith, Carl T. "An early Hong Kong success story: Wei Akwong, the Beggar Boy." Hong Kong: *Chung Chi Bulletin* (Chinese University of Hong Kong), no. 45: 9–14, December, 1968.
———. "Ng Akew, one of Hong Kong's 'Protected' Women." Hong Kong: *Chung Chi Bulletin*, no. 46: 13–17, 27, June 1969.
———. "The Chinese Settlement of British Hong Kong.", Hong Kong: *Chung Chi Bulletin*, no. 48: 26, 28–32, May 1970.
———. "The Emergence of a Chinese Elite in Hong Kong." *JHKBRAS* 11 (1971): 74–115.
———. "Notes on Chinese Temples in Hong Kong." *JHKBRAS* 13 (1973): 133–39.
Smith, Rev. George. *A Narrative of an Exploratory Visit to each of the Consular Cities of China and to the Islands of Chusan and Hong Kong.* 2d ed. London: Seeley, Burnside and Seeley, 1848.
Smith, Thomas C. *The Agrarian Origins of Modern Japan.* New York: Atheneum, 1966.
Stevens, Rev. H.J. *Cantonese Apothegms, Classified, translated and commented upon.* Canton: E-Shing, 1902.

Sung Hok P'ang. *Cantonese Conversation (with English Notes)*. Hong Kong: 1934.

———. "Legends and Stories of the New Territories: Part III, Kam Tin." *The Hong Kong Naturalist*, in six installments between December 1935 and March 1938. Reprinted in *JHKBRAS* 13 (1973): 110–32 and 14 (1974): 160–85.

———. "Ts'in Fuk (遷復), being an account of how part of the coast of South China was cleared of inhabitants from the first year of Hong Hei (康熙) 1662 to the 8th year of Hong Hei 1669." *The Hong Kong Naturalist* 9, nos. 1 and 2 (November 1939): 37–42.

Szczesniak, Boleslaw. *The Opening of Japan. A Diary of Discovery in the Far East, 1853–1856 (by Rear Admiral George Henry Preble, U.S.N.)*. Norman, Arizona: University of Oklahoma Press.

Takekoshi, Yosaburo. *Japanese Rule in Formosa*. Translated by George Braithwaite. London: Longmans, Green & Co., 1907.

Taylor, W.A. "A Note on Land Measurement and Tenant Rentals in Hong Kong." *JHKBRAS* 6 (1966): 165–71.

Thomas, J.S. *The Chinese*. Indianapolis: The Bobbs-Merrill Company, 1909.

Topley, Marjorie. "Chinese Religion and Religious Institutions in Singapore." *Journal of the Malayan Branch Royal Asiatic Society* 29, part 1 (May 1956): 70–118.

———. "The Emergence and Social Functions of Chinese Religious Associations in Singapore." *Comparative Studies in Society and History*, vol. 3, no. 3. The Hague, April 1961: 289–314.

———. "Hong Kong." In *The Role of Savings and Wealth in Southern Asia and the West*, edited by Richard D. Lambert and Bert F. Hoselitz. Paris: UNESCO, 1963, pp. 126–77. Also reprinted with new concluding note, 1967, in *Hong Kong: A Society in Transition; Contribution to the Study of Hong Kong Society*, edited by I.C. Jarvie in consultation with Joseph Agassi. London: Routledge & Kegan Paul, 1969, pp. 167–227.

———. "Capital, Saving and Credit among Indigenous Rice

Farmers and Immigrant Vegetable Farmers in Hong Kong's New Territories." In *Capital, Saving and Credit in Peasant Societies from Asia, Oceania, the Caribbean and Middle America*, edited by Raymond Firth and B.S. Yamey. London: George Allen and Unwin, Ltd., 1964, pp. 157–86.

———. "Chinese Occasional Rites in Hong Kong." In *Some Traditional Chinese Ideas and Conceptions in Hong Kong Social Life Today*, edited by M. Topley. Hong Kong: The Hong Kong Branch of the Royal Asiatic Society, 1967, pp. 99–117.

———, ed. *Some Traditional Chinese Ideas and Conceptions in Hong Kong Social Life Today, Week-end Symposium, October, 1966*. Hong Kong: *HKBRAS*, 1967.

———, with Hayes, James. "Notes on Temples and Shrines of Tai Ping Shan Street Area." In *Some Traditional Chinese Ideas and Conceptions in Hong Kong Social Life Today*, edited by M. Topley. Hong Kong: *HKBRAS*, 1967: 123–42.

———, compiler. *Anthropology and Sociology in Hong Kong, Field Projects and Problems of Overseas Scholars. Proceedings of a Symposium February 8–9, 1969*. Hong Kong: Centre of Asian Studies, University of Hong Kong, 1969.

———, compiler. "Published and Unpublished Materials on Hong Kong by Overseas Affiliated Scholars." *Journal of Oriental Studies* 8, no. 1 (1970): 219–25.

———. "Chinese Traditional Ideas and the Treatment of Disease: Two Examples from Hong Kong." *Man* 5, no. 3 (September 1970).

———, ed. *Hong Kong: The Interaction of Traditions and Life in the Towns. Week-end Symposium, November 1972.* Hong Kong: *HKBRAS,* 1975.

———. "Marriage Resistance in Rural Kwangtung" in *Women in Chinese Society*, edited by Margery Wolf and Roxane Witke, Stanford: Stanford University Press, 1975.

Tregear, Thomas R. *Land Use in Hong Kong and the New Territories.* Hong Kong: Hong Kong University Press, Geographical Publications Limited, 1958.

Turner, Rev. J.A. *Kwang Tung or Five Years in South China.* London: S.W. Partridge & Co., n.d. but preface dated 1894.

Tyau, Min-chien, T.Z. *China Awakened.* New York: The Macmillan Co., 1922.

Vaillant, L. "Contribution a l'étude anthropologique des chinois Hak-ka de la province de Moncay (Tonking)." *L'Anthropologie* 30 (1920).

Vansina, Jan. *Oral Tradition, A Study in Historical Methodology.* Translated by H.M. Wright. London: Routledge and Kegan Paul, 1965.

Wade, Thomas Francis. *Wen-chien Tzu-erh Chi, a Series of Papers selected as Specimens of Documentary Chinese designed to assist Students of the Language as written by the Officials of China.* London: Trübner & Co., 1867.

———, and Hillier, Walter Caine. *Yü Yen Tzu Erh Chi, A Progressive Course designed to assist the Student of Colloquial Chinese.* 3 vols. 2d ed. Shanghai: Inspectorate General of Customs, 1886.

Wakeman, Frederic Jr. *Strangers at the Gate: Social Disorder in South China 1839–1861.* Berkeley: University of California Press, 1966.

Waley, Arthur. *The Opium War through Chinese Eyes.* London: Allen and Unwin, 1958.

Ward, Barbara E. "A Hong Kong Fishing Village." *JOS* 1 (1954): 195–214.

———. "Varieties of the Conscious Model: The Fishermen of South China." In *The Relevance of Models for Social Anthropology.* A.S.A. Monographs 1. London: Tavistock Publications; New York: Frederick A. Prager, 1965, pp. 113–37.

———. "Chinese Fishermen in Hong Kong: Their Post-Peasant Economy." In *Social Organization: Essays Presented to Raymond Firth*, edited by M. Freedman. London: Frank Cass & Co., Ltd., 1967, pp. 271–88.

Watt, John R. *The District Magistrate in Late Imperial China.* New York: Columbia University Press, 1972.

Waung, W.S.K. *A Short History of Modern China from 1900 to*

1970. Hong Kong: Heinemann Educational Books (Asia), 1971.

Weber, Max. *The Religion of China, Confucianism and Taoism.* Translated and edited by Hans. H. Gerth, with an Introduction by C.K. Yang. New York: The Free Press, Paperback Edition, 1968.

Welsby, G.E. *A History of the Preventive Service, 1909–1939*. An account compiled by a serving officer post-1956, and authorized by the Department of Commerce and Industry, Hong Kong.

Werle, Helga. "Swatow (Ch'aochow) Horizontal Stick Puppets." *JHKBRAS* 13: 73–84.

Werner, E.T.C. *China of the Chinese*. London: Pitman's, 1920.

Wesley-Smith, Peter. "The Walled City of Kowloon: Historical and Legal Aspects." *Hong Kong Law Journal* 3, no. 1 (1973): 67–96.

———. "The Walled City of Kowloon and its Law Today." In *Hong Kong: The Interaction of Traditions and Life in the Towns*, edited by M. Topley (Brochure for symposium held on 25–26 November 1972). Royal Asiatic Society, Hong Kong Branch, 1975, pp. 119–29.

Wiens, Herold J. *Han Chinese Expansion in South China*. Hamden, Conn.: The Shoe String Press, Inc., 1967. Originally published in 1954 under the title *China's March towards the Tropics*.

Williams, E.T. *China Yesterday and Today*. London: Harrap & Co., 1923.

Williams, Frederick Wells. *The Life and Letters of Samuel Wells Williams, LL.D., Missionary, Diplomatist, Sinologue*. New York: G.P. Putnam's Sons, 1889.

Williams, S. Wells. *Tonic Dictionary of the Chinese Language in the Canton Dialect*. Canton: Office of the Chinese Repository, 1856.

———. *The Middle Kingdom: a Survey of the Geography, Government, Education, Social Life, Arts, Religion etc., of the Chinese Empire and Its Inhabitants*. 2 vols. 4th ed. New York: John Wiley, 1861.

———. *The Chinese Commercial Guide, Containing Treaties,*

Tariffs, Regulations, Tables etc. useful in the Trade to China and Eastern Asia. 5th ed. Hong Kong: Shortrede & Co., 1863.

———. *The Middle Kingdom, A Survey of the Geography, Government, Literature, Social Life, Arts and History of the Chinese Empire*. 2 vols. Rev. ed. London: W.H. Allen and Co., 1883.

Willmott, Donald Earl. *The Chinese of Semarang, A Changing Minority Community in Indonesia*. Ithaca, N.Y.: Cornell University Press, 1960.

Willmott, William E. *The Chinese in Cambodia*. Vancouver: University of British Columbia Press, 1967.

Wong, Aline K. "Chinese Voluntary Associations in Southeast Asian Cities and the Kaifongs in Hong Kong." *JHKBRAS* 11: 62–73.

———. *The Kaifong Associations and the Society of Hong Kong*. Asian Folklore and Social Life Monographs, vol. 43. Taipei, Orient Cultural Service, 1973.

Wood, Winifred A. *A Brief History of Hong Kong*. Hong Kong: South China Morning Post, Ltd., 1940.

Woodside, Alexander Barton. *Vietnam and the Chinese Model, A Comparative Study of Nguyen and Ch'ing Civil Government in the First Half of the Nineteenth Century*. Cambridge, Mass.: Harvard University Press, 1971.

Wu, Nelson I. *Chinese and Indian Architecture*. New York: George Braziller, 1963.

Yang, C.K. *A Chinese Village in Early Communist Transition*. Cambridge, Mass.: The M.I.T. Press, 1959.

———. *Religion in Chinese Society, A Study of Contemporary Social Functions of Religion and Some of Their Historical Factors*. Berkeley and Los Angeles: University of California Press, 1967.

Yang, Lien-sheng. *Money and Credit in China. A Short History*. Cambridge, Mass.: Harvard University Press: 1952.

Young, John A. *Business and Sentiment in a Chinese Market Town*. Asian Folklore and Social Life Monographs, vol. 60. Taipei, Orient Cultural Service, 1974.

Official Reports

Colony and Departmental

Annual Departmental Reports from 1946 on. Hong Kong: the Government Printer.

Administrative Reports, being annual departmental reports, 1909–40. Hong Kong: the Government Printer. Library of the Colonial Secretariat, Hong Kong.

Earlier annual reports by departments bound into *Sessional Papers* (Papers presented to the Legislative Council of Hong Kong). Hong Kong: the Government Printer. Library of the Colonial Secretariat, Hong Kong.

Annual *Colony Reports* from 1946 on. Hong Kong: the Government Printer.

Connected with Land

Land and N.T. Reports are *italicized*, for ease of reference. Wherever possible, *Gazette* entries are given as well as SP references, since page numbering can differ in different bindings.

Anglo-Chinese Land Commission, 1862. *Report of the Commissioners appointed under the VI article of the Convention of Pekin to investigate the Claims of the Chinese on the Kowloon Territory*. Attached to a dispatch from Sir Hercules Robinson to Lord Newcastle, Secretary of State for the Colonies, no. 82 of 30 April 1862, in CO 129/85, PRO London.

Report from the Hong Kong Land Commission of 1886–87 on the History of the Sale, Tenure and Use of the Crown Land of the Colony. In *Sessional Papers* 1887: xxvi–xxvii.

Summary of Report of the Squatters Commission, 1891–1906. A collection of detailed evidence taken down at various hearings. Library of the Colonial Secretariat, Hong Kong.

Memorandum on Land. Appendix No. 3 to *Hong Kong, Report on the new Territory during the First Year of British*

Administration. Hong Kong: Noronha & Co., Government Printers, 1900: 15–18.

Some Notes on Land Tenure in the New Territory. Appendix No. 1 to *Hong Kong, Report on the New Territory for the Year 1900*, in SP 1901: 565 et seq., and at Government Notification 446 in *HKGG*, 17 August 1901.

Memorandum of Work done in the Land Office, Hong Kong, in respect of the New Territories for the year 1899. Appendix No. 8 in *Hong Kong, Report on the New Territory during the First Year of British Administration* (as above): 26–28.

Report on the Work of the Land Court for the Seven Months ending December 31st 1900. Being Appendix No. 1a to the *Report on the New Territory for 1900.* In *HKGG*, 11 May and 17 August 1901. Signed H.H.J. Gompertz, Member of Court.

Report on the Work of the Land Court up to the 31st December, 1901. Being Appendix No. 1 to the *Report on the New Territory for 1901.* In *SP 1902*: 557–61. Has an Appendix A, Demarcation Rules, pp. 561–65.

New Territories: Land Court, Report on Work from 1900 to 1905. By J.R. Wood, with reports by C. McI. Messer, Cecil Clementi, and J.R. Wood. See *SP 1906:* 143–52.

New Territory/New Territories

Report on the New Territory at Hong Kong, by J.H. Stewart Lockhart, Special Commissioner, n.d. See *SP 1899*: 181 et seq. Also *HKGG* 8 April 1899: 535–52.

Despatches and Other Papers relating to the Extension of the Colony of Hong Kong. Hong Kong: Noronha & Co., Government Printers, 1899, pp. 1–69.

Report on the New Territory during the First Year of British Administration. Hong Kong: Noronha & Co., Government Printers, 1900, pp. 1–41.

Report on the New Territory for the Year 1900. In *SP 1901*, No. 38, 565 et seq. Also in *HKGG* 17 August 1901, GN 446.

Report on the New Territory for the Year 1901. In *SP 1902*, No. 22, 663 et seq. Also in *HKGG* 2 May 1902, GN 264.

Report on the New Territory for the Year 1902. In *SP 1903*, No. 27, 337 et seq. Also in *HKGG* 7 August 1903, GN 498.

Report on the New Territories for the Years 1899 to 1912. By G.N. Orme, district officer. In *SP 1912*, No. 11. Also published separately by Noronha & Co., Government Printers, 1912, pp. 1–21.

Other Printed Material

Blue Books. These are a form of printed report, produced annually as a supplement to the Colony Annual Report, and containing, in the main, statistical information arranged under various heads. The early Blue Books can be found appended to the Hong Kong annual reports contained in the *Reports on the Past and Present State of Her Majesty's Colonial Possessions*, published yearly in the 1840s by Clowes & Sons for H.M.S.O.; e.g., as for those for 1846. The later Blue Books were published in Hong Kong, and are available in the library of the Colonial Secretariat from 1871 onwards.

Colonial Estimates. The Hong Kong annual estimates were published annually by the Government Printer and are available in the library of the Colonial Secretariat, Hong Kong.

Hong Kong Hansard. The proceedings of the Legislative Council of Hong Kong were published in yearly volumes under this title from the early 1890s on by the Government Printer. Earlier proceedings were published in the local press, and are also available at the PRO London, Series CO 131.

Hong Kong Government Gazette. This important publication has been available since 1853. Between 1845 and 1853 official notices appeared in the *China Mail*, a Hong Kong newspaper. There was a gazette before this. Details are incomplete.

Miscellaneous

Eastern No. 88. Correspondence relating to the Kowloon-Canton Railway. London: Colonial Office, 1907.

Imperial Maritime Customs. Imperial Maritime Customs Special Catalogue of the Chinese Collection of Exhibits for the International Fisheries Exhibition 1883. Shanghai: Inspector General of Customs.

Parliamentary Papers, China 1861–66. Report on the Sanitary Condition of Hong Kong and Kowloon for 1864...presented to both Houses of Parliament by Command of Her Majesty in 1865.

Official Papers (Manuscript)

Series Colonial Office (CO) 129. Dispatches from the Governor of Hong Kong from the early 1840s on.

Series Foreign Office (FO) 233. Volumes 185–87 include the Chinese papers of the Hong Kong government, including petitions, for 1844–48.

Authorities. Leather bound volumes kept in the library of the Colonial Secretariat, Hong Kong, containing correspondence between the Colonial Secretary's Office and departments in the years 1857–87.

Land files of the Colonial Secretary's Office. These relate, *inter alia*, to the taking over, land survey, and settlement of titles to land, and sale and administration of land in the New Territories, 1898–1907. Now in the Public Records Office of Hong Kong, as Hong Kong Record Series 58.

Private Papers (Manuscript)

An assemblage of Chinese land deeds, mainly of sale, from Lantau Island. With a few exceptions these are for the second half of the 19th century, and relate to land at Pui O and Shek Pik on South Lantau. (Originals and copies in my possession.)

Other deeds of the same date and place are mentioned, without full text or supporting detail, in a property book belonging to a local landlord, who took it over when he purchased from the previous owner during the Japanese occupation of Hong Kong, 1941–45. Full texts, but in transcription, from the financial/property record of a clan trust (*t'ang*), are available for another small group of deeds from Pui O, South Lantau. (Copies in my possession.)

Family records in manuscript have been loaned by a number of lineages of the Southern District of the New Territories, including New Kowloon: see the Chinese bibliography.

Other Materials

Inscriptions on family graves, particularly on those of founding ancestors of lineages or branch heads, have been copied from a number of local graves. They are often of great assistance in determining length of settlement, and give both origins and descent lines in the better examples.

Licences and permits to occupy land for various purposes from the earlier period of British administration in the New Territories, printed in English and Chinese, are sometimes illuminating for the way in which they seem to take note of Chinese rural custom. I have made a small collection of such papers covering village forest lots, pineapple cultivation, other cultivation, structures and grave permits, now kept in the District Office, Tsuen Wan, New Territories Administration, Hong Kong.

Temple fittings often carry inscriptions naming donors of individual items of furniture, cast-iron bells, commemorative boards, etc. There are also slatelike tablets—which C.K. Yang calls "steles" (*Religion in Chinese Society*: 175–77)—that provide information on donors at the time of a major reconstruction and hence throw light on local society and its outside contacts. Such tablets are also found at the site of bridges or in schools and community offices. Occasionally they relate not to the structure, but to an official decision in a local dispute over land or rentals. In such cases they were placed there because these were public places, well patronized by large numbers of the inhabitants at certain times of the year.

Specimens of customary deeds relating to land and buildings can be found in *Manuals for Everyday Use*, usually styled 日用百科全書. Those I have seen so far, through collecting them in Hong Kong, are all published by various firms in Shanghai and date from the early and mid-Republican period. There must, however, be others from other publishing centres and earlier times; and in our case it would be interesting to have works from Canton and Foochow, which might show the regional types more plainly.

Those seen to date in the Shanghai publications indicate the importance of the customary deed in the early modern China context: but presumably they only represent the norm or that obtaining round Shanghai. However, the specific social, geographic and historical factors found in different regions must be reflected in the type and wording of the local forms of customary deed. Descriptions of different types of field and tenure will undoubtedly be used, together with local measures, and there will be statements that will reflect the local practise in regard to the use and ownership of land. This is what would make the preservation of manuals from other parts of the country, and for us particularly from the South, so interesting. We shall then be able to estimate the extent to which the norms vary in the manuals: and, with the aid of local deeds that still survive, the extent to which the latter coincide with, or depart from the norms.

How long have such guides to the form of customary deeds been published? Niida Noboru has found tenancy contract forms in "encyclopedia of daily use" from Ming editions (Rawski 1972: 16, 263), so that there seems every likelihood that they may be found in surviving books of this kind of intermediate date. Others may perhaps be found in earlier editions still, where such exist.

In Chinese

Association of Hui-chou natives in Hong Kong 僑港惠州同鄉總會. Bulletin of the Association of Hui-chou natives in Hong Kong 僑港惠州同鄉總會會刊. Hong Kong: 1964.

Chang lineage of Pui O, South Lantao, Hong Kong 香港大嶼山南段杯澳張族. Family Record 張氏族譜. Copied in manuscript in the 1930s from an earlier version.

Chang lineage of Pui O, South Lantao, Hong Kong 香港大嶼山南段杯澳張族. Family Record (not identical with the above as it came from another branch of the family) 張氏族譜. In manuscript. Last compiled in 1927.

Chang Ming-en 張銘恩. An account of the Tung-i T'ang of Tung-kuan natives in Hong Kong 駐港東莞東義堂事略. Hong Kong: 1931.

Chen Ching-ho and Tan Yeok-seong 陳荊和, 陳育崧. A Collection of Chinese Inscriptions in Singapore 新加坡華文碑銘集錄. Hong Kong: The Chinese University of Hong Kong Press, 1970.

Ch'en Hung-mou 陳宏謀. Instructions from bequeathed Teaching 訓俗遺規. 4 chüan. Canton: Chia Ch'ing reprint of 戊寅 year 1818–19 of original of 1742.

Ch'en Meng-lei 陳夢雷, Chiang T'ing-hsi, and others 蔣廷錫等. Synthesis of Books and Illustrations: Past and Present (The Imperial Encyclopedia) 古今圖書集成. 10,000 chüan, 1st ed. 1725.

Cheng Jo-tseng 鄭若曾. An Edited Collection of Plans of Coastal Regions 籌海圖編. Edition of 1802–03 (original edition 1561–62).

Chin Wen-mo (preface) 靳文謨. Gazetteer of the Hsin-an District 新安縣志. 13 chüan, rev. ed. 1688.

Chou K'uang 周廣. Ch'eng Yeh-chung, and others 鄭業崇等. Summary of historical researches on Kwangtung 廣東考古輯要. 46 chüan. 1894.

Chu Ch'in-shih 仇池石. Notes on the History of Canton 羊城古鈔. 8 chüan, Chia Ch'ing 丙寅 year, 1806–1807.

Ch'ü Ta-chün 屈大均. A New Notice of Kwangtung 廣東新語. Hong Kong: reprinted by Universal Book Co., c. 1965.

Editorial Committee for Kwangtung Literature 廣東文獻編輯委

員會. Quarterly Journal of Kwangtung Literature 廣東文獻季刊. Taipei, from 1972 on.

Hsieh Chin 解縉, Yao Kuang-hsiao 姚廣孝, and Liu Chi-ch'ih 劉季箎. Yung Lo Encyclopedia 永樂大典. Compiled in manuscript 1403–1408. Surviving portion printed by World Book Company, Taipei, 1964. See vol. 64 for *Kuang-chou-fu*.

Hsin-an Hsien-chih 新安縣誌. For information on all editions see K.M.A. Barnett in *JHKBRAS* 4 (1964): 66–67.

Huang Pen-chi 黃本驥. A historical record of Official Posts 歷代職官本. 6 chüan. Shanghai: 1883 (reprint of edition of Ch'ien Lung 45).

Hung Liang-chi and others 洪亮吉等. Concise General Gazetteer of the Ch'ing Dynasty 大清一統要. 50 chüan. Edition republished by Hung's great-grandson. n.d., but *c.* 1890.

Jao Tsung-i 饒宗頤. Kowloon in Historical Records of Sung Dynasty 九龍與宋代史料. Hong Kong: Universal Book Co., 1959.

Jen Yu-wen 簡又文. A critical appraisal of Kwangtung calligraphy and paintings (2 parts) 廣東書畫鑒藏記. Taipei: Quarterly Journal of Kwangtung Literature, 2, no. 4 and 3, no. 1 (1972–73).

———, compiler. Sung Wong Toi: A Commemorative Volume 宋皇臺紀念集. Hong Kong: Chiu Clansmen's Association, 1960.

Juan Yuan and others 阮元等. Gazetteer of the Kwangtung Province 廣東通志. 334 chüan. rev. ed. 1823.

Kung lineage of Yee O, Lantau, Hong Kong 香港大嶼山二澳龔族. Record of properties by lot numbers 各號田土地段號數. In manuscript, dated 庚申 year 1920–21.

Li Chin-wei, ed. 黎晋偉主編. Centenary History of Hong Kong 香港百年史. Hong Kong: Nan Chung (南中) Printing House, c. 1947.

Li Hsien and others 李賢等. General Gazetteer of the Ming Dynasty 大明一統志·萬壽堂 edition, mid Wan-li period.

Li Tiao-yüan 李調元. Sketches of Kwangtung 粵東筆記. 16 chüan. Reprinted, Shanghai: 1917. (Original about 1780.)

Lien-chiang T'ang of the Chang lineage of Pui O 香港大嶼山杯澳張族蓮江堂. Financial Record for the 23rd–24th years of

Kuang-hsü 1897–99 蓮江堂紀號進支部壹本. In manuscript.

Lin T'ien-wei 林天蔚. "A Chronological Account of the Yao Uprisings in the Sung Period" in Essays in Chinese Studies presented to Professor Lo Hsiang-lin (Festschrift); 135–51 宋代猺亂編年紀事. Hong Kong: 1970.

———. "An attempt to prove that Lantau was a Yao area in Southern Sung times" 南宋時大嶼山爲傜區之試証. Hong Kong: *Chung Chi Journal* (崇基學報) (Chinese University of Hong Kong), 3, no. 2 (May 1964): 175–89.

Lo Hsiang-lin 羅香林. "An Investigation of the Origin and Movements of the Hakka." Thirty Years of Tsung Tsin Association 客家源流考崇正總會三十週年紀念特刊. Hong Kong Tsung Tsin Association, 1950, pp. 1–106.

———. A Study of Chinese Genealogies 中國族譜研究. Hong Kong: Institute of Chinese Culture 中國學社, 1971.

———. Historical Sources for the Study of the Hakkas 客家史料滙篇. Hong Kong: Institute of Chinese Culture 中國學社, 1965.

———, and others. Hong Kong and Its External Communications before 1842, the History of Hong Kong prior to British Colonization 一八四二年以前之香港及其對外交通. Hong Kong: Institute of Chinese Culture 中國學社, 1959.

Lo Po-kwan 盧寶均. Family record of the Lo Lineage of Lo Pin, Chiu-lin subdistrict of Hsin-hui [Kwangtung] 新會潮連蘆鞭盧氏族譜. 26 chüan, apparently 1948 rev. ed.

Mai Ying-jung 麥應榮. "An account of the clearance of the coast of the Five Districts round Canton" 廣東五縣遷海事略 in Kwangtung Culture 廣東文物, 2: 408–17. Hong Kong: 1941.

Mao Hung-pin 毛鴻賓 and Jun Lin 瑞麟. Atlas with Commentary of Kwangtung 廣東圖說. 92 chüan, Canton: about 1865.

Mao Yuan-i 茅元儀. Record of Military Preparations 武備志. 240 chüan. Canton: late Ch'ing reprint of original of 1620.

New Territories Weekly 香港週報. Hong Kong. 1962 on.

Pang lineage of Shek Pui Ling, Pang Tong, Tung-kuan County, Kwangtung 廣東 東莞縣 彭塘 石背嶺 彭氏族譜 Manuscript copy in my possession, apparently circa 1905–10.

Shu Mou-kuan 舒懋官 and Wang Ch'ung-hsi 王崇熙. Gazetteer

of the Hsin-an District 新安縣志. 24 chüan. rev. ed. 1819.

Shui Shang Tong of Tai O, Lantau, Hong Kong 香港大嶼山大澳逐生堂. Financial Record. In manuscript. The Tong was apparently founded in the mid 19th century but the surviving yearly statements of income from field rentals date from 庚辰 year, 1940–41.

So lineage of So Uk, Kowloon, Hong Kong 香港九龍蘇屋蘇族. Family record of ancestor (Su) Tso-chün (蘇) 佐君公家族譜. In manuscript, copied prewar from an earlier version.

Sun Y'uan-p'o 孫完璞. Kwangtung Customs 粤風 in Kwangtung Culture 廣東文物 3: 892–902. Hong Kong: 1941.

Tai Chao-chen and others 戴肇辰等. Gazetteer of the Canton Prefecture 廣州府志. 163 chüan. Canton: rev. ed. 1880.

Teng lineage of Tong Fuk, South Lantau, Hong Kong 香港大嶼山南段塘福鄧族. Family record 鄧氏族譜. In manuscript, copied prewar from an earlier version.

T'ung Shih-hsiang 童世亨. New Atlas of the Chinese Republic 中華民國區域圖. Shanghai: Commercial Press, 1915.

Tung-kuan Hui-so (Cheung Chau Branch) 長洲東莞會所. Historical Record compiled in the mid 1920s. In possession of the association.

Wong Lineage (of Nam Tau and Cheung Chau 南頭長洲黃族). *Huang-shih Tsu-p'u* 黃氏族譜. Woodblock edition of the T'ung Chih period. In private ownership.

Wong Wai Tsak Tong (of Cheung Chau) 長洲黃維則堂 Directory and Record for 1958 黃維則堂徵信錄戊戌歲十二月結日. Privately printed.

Wu Clan of Nga Tsin Wai, Kowloon, Hong Kong 香港九龍衙前圍吳族. Family record 吳氏族跋. In manuscript, copied prewar from an earlier version.

Index

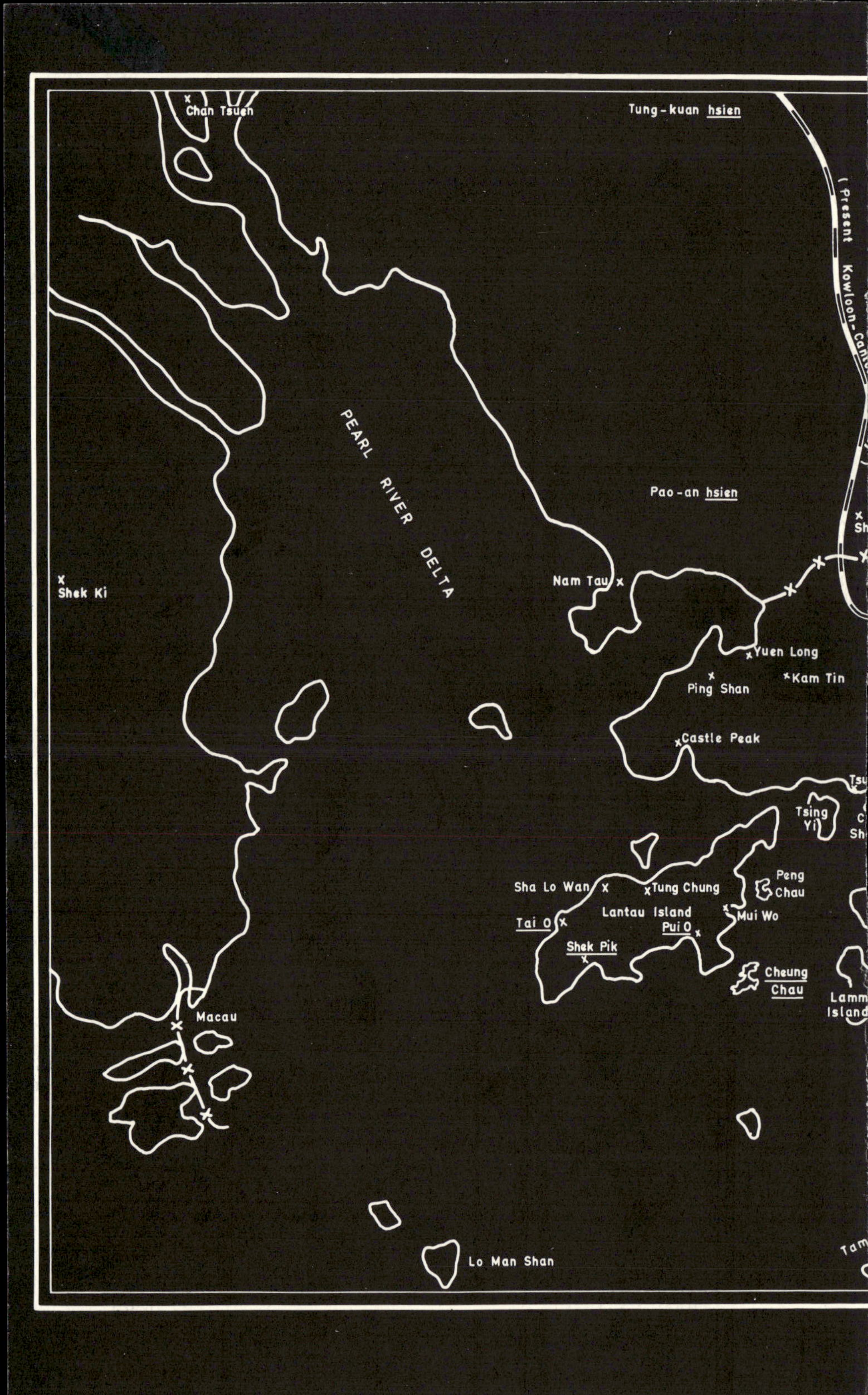
Chan Tsuen
Tung-kuan hsien
(Present Kowloon-Canto
PEARL RIVER DELTA
Pao-an hsien
Shek Ki
Nam Tau
Yuen Long
Ping Shan
Kam Tin
Castle Peak
Tsing Yi
Sha Lo Wan
Tung Chung
Peng Chau
Lantau Island
Tai O
Pui O
Mui Wo
Shek Pik
Cheung Chau
Macau
Lo Man Shan